JUNIOR TRANSLATION FROM FRENCH

JUNIOR TRANSLATION FROM FRENCH

BY

R. L. GRÆME RITCHIE, M.A., D.LITT.

Docteur de l'Université de Paris: Lauréat de l'Académie Française: Professor of French in the University of Birmingham

AND

JAMES M. MOORE, M.A.

Lecturer in French in the University of Edinburgh

CAMBRIDGE

AT THE UNIVERSITY PRESS

1928

CAMBRIDGE
UNIVERSITY PRESS

University Printing House, Cambridge CB2 8BS, United Kingdom

Cambridge University Press is part of the University of Cambridge.

It furthers the University's mission by disseminating knowledge in the pursuit of education, learning and research at the highest international levels of excellence.

www.cambridge.org
Information on this title: www.cambridge.org/9781316612576

First published 1928
First paperback edition 2016

A catalogue record for this publication is available from the British Library

ISBN 978-1-316-61257-6 Paperback

PREFACE

This book deals with translation from French into English, from the beginnings up to the standard of the School Certificate Examinations. It requires no excuse. On the one hand no other such book exists, except our own advanced *Translation from French*. On the other hand the examination papers in French, which contain—and always will contain—passages for translation into English, are being attempted by candidates without any real instruction in the art.

It is too often assumed that special training is not essential, that the exercise can be safely left to the inspiration of the moment in the examination room, and that, in the limited time available, attention is more profitably devoted to other things. The results show this assumption to be entirely false. More candidates fail because of weakness in translating into English than because of weakness in any other part of the papers. In the case of those who do pass, the pass is often unsatisfactory to everyone concerned. Of the very numerous failures many are caused not by ignorance of French but by inability to translate it.

It is in fact clear that while translation into French is well taught in our schools, translation into English is neglected. In French Composition the School Certificate scripts usually give evidence of careful teaching. The exercise is performed with adequate, often with complete, success. It is essentially one of exact application of grammatical rules. The passage set was probably chosen for its simplicity, and then simplified still more. Translation from the known to the unknown is in a sense the easier exercise, since the standard of French demanded from English children must always be lower than the standard of English. While translation into French is thus a test of accuracy, translation into English is a test of intelligence, judgment and taste. It tests comprehension of a passage which, even after considerable simplification, remains 'literature', and it involves the handling of English as a means of expressing ideas.

In translating from French the average School Certificate candidate shows such unwillingness to come to grips with the passage, such inability to clothe French ideas in suitable English words, such disregard of French usage and of the King's English as almost to warrant the belief that he has never heard what translation into English really means.

It means, among other things, learning—and practising—an art which, like any other art, has its own principles, rules and methods. Translation requires knowledge of the foreign language, but knowledge of a special kind, for good linguists may be bad translators. It demands three qualities: power to understand the exact sense of foreign words, power to *see* what they describe or to grasp the idea they convey, and power to express this correctly in English. These three qualities are not acquired by the light of nature. The first two are acquired by using not one but many methods. The third presupposes knowledge of certain guiding principles, constant practice, and the gradual acquisition of clear notions as to the relative force and values of French and English words and phrases.

Translation into English is thus one of the most complex processes in language-learning. It is also one of the most fascinating and most instructive. It opens in the foreign language vistas which would otherwise remain closed. It forces us to clear up difficulties of interpretation which without it would simply have been ignored, and thus to learn necessary facts of language which nothing else can teach. Of the many roads which at one time or another we must follow in our approach to French, translation into English is perhaps the most obvious, and it has over all others this advantage that, while it takes us a long way towards mastery of French, it also takes us a long way towards mastery of English. But it is a road which has been too often avoided or misused.

The foreign teachers to whom the French classes were so long entrusted shunned it, because for them it was full of pitfalls subversive of discipline. The older school of British teachers misused it when in class-reading they translated every line, every word, however simple. The first exponents of the newer methods would not use it themselves and warned everyone else against it, maintaining that it perpetuated the bad habit of interposing English between the French word and the idea it expresses. Examining bodies, however, retained their faith in the value of translation into the mother-tongue as a test of linguistic knowledge. And well they might, for no one has yet devised a more satisfactory practical means of testing exact and full comprehension of a passage written in a foreign language. But by setting incredibly long passages, to be translated in an incredibly short time, they showed that they underestimated the difficulty of the exercise and mistook its nature.

Sounder views now prevail. It is being recognized that even if the exact sense of all French expressions could be taught by the exclusive use of French in the classroom, translation would still have its place in language study, that while rapid translation, done orally in class and necessarily very rough, is apt to result in waste of time, careful translation is highly instructive. Now that the teaching of French in this country is being steadily reduced to order and common-sense we make here our contribution to that process, as follows:

Since translation cannot begin at the very beginnings of French, we assume that those who use this book are able to understand roughly the meaning of simple French. The preliminary instruction which they require before they can profitably embark on translation is given in an Introduction embodying the experience acquired in examining many thousands of candidates at the School Certificate stage. In it we discuss the general principles and the special difficulties involved in translation from French, classify the errors most commonly made and draw attention to those points in French grammar with which translation is most concerned. The examples utilized for these purposes are as a rule drawn from the 120 passages in this book. The information supplied in the Introduction could of course be extended indefinitely. But these are not chance passages. They are the siftings of hundreds which we have ourselves tested and at least one-third of them have been actually set in School Certificate Examinations. We are confident that they contain the bulk of the language-material of which passages set at this stage must always be composed.

The necessary practice is provided in eighty passages accompanied by Vocabularies and Notes. What we try to teach here is not the meaning of individual words, but the process of translation. The Vocabularies give, in the order in which the words occur in the French text, the meanings unfamiliar to pupils at the stage concerned. The English terms suggested are not necessarily those which best translate the French. Others, better suited to the context, will often be found by the pupil himself. Frequently several possible variants are suggested in order to afford practice in the very essential art of selection. The Notes draw attention, interrogatively where possible, to important points which a translator might easily miss. All the French words translated or discussed are collected in an Index at the end of the book.

Systematic progress from the easier to the more difficult stages is ensured by exact grading of the passages within four Sections; I and II contain none beyond the standard of Matriculation and First School Certificate, III and IV lead up to that of the University Entrance, Scottish Leaving Certificate and the various Higher School Certificate Examinations. From Section to Section less and less elementary help is offered.

To show what the difficulties are, and how they are practically met, we have written six Model Lessons. Sections I and II are each introduced by two of these, Sections III and IV by one.

For Unseen Translation, i.e. translation considered as a test, material for practice is provided in the forty graded pieces of Section V. Here also the meaning of uncommon words is given, but the help of Notes is withheld. The Unseen is essentially a test. The general preparation for it is wide reading; the special preparation is that given in the Introduction and the four corresponding Sections.

We suggest that after pupils have translated a passage they should be examined in its vocabulary. This seems to us one of the best ways of learning words whether for composition or for translation purposes.

Attention has just been fixed on them, not as isolated units but in a context, and their precise sense has been ascertained. They should now be committed to memory, with their gender and spelling, more particularly the words given in the Vocabularies. All of these are not only words likely to recur in examination papers (since that is precisely where we found them), but words which anyone wishing to know French must learn, ammunition indispensable in the minor war with examiners and in the major war with French writers whose meaning must be extorted by force.

Translation, unlike Mathematics, has no final standard of truth. A passage means something slightly different to each reader. We cannot hope to have dealt with each and all of the points which will arise in the practical use of this book, and we should welcome comments or suggestions from teachers. That they appreciate our efforts we are now well aware, and we are very grateful. Henceforth we shall be even more grateful to those who will kindly point out to either of us the shortcomings in this or in any other of our books.

R.L.G.R.
J.M.M.

July 1928

CONTENTS

INTRODUCTION

§ 1. UNSEEN TRANSLATION

The object of any general examination in French is to ascertain how much French the candidate knows and how well he knows it. Looked at broadly, the only questions he can be asked, and must be asked, are four in number: 1. 'How well can you *speak* French?' 2. 'And *write* it?' 3. 'How well can you understand it when *spoken*?' 4. 'And when *written*?' Questions 1 and 3 are put in Dictation and Oral. Question 2 is put in Composition. Question 4 is put in Translation, and with it alone we are here concerned.

It takes the form of one or more passages, usually Unseen, printed under the legend 'Translate into English'. This imperative denotes an order which must be obeyed without question or delay, under penalty of failure in the examination. But now there can be no harm in inquiring into the reasons for the order.

The examiners are evidently anxious to test the candidate's power of understanding French when written (or printed). For that purpose what means are at their disposal? They might say, 'Read this passage and then give us the gist of it. Tell us in a general sort of way what it is about, what is described in it, what happens in the narrative, etc.' They might say, 'Make a paraphrase of it' or, 'Write an Essay on it'. If they took any of these courses they would certainly test the power of ready or rapid or rough or general comprehension of a French passage—a very useful accomplishment and one which has its own place in language-learning. But they would have the greatest difficulty in valuing the answers, whether given in English or in French, orally or in writing. And they would not have tested the power of *exact* and *full* comprehension—a more necessary and a far finer thing than facility in rough-and-ready approximations. The only known practical method of testing this exact and full comprehension is by translation. That is why the examiners say 'Translate into English', meaning thereby 'Say to us in English *exactly* what the French author says in French. Do not add to it, nor subtract from it, nor embellish it nor spoil it, but write what the author would presumably have written had he been an Englishman'.

For another reason translation into English appears —and always will appear—in French examinations. It is an invaluable means of learning French—*and* English. By compelling us to look closely at the French, it draws our attention to difficulties of meaning which remain unnoticed even in careful reading. Things which appeared easy become difficult when we really have to understand them. Thus we come to realize that we do not know French nearly so well as we had imagined.

And soon we make another discovery, equally unpleasant, but equally good for us. We do not know English nearly so well as we should. For even when we do grasp the French author's idea, we often find ourselves unable to express it in natural English. Then, if not before, we see what light the study of a foreign language throws upon our own, and understand at last the full force of a line slightly adapted to the present purpose: 'What does he know of English who only English knows?'

Translation from French is not an easy exercise.

Examination candidates in the past thought it was. That is one reason, perhaps the chief reason, why they did it so badly, so much worse than they need have done. Mistakes due to ignorance are good honest mistakes. But at least one-half of the errors hitherto made in Unseen translation from French the candidates could easily have avoided, and would themselves have corrected, had they been given a second chance. These were silly mistakes, mistakes of candidates who would not make the necessary effort, who did not utilize to the full their own knowledge of French and of English, who sometimes knew every word, every construction, of a French passage and yet made nonsense of it. Many were nevertheless so well pleased with what they had done that they left the Examination Hall half-an-hour before the end of the time allowed. Why? Because when they read the instruction 'Translate into English' they did not really understand either what was meant by 'Translate' or what was meant by 'English'.

What these two words mean it is the aim of this book to show. The Introduction, containing more necessary facts than can be mastered at one reading, should be first read without the detailed lists, then read in full, re-read and gradually assimilated. The better it is known, the less difficulty will be found with the Passages for Translation. The Model Lessons can be taken as the reader proceeds through the book. In translating the Passages, there will be further opportunity for revising the Introduction until the facts stated therein become familiar. They will not only help the reader to pass his examination, but—what is much more important, since examinations are only a means and not an end in themselves—they will help him to understand French.

§ 2. FOR THOSE WHO, HAVING EYES, SEE NOT

Translation is a threefold process: 1. Understanding the foreign words; 2. Seeing what is described; 3. Describing in English what has been seen. The youthful translator is only too apt to get no further than process 1. He substitutes an English word for each foreign one. He does not *translate.*

To take a very simple instance, how does he 'translate' *un petit chat*? He recognizes the foreign words at a glance, says to himself *un* = a, *petit* = little, *chat* = cat, writes down 'a little cat', and thinks no more about it. He has seen nothing—nothing except three French words and three English words. If he had seen what was described, he would have seen a kitten. That is what a French reader sees in the words *un petit chat.* No doubt the correct translation could have been arrived at by other means. Anyone who had learned *un petit chat* as a complete phrase, equivalent to 'kitten', would have avoided error here. But he would have learned something not quite true, because in a few cases, let us say one in a thousand, *un petit chat* may mean a fully grown but undersized cat. When an effort is made to *see* what is described, it becomes clear from the circumstances whether 'a kitten' or 'a small cat' is intended.

When the French is more difficult than in the above phrase, the translator is apt to peer at each word instead of trying to get a little away from it and take a general view of its surroundings. To look at the French sentence as a whole would repay him better. He must in fact form a mental picture. In order to translate *Le vaincu rentrait chez lui l'oreille basse* it is not enough to know that *oreille* = ear, and *basse* = low. We must try to *see* the home-coming of the vanquished one. Then we realize that he was what we call 'crest-fallen' or 'chop-fallen'.

§ 3. FOR THOSE WHO, HAVING EARS, HEAR NOT

Here is another sentence, from another story: *Il ôte d'abord devant lui sa casquette.* Those who deal not in mental pictures but only in words write down 'He takes off at first before him his cap'. Those who not only see but *hear* picture up the circumstances, and then ask themselves how these circumstances would naturally be described in English, and say naturally, 'He first takes off his cap to him'. Every time *le lion rugit* appears in a First School Certificate Examination large numbers of the candidates state that 'the lion blushed'. Have they tried to *see* him blush? Do they not *hear* any difference between *rugir*, = to roar, and *rougir*, = to blush?

We must represent to ourselves the whole situation, sound as well as sight. The sound of *crier* varies according to circumstances. It is not the same in *les hommes criaient* as in *les femmes criaient*, or as in *les bébés criaient.* Yet in each case nine School Certificate candidates out of ten say 'cried'. Either they do not know that *crier* means also 'to shout' and 'to scream' and 'to yell', and merely 'to call out', or else they do not think. There is a great difference between *L'enfant ne* criait *plus* and *Allons! faites donner la Garde*, cria-*t-il*, and there are cases where such a difference must be shown in translation. Again, the word *grincer* means variously 'to creak', 'grate', 'grind', 'rasp'; everything depends on what makes the sound—a door, a file, etc. If in translating *le bruit de la plume* we only listened to the sound we are making ourselves we should certainly erase 'the *noise* of the pen' or 'the *sound* of the pen', and write 'the *scratching* (or 'the *scraping*') of the pen'.

§ 4. ON ACQUIRING THE NECESSARY STOCK OF WORDS

The translator, as has just been shown, must not be the slave of French words. He must be the master of as many as he can, must know at least their usual meanings. Vocabulary is his initial difficulty. It will not be his main difficulty, far from it. Errors in construction are much more deadly. It is possible to know the meaning of all the words in a passage and yet completely miss the sense of the whole. But individual words are the material of which the sentence is composed and the translator must know the meaning of ordinary French words. He requires a minimum stock of these before he can begin translation at all. It should be a constantly growing stock, increased by every means in his power.

For purposes of translation, word-lore can be acquired much more rapidly than for purposes of composition. The words have only to be recognized. They require only passive knowledge. They need not be part of our active vocabulary. To be able to recognize the French for, say, 'The Field of the Cloth of Gold' when we see it in print is very much easier than to be able to supply it ourselves, viz. *Le Camp du Drap d'Or*. In translation, many of the difficulties attending composition are non-existent. The thorny problems of spelling, gender, verbal forms, Mood, Tense, agreement of Participles, Adjectives, etc., choice and order of words, have all been settled for us by the French writer. We have only to recognize his words, not to select or to use French words ourselves. So far as translation into English is concerned, it is thus with a comparatively light heart that the learner proceeds on his way, picking up words in the course of reading.

§ 5. EVERYDAY WORDS: COMMON WORDS: RARE WORDS

The vocabulary of French falls, for the purposes of translation, into three classes: 1. Elementary everyday words. These are of limited number, but they recur at every moment. They include, besides names of ordinary things and ordinary ideas, those essential parts of speech which, like Prepositions and Conjunctions, indicate the relationship between things or between ideas. They are all of prime necessity. Without them one cannot grasp the sense of any French passage. Until they have been learned it is useless to begin translation and therefore they are not treated in this book.

2. Common words, almost certain to occur in any French text, even in the very simplest. They are those learned in the ordinary course of reading during the first three or four years of French. Any which the reader may happen to have missed will be learned before he has gone far in this book. The less common are given in the Vocabularies to the passages.

3. Rare words. They are by far the most numerous, because by 'rare' we mean here those which pupils cannot reasonably be expected to have learned in three or four years. These are given in the Vocabularies or discussed in the Notes to passages, because the

purpose of this book is not to test knowledge of vocabulary, but **to teach how to translate.**

Such words are not always names of rare things, nor do they always express uncommon ideas. But it is quite possible to read a great deal of French at school without coming across them. They are not necessarily rare to a French boy or girl or even to a French baby. The word *dodo* (m.), = bed, is extremely familiar to everyone in France and in Navarre and in the French dominions beyond the seas, from the age of six months or under. But in literary texts it is very rare. To breathe the air of France for many months without learning the word *goudron* (m.), = tar, would be difficult. But of twelve hundred Higher Certificate candidates in 1926 only a few knew *goudron*, because it was beyond their school reading.

§ 6. HOW TO ASCERTAIN THE MEANING OF 'RARE' WORDS

Now in any examination some 'rare' words will occur in the passage set for Unseen Translation. The fewer there are, the more credit due to the person who set it. A badly chosen passage is one containing a large number of words which candidates cannot possibly know and have no means of guessing, or one of which the sense depends entirely on a single difficult keyword. A good passage is one, interesting and complete in itself, containing few words which are unfamiliar, but constructions which have to be thought out and sentences which test intelligence. To translate it properly calls for the exercise of judgment and taste. If it contains one or two words which only the better candidates know, this is only fair. It is a legitimate method of rewarding merit and encouraging pupils to learn as many words as possible. In the search for such passages an examiner may read book after book in vain, because literary treatment of any subject nearly always demands some departure from the commonplace and the use of some words which in an examination sense are 'rare'. Such words are learned by wide reading, especially of anthologies, where the frequent change of author and subject necessarily makes the vocabulary extensive and varied. But reading can be supplemented very profitably by translating carefully the passages in this book.

§ 7. SPELLINGS AND GENDER

Before tackling 'rare' words we must make sure of the words we do know and, in particular, take care not to confuse them with others which look somewhat like them. Words similar in spelling are often confused, sometimes with disastrous consequences. Such are: *le besoin* = need, *la besogne* = work; *baiser* = to kiss, *baisser* = to lower; *embraser* = to set on fire, *embrasser* = to embrace; *poison* = poison, *poisson* = fish; *rougir* = to blush, *rugir* = to roar; *le sort* = fate, *la sorte* = the sort; *la veille* = the night before, *la vieille* = the old woman. When two words have the same spelling the context shows which one is intended: otherwise *les fils* might just as well be translated by 'the threads' as by 'the sons', since the difference in pronunciation does not appear; *je suis* is either 'I follow' or else 'I am', according to the context: *D'un œil triste je* suis *au loin son blanc sillage* must mean 'With a sad eye *I follow* afar her white wake'. Similarly *je vis* means 'I live' and 'I saw'.

In some such cases difference of gender makes the error inexcusable. The most notable are perhaps *le manche* = the handle, *la manche* = the sleeve (which is easily remembered from *La Manche*, the sleeve-shaped 'English Channel'); *le mort* = the dead man, *la mort* = death; *le poste* = the situation, *la poste* = the post-office; *un tour* = a turn, a trick, *une tour* = a tower; *le vase* = the vase, vessel, *la vase* = mud, slime; *le voile* = the veil, *la voile* = the sail. An accent indicates the distinction between *une tache* = a stain, and *une tâche* = a task (so *tacher* = to spot, and *tâcher* = to try).

Failure to note the conjugation adds considerably to the offence; e.g. confusion of *jouer*, = to play, with *jouir*, = to enjoy, or *bâti*, = built, with *battu*, = beaten.

Other, less deadly, errors are the confusion of *définitif* with *défini*: *définitif* means not 'definite' but 'final', and is used of something against which there is no appeal; and the failure to distinguish *la justice*, = justice, from *la justesse*, = exactness; *part* from *parti* and *partie*: *une part* = a share—*Que chacun de vous se contente de* sa part, 'Let each one of you be content with his share', *une partie* = a part, *un parti* = a party, often a political one, e.g. *le parti conservateur*.

§ 8. INTELLIGENT GUESSING

When a candidate meets an unfamiliar word, ought he to leave a blank? To do so is a confession of despair, not to be made till all possible avenues of escape have been explored. By what means can he hope to find out the meaning? By applying reason, that is, by intelligent guessing. If he understands the passage as a whole and applies his knowledge to a small part of it which he does *not* understand, he will often arrive at the correct meaning, or at a very close approximation, for which sensible examiners will give him due credit. He can at least find a word which does not make nonsense.

To take a recent instance, in the lines in which Coppée says that Winter

> '...vient balayer de son dur râteau
> Les espoirs brisés et les feuilles mortes',

râteau proved a stumbling-block to many candidates. It was, for almost all, a 'rare' word, although it is the name of an implement as 'common', indeed as 'garden', as any implement can well be, since *un râteau* is 'a rake'. Some gave it up without an effort. Others asked themselves 'What does a man use to *balayer* or "sweep up" dead leaves?'—and answered: 'a broom'. They were wrong, but the fault was partly Coppée's, for *balayer d'un râteau* is just as odd in French as 'to sweep with a rake' would be in English. They deserved—and received—some credit for using their heads.

Intelligent guessing is to be encouraged. It is reasoning from the known to the unknown. It develops the logical faculties. It has all the interest of a missing-word competition. But it will not solve all difficulties. In a sentence enumerating, say, various birds or flowers or trees, there may be no means of arriving by any process of reasoning at the conclusion that *une alouette* must be a lark, or *un rossignol* a nightingale; that *le nénuphar* is the water-lily or *le réséda* the mignonette; that *le frêne* is the ash, *le hêtre* the beech, *le sapin* the fir. We can, however, at least refrain from writing down a word which could not possibly have any connection with birds or flowers or trees and which we know must be wrong. If, unhappily, we are unaware of the meaning of *alouette* and *rossignol*, we can surely make use of such information as we do possess, for instance, that larks do not usually sing in a forest at midnight, nor nightingales high in the heavens on a bright summer morning!

It is astonishing to find how far reason and common-sense can sometimes take those who are willing to follow them. The intelligent translator of an Unseen meets the strange term, *le mélèze*, in the description of a walk on the mountains. He knows the other trees mentioned in the passage: *le pin*, = pine, *le sapin*, = fir, *le hêtre*, = beech. He asks himself, What tree is likely to be found in such company on such a mountain-side? And if he knows anything about trees, there is a fair chance that he will answer correctly 'the larch'.

In many ways translation into English is one of the best types of examination in General Knowledge and Common-sense.

§ 9. ABSURD MISTAKES

There are degrees in mistranslation, as there are degrees in murder. The lowest degree is that which was represented, for the time being, by a young man who, in a poem on Evening recently set for translation in a University Entrance Examination, rendered *Les minces peupliers frissonnaient dans la nuit* by 'The nations were frying mince in the night'. He thought that *peupliers* were *peuples* or 'peoples', 'nations', and there is in fact considerable likeness between these words. He did not know *frissonner*, = to shiver, but he did know an English word which at least begins with the same letters, perhaps he even knew a French word *frire* which undoubtedly means 'to fry'. The nations seemed thus to be engaged in frying something in the night. It is not very probable as a national occupation, but what were they frying? *Les minces*. This presents a remarkable likeness to 'mince' and he therefore concluded that: 'The nations were frying mince in the night'. Apart from the errors of construction and vocabulary, the apparent belief that a poem on evening is likely to contain allusions not only to sunset and evening star but also to frying operations on an international scale suggested that the candidate was qualifying for admission not to a University, but to another institution where such visions are perhaps more commonly seen.

To a higher degree belongs the offence of a second young man who translated *L'aïeule penchait sa tête ridée* as 'The owl scratched her feathered head'. *L'aïeule*, = the grandmother, *pencher*, = to droop, and *ridé*, = withered, were unknown to him. The only words he did know were *sa* and *tête*. *L'aïeule* may sound something like 'owl', if it is pronounced badly enough. The error is no worse than the translation of *cigale* by 'seagull' by large numbers of candidates in another examination, most of whom probably knew by heart La Fontaine, *La Cigale et la Fourmi*, 'The Grasshopper and the Ant'. This type of error, due to thinking of the sound of an English word, is very common, e.g. *blesser*, = to wound, *dresser*, = to train, *rester*, = to remain, *traîner*, = to drag, are often confused with the English verbs which have approximately the same sound, but quite a different meaning, and which usually make nonsense. In this passage, however, the old lady in question was far from beautiful, indeed somewhat like a witch, and an owl might quite well be one of her familiars. If we start from the assumption that the subject of the sentence is an owl and reflect that an owl does have a 'feathered head', then it is reasonable enough to conclude that 'The owl scratched her feathered head'.

There is even some slight merit in the error of a third young man who took *Une longue suite de jours prospères* to be 'A lounge suit that had seen better days'. His rendering had a fine English flavour about it, and suited the context admirably. It deserved a better fate. Unhappily the French author was not, for the moment, thinking about lounge suits, but about 'A long series of prosperous days'.

§ 10. ETYMOLOGY AS AN AID

Words fall naturally into groups, and for Translation as for Composition it is best to learn them in these groups, as explained in our *Junior Manual of French Composition*, § 3. The derivation of words helps us to translate them exactly. The French vocabulary is partly derived from Latin and partly from the Germanic languages, including English. The Latin or the Germanic form of a word may happen to be well known to us though the French form remains effectually disguised. When dealing with an unknown French term, it is therefore useful to think of its possible origins. What sometimes alters the appearance of a French word is the loss of *s*, whether Latin or Germanic; thus *pâtre* stands for Latin *pastor* = a shepherd, and *dépouillé* corresponds to our 'despoiled'; *bifteck* is 'beefsteak' and *beaupré* is 'bowsprit'. Remembering this, we can decipher the perhaps strange word *cloître* as 'cloister' and safely translate *un cheval rétif* by 'a restive steed'. Since *exprimer* means 'to express', *opprimer* will mean 'to oppress', from which we may draw the conclusion that French often forms its verbs from the Latin Infinitive (*ex-primere*, etc.), whereas English prefers the Past Participle (*expressum*). On the strength of this etymological fact, when we come across the possibly unfamiliar *déprimé* we may confidently render it as 'depressed'.

Memories of Latin will suggest more precise renderings of words, because French as a rule keeps very close to the original Latin sense. Thus *superbe* retains more of the force of Latin *superbus*, = proud, than does our 'superb' and may often require to be translated by 'proud' rather than by 'superb'. *Un vain mot* is more likely to be 'an empty' (Latin *vanus*) than 'a vain word'.

Etymology is not to be despised as an aid to translation. Its rules may be used to help us out of difficulties. To know that Latin *p* between vowels becomes *v* in French might help us with a word like *sevré*. What does *sevré* come from? It comes from Latin *separatus*, Vulgar Latin *seperatus*, and therefore means 'separated', 'cut off from', and is said, more especially, of a child 'weaned' from its mother.

§ 11. THE ORIGIN OF WORDS AS A GUIDE TO THEIR SENSE

We make a long step forward in the study of French when, instead of looking upon words as ready-made units, we acquire the habit of noting how they are formed. That is the best way of realizing their exact sense. It is also the best way of arriving at a correct translation. Thus *Un ménestrel cheminait seul* fails to yield its full meaning till we reflect that *cheminer* is just *chemin* (= way) + *-er* (verbal termination), and consequently means '*way*-faring'. This suggests a good translation: 'A minstrel was faring on his lonely way'. Similarly, *doter* conveys little meaning unless it is divided as *dot-er*, when it becomes apparent that if *dot* means 'dowry' then *doter* means 'to endow'; *denteler* is to 'notch', 'indent', 'jag', *des rochers dentelés* are 'jagged rocks' and we fully understand this epithet when we think of *dentelle* = lace, or lace-work pattern.

In a list of trees with unfamiliar French names we come across *le tremble.* Few will know the Latin word which it comes from, *tremulus* = an aspen, but even those who know no Latin will get a broad hint from *trembler* = to tremble, and come safely, though not by the true etymological route, to the trembling, quivering 'aspen'. In a sentence like *Je fus flatté de cette ouverture* the English 'opening' will not help us very much. But the wary will bethink themselves that our English 'overture' is probably just French *ouverture,* and that, if so, the French word must mean 'overture' as well as 'opening'.

§ 12. BREAKING UP A WORD INTO ITS COMPONENT PARTS

By breaking up words into their component parts, we may arrive not only at their meaning but at the exact English equivalent. The manœuvre implied in *Le vaisseau aborde* may not be very clear. Break up *aborder* into *a-bord-er*, *a* being *à*=to, and *bord*=edge, or side, and you obtain both a clue to the sense and a broad hint as to the translation: 'The ship heaves (or draws) alongside'. A poet refers to Napoleon at St Helena as *Cette grande figure en sa cage accroupie.* Break up *accroupi* into *ac* = *à* + *croupe* + *-i*, *croupe* being as in *la croupe d'un cheval*, and you are not far from the translation 'squatting' or 'huddled'. *Nos devanciers* discloses its meaning when divided as *nos devan-ciers, devan* representing *devant.* It means 'those that were before us', 'our predecessors'. So *assaisonnement* = *as-saison(ne)-ment* = seasoning.

This method is particularly helpful in unearthing an adjective from its lair in the midst of an unintelligible word. Thus, in the sentence *Le baume assainit la blessure* we may find *assainir* difficult. Let us look at it more closely. We see that *-ir* is only the verbal ending and that *as-* is only the prefix *ad*, assimilated, as usual, to a following *s*. The word is thus *ad-sain-ir*; *sain*, = healthy, stands forth from its disguise; the whole is seen to mean 'to make healthy', 'to heal', and the sentence means 'The balm heals the wound'. In like manner *agrandir*, *allonger*, *anoblir*, *arrondir*, *élargir* conceal the familiar adjectives *grand*, *long*, *noble*, *rond* and *large*. To realize that fact is often to find an exact translation in difficult circumstances, as in the instance in Model Lesson I B, p. 96. So also *épaiss-ir* = to make thick, to thicken, *blanch-ir*, *jaun-ir*, *roug-ir*, *verd-ir* = to make (become) white, yellow, red, green or to whiten, to make yellow, to redden, to make green, and *éclair-cir*, *noir-cir*, *obscur-cir* = to lighten, to darken, to obscure.

§ 13. THE PREFIX OF VERBS

The prefix of verbs is an essential factor in their meaning. Thus, while *se lever* means 'to rise', *s'é-lever* means something more—'to rise out' or 'rise up': *Le vent se lève*, 'The wind rises' after calm; *Le vent s'élève*, 'The wind freshens', i.e. has been already blowing, but now rises higher. *Sou-lever* (= *sous* + *lever*) is 'to raise from underneath', 'to heave up'; *re-lever* is 'to raise again'. There is a great difference between *porter* = to carry, *ap-porter* = to carry here, bring, and *em-porter* = to carry away, or take away, and between *mener* = to lead, *a-mener* = to lead up, bring, and *em-mener* = to lead away, or take away. A verb with a prefix cannot have quite the same sense as the simple verb, e.g. *entraîner* cannot be quite the same as *traîner* = to drag; it means 'to drag along'. Note also here *jouir de* = to enjoy, *se réjouir de* = to rejoice at; they are often confused.

The prefix *dé-* corresponds generally to English 'dis-'. Thus *découvrir* is, in an etymological sense, the same thing as 'to discover'. But 'discover' has various shades of meaning. 'America was *discovered* by Columbus' is not the same thing as 'Land was *discovered* on the lee-bow'. Most of these shades are found in *découvrir*, but there comes a point when it can no longer be translated by 'discover' and we must say '*un*cover'. When the meaning becomes yet more specialized, we must use a different word altogether. Thus *se découvrir* means 'to take off one's hat', the opposite of *se couvrir*, in, e.g., *Couvrez-vous, Monsieur, je vous en prie*, as French ladies considerately say when one has stood in their presence for a few moments, as is the custom, bareheaded in the open air.

Similarly, *déformer* means 'to put out of shape', 'to distort'; hence *déformé* is 'distorted', not 'deformed', which is *difforme*.

In *découper*, = to cut out, *dé* has the force of 'out' and suggests, for instance, cutting out in paper. In descriptions of scenery *se découper* is used of anything sharply silhouetted on a background: *à l'horizon des montagnes commençaient à se découper*, 'on the horizon mountains began to stand out'.

In *détourner*, *dé* suggests 'away': *Il détourna la tête,*

'He looked away', *Il se détourna*, 'He turned aside', whereas *Il retourna la tête* means 'He looked round' and *Il se retourna* means 'He turned round, wheeled round'.

A verb with *em-* (*en-*) is generally the exact opposite of a verb with *dé-*. Thus em*barrasser* = to encumber, dé*barrasser* = to rid, free, clear: *Le sol avait été débarrassé de broussailles*, 'The ground had been cleared of brushwood'; em*mêlé* = tangled, ravelled, dé*mêlé* = disentangled, unravelled; *s'*en*gager* = to enter, *se* dé*gager* = to extricate oneself; en*raciné* = rooted, dé*raciné* = uprooted.

é- means 'out' or 'away'; *crouler* = to crumble, *s'écrouler* = to crumble away; *éloigner* = to send away, or drive away.

entre- means 'between' or 'through' as in *entrevoir* = to catch a glimpse of, originally to see between some obstacles; *entr'ouvert* = half-open, ajar.

re- means properly 'again', e.g. *remonter* = to go up again; *reparaître* = to appear again, to re-appear; *reprendre* = to resume, take up the conversation again, continue the conversation. This sense is as a rule present in compounds, and must not be overlooked. It gives point, for instance, to the line in which Rostand describes the red combs of Chantecler's hens as ap*paraissant*, dis*paraissant*, re*paraissant* amid the green corn. We must be ready to recognize *re* in words where its *e* is elided, such as *rallumer* (= *r'allumer*) = to light up again, or, as Othello says, 'to relume', *rappeler* (= *r'appeler*) = to recall, *se rassurer* (= *r'assurer*) = to pluck up confidence (again). It has two other senses, 'back' and 'duly', which are both present in the same verb, *remettre* = (1) 'to put back', also 'to put off to another occasion', (2) 'to give to the proper person': *remettre une lettre à quelqu'un*, 'to hand someone a letter'. Note also *rapetisser* = to make smaller (*petit*), and *rapiécer* = to patch, i.e. to add a new piece (*pièce*); *recouvert* = covered over, covered completely; *revêtu* = clad: *une tour* revêtue *de lierre*, 'an ivy-mantled tower'; *rembruni* (from *re* + *en* + *brun* + *-i*) = made completely dark: *un ciel rembruni*, 'a sky turned to dusk all over', i.e. overspread with dusk.

sur- means 'on' or 'over': *survenir* is 'to come on the scene', as does La Fontaine's Fly (see p. 76, § 59, *Une Mouche survient*); *surmonter* = to overcome; *surplomber* (from *sur* + *plomb* = lead) = to overhang (said, for instance, of rocks overhanging so that a lead-line dropped from the summit would fall clear of the sides).

§ 14. FRENCH VERB = ENGLISH VERB + ADVERB

In the preceding paragraph it will have been noticed that the sense which in French is conveyed by a prefix is in English often conveyed by an adverb, e.g. *entraîner* = to drag *along*. Our free use of adverbs to eke out the sense of a verb extends to verbs whose French equivalent requires no prefix. Hence translation of a French verb by an English verb alone tends to produce an odd effect. Our usual way of saying *s'approcher de quelqu'un* is not 'to approach' but 'to go *up* to': *La cuisinière* regagna *sa cuisine* is 'The cook *went back* to her kitchen'.

To ignore this difference between the two languages often causes misapprehension of the meaning. Thus *balayer* may be merely 'to sweep', but it may mean much more, e.g. 'to sweep out' or 'to sweep away', and neglect of this fact leads to serious errors such as that which we have noted on p. 119. Similarly, *boire* means 'to drink', but also 'to drink in': *l'enfant* boit *toutes mes paroles*, 'the child *drinks in* everything I say'; *ôter* is 'to take off', or 'to take away': *Otez ce chapeau*, 'Take *off* that hat'; *Otez-moi ce hochet*, 'Take *away* that bauble'. In translating a French verb it is always well to ask oneself whether some expansion is not required; *donner tout ce qu'on a à un brigand* is 'to hand *over*'.

For *Les étoiles fuient*, 'The stars flee' is not enough. 'The stars flee away' may be a better rendering; for *rouler* we often have to say 'roll up', 'roll along', or 'wheel up', 'wheel along'; for *tourner la page* no doubt 'turn the page' could be said, but *Tournez s'il vous plaît* is 'Turn *over*', and 'over' seems so important an element of the phrase that even in abbreviations we retain it, and for T.S.V.P. use P.T.O. or simply OVER.

In revising a translation from French it is always useful to look at the verbs and consider whether some of them do not require a little supplementing to bring them up to proper strength.

§ 15. SOME SUFFIXES

As regards nouns, the sense of the following terminations should be carefully noted for translation purposes:

-AGE: collective: *la corde* = the rope, *les cordages* = the rigging; *la langue* = the tongue of a nation, *le langage* = the words used by a particular author, diction.

-ÉE: denoting (1) content of: *poing* = fist, *poignée* = handful; so *une bouchée* = a mouthful; *une pelle* = a spade, shovel, *une pelletée* = a spadeful; (2) space of time with special reference to the events which took place in it: *dans votre journée* = in your day's work.

-OIR: indicating place where: thus *le boudoir* = *l'en-*

droit où l'on boude ('sulks'), *un couloir* is a passage (through which a stream of people flows or might flow: *couler*), *le fumoir* = the smoking-room, *le séchoir* = the drying-loft.

-TÉ: denoting an abstract quality: *bonté* = goodness, kindness, *cher-té* = dearness.

-URE: collective: *ramure* = branches (*rameaux*) collectively; *mâture* = the masts (*les mâts*); *voilure* = the sails (*les voiles*).

Diminutive endings must never be overlooked; *un îlot* is not 'an island' but 'an islet'; *une tourelle* not 'a tower' but 'a turret'; *une faux* is 'a scythe', *une faucille* is only 'a sickle'; *une vallée* = a valley, *un vallon* = a vale; *l'aigle* = the eagle, *l'aiglon* = the eaglet. This termination *-on* gives point to the line in which, telling how Napoleon became the prisoner of England and his son the King of Rome became the prisoner of Austria, Victor Hugo says:

L'Angleterre prit l'aigle *et l'Autriche* l'aiglon.

As regards adjectives, *-ard* (pejorative—e.g. *criard* = unpleasantly loud, harsh) and *-âtre* (of colour) = -ish, e.g. *rougeâtre* = reddish, are to be noticed. But it should be added that adjectives of the former class are less common than might be supposed, and that adjectives of the latter class are sometimes indistinguishable in sense from the simple form, the normal English for *verdâtre* being often not 'greenish' but merely 'green'.

§ 16. FRENCH AND ENGLISH HOMONYMS

To the meaning of French words English is a treacherous guide. It very often helps us, but just as often leads us astray. French is very like English. That is why it is in appearance so easy, in reality so difficult. Any intelligent British citizen who has not had the advantage of learning French at school can tackle an apparently simple passage with a reasonable prospect of arriving at half the meaning. At the other half—usually much the more interesting half—he never arrives. Neither do those who say that French is easy. They think they understand when they do not. So deceptive is the similarity of the two languages that everybody is at one time or other deceived. The wise are the sooner undeceived—generally as the result of their experiences in translation. In the practice of that art disquieting facts come to light. In particular, words which in form are identical in both languages turn out to be in some subtle way different in sense. On these words, called 'homonyms', two pieces of advice may be here given:

1. In translating, be very suspicious of an English word which closely resembles the French word. Consider whether in the circumstances a different English one would not perhaps be more natural.

You may in the end have to come back to the homonym for want of a better word. But it should not be used till all other possibilities have been exhausted.

2. Commit to memory the following list of the most common homonyms:

HOMONYMS

ACCIDENT (m.): 'accident', but also 'irregularity' (of ground), e.g. *les accidents du terrain*: cp. *un terrain accidenté*, 'rough ground'; *un pays accidenté*, 'hilly country'.

ANCIEN: 'ancient', but also 'former', e.g. *notre ancien professeur*, 'our former teacher'.

ANGOISSE (f.): occasionally 'anguish', but usually mental 'agony': *plein d'angoisse*, 'sick at heart'.

ANTIQUE: 'ancient', often 'old-world'.

APPARTEMENT (m.): 'a suite of apartments', 'a flat'.

AVIS (m.): 'opinion': *à mon avis*, 'in my opinion', 'warning'.

CLASSE (f.): 'class' or 'class-room'.

CLIENTS (m.): 'clients', used also of those who deal not with a lawyer but with a doctor, = 'patients'; with a shopkeeper, = 'customers'.

COLLÈGE (m.): 'college' in the sense of a Secondary School, High School, not 'University': *au collège*, 'at school'.

DEMANDER: not 'to demand', which is *exiger*; 'to ask'.

DISTRACTION (f.): 'distraction', i.e. interruption during work; also 'amusement', i.e. interruption of work for purposes of play or recreation.

ENFANT (m. and f.): 'infant', 'child'; 'boy', 'lad'; 'girl'.

FIGURE (f.): 'face', but often also 'figure'.

FLEUR (f.): 'flower', also 'blossom', e.g. *des fleurs d'oranger*, 'orange-blossom'.

FONTAINE (f.): 'fountain'; but also 'spring' or 'well'.

FRAIS: 'fresh', also 'cool': *Goûtez cette boisson, elle est* fraîche; 'new': *du pain frais*, 'new bread'; *des œufs frais*, 'new-laid eggs'.

GAGNER: 'to gain', also 'to earn': *Il* gagne *trente shillings par semaine*; 'to reach', 'win', 'go to', 'get to': *gagner la gare*, 'to get to the station'.

GOUFFRE (m.): 'gulf', in the sense not of the 'Gulf' of Mexico (*le Golfe du Mexique*), but of the 'gulf' fixed between the Rich Man and Lazarus; *le gouffre amer*, 'the briny depths of the sea'.

GRACIEUX: 'gracious', also 'graceful'.

HERBE (f.): 'herb', 'grass', 'weed'.

HEURE (f.): 'hour', also 'time': *C'était l'heure où.*

IGNORER: not 'to ignore' (*passer sous silence*), but 'to be ignorant of': *vivre ignoré*, 'to live unknown (obscure)'.

INTÉRIEUR (m.): 'interior'; also 'home': *une femme d'intérieur*, 'a home-loving woman'; *le Ministère de l'Intérieur*, 'the (French) Home Office': *la guerre à l'étranger, la paix à l'intérieur*, 'war abroad, peace at home'.

JUSTE: 'just', but often 'exactly', 'right': *juste devant lui*, 'right in front of him'.

LABOUR (m.): not 'labour' (*le labeur*), but 'ploughing', 'plough-land'.

LABOURER: not 'to labour', but 'to plough': *labourer les champs*.

LABOUREUR (m.): not 'labourer', but 'tiller of the soil', 'peasant', 'farmer'.

LANCER: 'to launch'; also 'to throw', 'hurl', 'fling': *lancer des obus*, 'to fire shells'.

LARGE: very seldom 'large', usually 'broad', 'wide': *une route large*, 'a wide road'.

MEURTRI(R): not 'to murder', but only 'to bruise'; so *meurtrier* (adj.), 'murderous', 'deadly': *un coup meurtrier* may be a very deadly blow, but it does not necessarily kill, still less 'murder' anyone, whereas *un meurtrier* really is 'a murderer', though the usual term is *un assassin*.

OBSCUR: 'obscure', but usually with the full etymological sense of 'dark' (as in *camera obscura*): *une rue obscure*, 'a dark street'.

OCCASION (f.): not usually 'occasion', but 'opportunity', 'chance'.

OPPORTUNITÉ (f.): rarely 'opportunity'; usually 'opportuneness'.

ORAGE (m.): not 'storm', but 'thunder-storm', as opposed to *la tempête*, 'wind-storm'.

PARENT: not often 'parent'; usually 'relative', 'relation'.

PEINE (f.): 'mental pain'; 'effort', 'trouble'.

PEUPLE (m.): 'people', but in the sense of 'nation': *les peuples étrangers*, 'foreign nations'; or 'the common people': *un homme du peuple*, 'a man of humble birth'.

PLACE (f.): often 'a public square'.

PLAISANT: not 'pleasant' (*agréable*), but 'amusing': *un livre plaisant*, 'an amusing book', which may contain *des plaisanteries*, 'jokes', 'pleasantries'.

UN POINT: 'a point', 'a speck'.

LA POINTE: 'the sharp point' of something.

POURPRE: sometimes 'purple'; usually 'red', 'crim son'; so *empourpré*: *la joue empourprée* ('rosy') *de la jeune fille*; and *s'empourprer*: *quand l'horizon s'empourpre*, 'when the horizon reddens'.

PRAIRIE (f.): not 'prairie' except in stories of the Far West, etc., but 'meadow'.

PRÉTENDRE: not 'pretend' (*faire semblant*), but 'to maintain': *Le père de Jean* prétend *qu'il ne travaille pas assez*, 'John's father *maintains* (alleges) that he does not work hard enough'; *prétendre à*, 'to claim the right to', 'to aspire to', 'to presume'.

PRÉVENIR: not 'prevent', but 'warn', 'inform'.

RELATION (f.): not 'relations' in the sense of 'relatives' (*parents*), but 'business relations', etc., 'family connections', 'influence'; *Il se vante de ses hautes relations.*

RÉPROUVER: not 'reprove' (*blâmer*), but 'to disapprove of', 'condemn': *les fêtes païennes que Dieu réprouve.*

RESPECTABLE: 'worthy of respect', 'venerable'.

REVERS (m.): 'reverse', also the 'slope' of a hill.

RUMEUR (f.): not 'rumour', but 'a confused sound', 'murmur', 'dull roar': *la rumeur de l'Océan.*

SON (m.): 'musical sound', as opposed to *un bruit*, 'an unmusical sound': *pas un bruit, pas un son*, 'not a sound, not a note'.

VASE (m.): 'vase', also 'vessel'.

VERS (m.): not 'verse' (*une stance*), except in the plural, *les vers*, but 'line': *un beau vers* is 'a splendid line'; *de beaux vers* may be 'fine lines' or 'beautiful verse'; *faire des vers* is 'to write verse'.

VIL: sometimes 'vile'; usually 'worthless', 'cheap': *acheter à vil prix*, 'to buy at a low price'; 'common': *un sang vil*.

VOLONTAIRE: seldom 'voluntary'; usually 'masterful', 'wilful'.

§ 17. THE DANGER OF ATTACHING TO A FRENCH WORD ONE MEANING ONLY

To know the full and precise meaning of French terms is indispensable in translating. To know which English terms *usually* correspond to them and have roughly the same general meaning, is convenient. But to assume that any given French word has a fixed English equivalent is a fatal mistake. No French word carries with it quite the same associations as any English word, nor is it invariably used in quite the same way. It is possible to give with English words the exact equivalent of a French sentence, but from sentence to sentence they will vary indefinitely. In different sentences the same French words require different English words. Since words have an immense variety of meanings and these are not all found in both languages, to attach to a French word one fixed meaning makes error inevitable.

Thus pupils learn at an early stage that *porter* is 'to

carry'. When they begin to translate, they are apt to write down 'carry' whenever they see *porter*. In translating *Portez cette lettre à la poste* it seldom occurs to them that the English equivalent in this connection is not 'carry' but 'take'. The word for 'take' is, so they have learned, *prendre* and they translate *L'aubépine a pris sa robe* by 'The hawthorn has taken her robe', where the meaning clearly is 'has put on', 'has donned'. Having also learned that *à* is 'to', they write down for *J'ai pris mes lettres à la poste* the very opposite of what the sentence means, which is 'I have called at the Post Office for my letters'.

All well-trained pupils know, almost from the outset of their career, that *ce* means 'that' as well as 'this' and *dire* is 'to tell' or 'to bid' as well as 'to say'. But in defiance of context and common-sense they use 'this' or 'say'. At the Higher Certificate stage, when after seventeen or eighteen winters we might expect youthful illusions to have vanished with Father Christmas, we find nearly half the candidates translating *vers trois heures du soir* as 'three o'clock in the *evening*'. Most know well enough that *soir* may be any hour between midday and midnight. But the *word* 'soir' calls forth the *word* 'evening', and the result is word-for-word nonsense.

An invariable meaning must not be attached to verbs whose sense varies, though sometimes only slightly, according to the context. In that respect, the following require special attention:

AIMER: 'to love', or only 'to like': *aimer mieux* = to prefer.

DÉFENDRE: 'to defend', or 'to forbid'.

ENTENDRE: 'to hear', or 'to understand', or 'to intend': *Voici comment j'entends faire.*

GOÛTER: 'to taste', 'to relish', 'to enjoy', 'to appreciate'.

LAISSER: 'to let', 'to leave', 'to allow'.

METTRE: 'to put', 'to set'; *se mettre à* 'to begin to'; also 'to take': *Combien de temps mettez-vous à venir?* 'How long do you *take* to come?'

PRIER: 'to pray', 'to beg', 'to beseech', 'to ask', 'to request'.

SENTIR: 'to feel', 'to smell': *Cette fleur sent bon.*

SONGER: 'to think', 'to dream', 'to muse'.

§ 18. ON AVOIDING HYPNOTISM

The plain fact is that as the meaning of a French word varies with the context, so must the translation vary. Thus *passer* is no doubt 'to pass', but just as often it is something quite different, e.g. 'to spend' (*Où avez-vous* passé *les vacances?*); 'to slip on' (*passer une robe* = to slip on a frock); 'to cross' (passer *une rivière*, passer *la frontière*). In *Le train de Paris* passe *à six heures* 'to pass' is the one thing that *passer* does *not* mean—fortunately for us if we are waiting for it. It means not 'passes' without stopping as on the London Underground, but 'comes in', almost 'calls', as in *Je* passerai chez vous *ce soir à six heures.*

Translation of this little word *chez* which we have just used, is not easy. It is not made any easier by clinging, in season and out of season, to the cut-and-dried rendering 'at the house of'. Through no fault of ours, the English phrase is clumsy compared with *chez*, though it often serves the turn. But the day comes when it leaves us in the lurch, as when we have to translate this sentence, by Madame de La Fayette: *Ses amies la voyaient* chez elle *et* chez le duc de Nevers, *son beau-frère, dont* la maison *était ouverte à tout le monde.* We cannot without utter disrespect for English make such a jingle-jangle as: 'at her own *house* and at the *house* of her brother-in-law whose *house*', etc. There is nothing for it but to consider other possibilities and give up the habit of talking about 'house' every time we see *chez*. Looking at the sentence with a freer mind, we might say, for instance: 'Her friends could see her at her own home, or at her brother-in-law's, for the Duke of Nevers kept open house'.

With such examples before our eyes, let us endeavour to avoid being hypnotized and to see French words in the light of their general meaning. The fact that *bon* sometimes makes us think of 'good' is no reason for closing our eyes to 'kind', 'worthy', 'honest', etc., which may be the proper translation. For *bonté*, 'kindness', is more likely to be correct than 'goodness'. Sometimes *un* grand *silence* may of course be 'a great silence', but more frequently it is 'a *deep* silence'; *Il y a* grande apparence *que*..., 'There is *every* appearance that...'; *un* jeune *chien* is generally 'a puppy'; *la* jeune *bergère*, 'the shepherd *girl*'; *des vues* justes are '*sound* views'; *un temps lourd* is 'sultry weather'; *ombre* is 'shade', or 'shadow', or 'gloom', or 'dusk'; *un ciel triste* is 'a dull (or gloomy) sky'.

§ 19. BLANK CHEQUES

Some words are like blank cheques which the translator is left to fill in for himself according to circumstances. Such is *coup*, which in French takes its meaning from the accompanying word, and in English must be variously rendered: *un coup de pied* = a kick; *un coup de pistolet* = a pistol-shot; *un coup de vent* = a gust.

Such also is *faire*, which means 'to make', but also

'to do' and a great many other things besides. When does *faire* mean 'to make' and when 'to do'? We know instinctively, though quite unable perhaps to supply a foreigner with the rules and regulations. No Englishman says 'make' when he ought to say 'do'—unless when he is translating from French. Then instinct itself seems powerless against the fixed idea that *faire* is always 'to make'.

Here is a simple experiment: Take twelve good schoolboys (or, if preferred, twelve good 'grown-ups'). Take one little sentence containing *faire*, such as *Il ne savait que* faire *de ce visiteur*. Ask for a translation of the sentence. Listen politely to 'He did not know what to *make* of that visitor'. Then point out that this idiom with *make* does not happen to be known to the French. They express the idea otherwise, e.g. *Il ne savait que* penser *de ce visiteur*. The proper translation is 'He did not know what to *do* with that caller'—a very different matter. This would be a suitable opportunity for noting that *faire une visite* is 'to pay a visit' (or 'to pay a call'), *faire un effet charmant*, 'to produce (have) a charming effect', *faire un repas*, 'to have a meal', *faire signe à quelqu'un*, 'to beckon to someone', *faire de l'esprit*, 'to be funny', sometimes even 'to be witty', etc.—also for mentioning that *esprit* is not only 'spirit', but 'mind', 'state of mind', 'intelligence', 'wit'.

§ 20. WORD-FOR-WORD TRANSLATION

No French word can be always, in each and every context, translated by the same English word. Though we must before all things be accurate and render in English the exact force of each item in the French sentence, that is a very different thing from capping each French word with the English one which we have come to associate with it. Word-for-word translation of this type is not translation at all. It must be avoided at all costs. The exact English equivalent we must determine for ourselves in each case. For *La mémoire de sa triste enfance le poursuivit jusqu'au jour de sa mort*, which is the better translation: 'The memory of his sad infancy pursued him until the day of his death', or 'The memory of his dreary childhood dogged him to his dying day'? Within the narrow limits of accurate translation there is always room for truth. Rendering *être dix heures à cheval* by 'to be ten hours on horseback', or *un de mes amis* by 'one of my friends', is speaking the truth. It gives what the French phrase means. But rendering these phrases by 'to be ten hours in the saddle' and 'a friend of mine' is also speaking the truth, and speaking the truth like an Englishman.

The danger of recommending freedom within the bounds of truth is that those who are inclined to desert the text and follow their imagination may go too far. For instance, in the poem (p. 163) where Sully Prudhomme speaks of how in later days of peace a soldier may feel an old wound in his side, 'lurks' is an excellent rendering of *gît*:

Le souvenir du fer gît dans ses flancs meurtris.

But to learn that *gît* means 'lurks' is just as injudicious as to learn that *gît* means 'lies', for when *Ci-gît Voltaire* appears in the School Certificate examination some simple souls will be sure to say 'Here lurks Voltaire'!

§ 21. TRANSLATION BY A DIFFERENT PART OF SPEECH

So far from being a mere matter of substituting an English word for a French one, translation often involves the use of a different form. It often happens that in given circumstances French people normally express themselves differently from us. They say *Vous êtes* victime *d'une erreur*; we say, 'You are *labouring under* a misapprehension'. They may use a prepositional phrase where we use an adverb: *avec éclat* = gloriously, brilliantly; *avec volupté* = voluptuously; *sans le savoir* = unconsciously. They may use two words where we use a compound: *peu probable* = improbable. The Present Participle *ayant* may be simply 'with': *J'aime à m'asseoir au coin du feu* ayant *mon chien auprès de moi*, 'I like to sit down by the fire-side *with* my dog near me'. Similarly, *un visage* féminin = a *woman's* face; *enflammé* = blazing; *la Tour* penchée *de Pise* = the *leaning* tower of Pisa; *Allez* chercher (trouver) *le médecin* = Send *for* the doctor; *Il courut* prendre *un marteau* = He ran *for* a hammer; *Venez me* prendre = Come *for* me; *Il* finit par *se rendre* = He *eventually* surrendered.

§ 22. MISPLACED 'ACCURACY'

Naturalness ought never to be sacrificed to misplaced 'accuracy'. Two examples will suffice:

When we read in a novel that a man speaking to a tramp *lui donna une pièce de dix sous*, we need not calculate the exact value of the donation in sterling. That depends on the current rate of exchange, which again depends on matters probably beyond our ken, such as the date of the incident or the date of writing. In 1914 the value was fivepence. Since then it has been considerably but variably less. But that has nothing to do with the case. To all intents and purposes the man bestowed on the tramp *une pièce blanche* and the novelist is not perhaps anxious to specify that it was a half-franc piece and not a franc. The English for that is 'he gave him a sixpence', a small silver coin of the realm, which as a matter of fact was perhaps a shilling, perhaps only a threepenny bit.

When we are told that walking on the hills in Auvergne, you can see heather extending *sur des lieues et des lieues*, it is sufficient to say 'for miles and miles'. It is true that *une lieue* is 'a league' or two and a half miles, but it is used in preference to the *kilomètre* (= five-eighths of a mile) when the distance is not given as exactly measured. For *un quart de lieue* 'half a mile' is accurate enough.

§ 23. NAMES OF PECULIARLY FRENCH THINGS

Many things are found in France which are not found in England. That each of these should have its own English name is too much to expect. In the Pyrenees one cannot walk very far without seeing *un gave*, a mountain torrent running in a deep narrow bed. Anywhere else in France one could walk for ever and not see one. The name for it is, like the thing itself, peculiar to the Pyrenees, and when Alfred de Vigny described them in *Le Cor* he had to borrow the local term, just as we have to do in translating his line:

Sources, gaves, *ruisseaux, torrents des Pyrénées.*

No French description of forest scenery seems complete without the word *futaie*. What is *une futaie*? It is a part of a forest where the trees are allowed to grow to maturity, e.g. for 120 years, before they are cut down. To render the word neatly and suitably in English is not possible because, among other reasons, our forests are not in the keeping of a Government Forestry Department which applies strict and definite regulations. When in the books of André Theuriet, himself at one time a member of this Department, we meet the term *la réserve* we cannot hope to find an exact English equivalent. We can only ascertain what *la réserve* is, viz. *un canton de bois qu'on a laissé croître en futaie*, and then give the sense as best we may.

National customs have national names. Many are the idyllic scenes depicted by the French poets under the title *La Veillée*. The term evokes suggestions which are not English: the elder members of the family sitting round the fire with the neighbours who have dropped in for a talk, the younger members reading for pleasure or busy with their school exercises. *La veillée* is not 'a party', it is not 'an evening gathering', it is not 'ingle-nook conversations'; it is not necessarily 'The Cottar's *Saturday* Night', nor is it quite 'an evening by the fire'; it is—*la veillée*, the way in which, especially in the country, large numbers of French people spend the hours between supper and bed-time—and the way in which large numbers of English people do not. In translation *l'Angelus* can often be called 'Angelus' or 'evening bell'. For the verb which is seldom far away, *tinter* (meaning properly the slow ringing of a bell with the clapper striking only one side), we can say 'tolls' or 'rings' or 'tones'. But *l'Angelus* is heard three times a day, morning, noon and night, wherever there is a church in France, and, national conditions being so different, it is doubtful if we can ever quite convey in English the exact impression which *l'Angelus tinte* conveys in French.

§ 24. ON OMITTING OR SUPPLYING WORDS

To omit or to supply a word is justifiable when it can be shown that English usage requires such a course. A very simple case first: *une petite fille de six ans.* We all know that *ans* means 'years', but the ordinary English is 'a little girl of six'. The characteristic use of *c'est* is not English: *Ce qui vous étonne* c'*est que...*, 'What surprises one *is* that...'.

When *et* regularly used connects two adjectives it is not *always* to be translated: *un soleil pur* et *doux*, 'pure, soft sunlight'.

When *et* connects an adjective and a relative clause it is *never* to be translated: *pauvre écolier rêveur*, et *qu'on disait sauvage*, 'a poor dreaming schoolboy, whom people called shy'.

Where the French say *le bon Dieu* we take the attribute for granted and the normal English equivalent is 'God' or 'Providence'. *Un bruit semblable* à celui *du tonnerre* is not really 'a noise similar to that of thunder', but just 'a noise like thunder'. The French cannot, but we can, omit pronouns, adverbs, etc. such as these: 'The man *whom* I saw at Legrand's yesterday said *to me that* you had been in the shop and *that you had* left your umbrella *there*'. The possibility of lightening a translated sentence should always be kept in mind.

On the other hand, some expansion may be not only justifiable, but necessary: *sur votre parole* is 'on your word *of honour*'; *donner sa parole* 'to give one's word *for it*'; *chasser* 'to go shoot*ing*'; *Je ne trouve pas mon* *chapeau* is exactly 'I *can*not find my hat'; *le soleil baissé* is '*when* the sun *had* gone down'; *le soir venu*, '*when* night *had* come'; *Quand la vie est mauvaise on la rêve meilleure*, 'When life is hard one dreams *it were* better'. In cases of apposition, where French usage is more abrupt than English, something may have to be supplied: *Beaucoup...y ont conduit leurs troupeaux*, troupeaux eux-mêmes *d'un ordre plus élevé*, 'Many... led their flocks, *though they* themselves *were only* flocks of a higher order'.

§ 25. THE USES OF ENGLISH SYNONYM

French has a much less wide vocabulary than English. Thus *un cheval* does duty for both 'horse' and 'steed', *un chien* for both 'dog' and 'hound', *attention* for both 'attention' and 'care'. It follows that there are cases where the proper translation for *un cheval* is not that which we habitually associate with the word, but one which at the critical moment we are prone to forget. If only we bear in mind both 'horse' and 'steed' we soon decide which to use. As a general rule, mistranslation is due not to difficulty in choosing, but to the absence of words to choose from. When members of a class are supplied with several words and asked to say which is the best translation, they are almost invariably right in their choice.

It is unfortunate that they themselves do not supply the possible variants, especially in the written exercise. The wooden effect so noticeable even in the more accurate School Certificate renderings is mainly due to reluctance to draw upon the resources of English synonym. We do not mean here the inexhaustible resources illustrated in Shakespeare or stored in the

Oxford English Dictionary, merely those of the average schoolboy's own vocabulary. He translates *ardemment* or *énergiquement* by 'ardently' or 'energetically', although 'eagerly' and 'strenuously' are equally well known to him and equally worth considering as possible translations. He gives *chercher à atteindre* as 'seeking to attain' when 'striving to reach' may be just as good, or slightly better. To him *un vallon désert* is 'a deserted valley'. What is it to a French poet? Surely a little more—possibly 'some sequestered vale', 'a lonely glen'; and there are poems in which *désert* has all the haunting beauty of 'forlorn'.

French *force* may be English 'force', but may it not also be 'strength'? The verb *forcer* may be 'to force', 'to compel' or 'to oblige'. French *humble* is often English 'humble', no doubt, but it is also 'lowly'; *humilité* may be, besides 'humility', 'humbleness' or 'lowliness'. *Un instant* may be 'an instant', but it is perhaps more likely to be 'a moment' or even 'a minute'. *Attendez deux instants!* is almost certain to be 'Wait two minutes!' What is *rapide* if not 'rapid'? Sometimes 'swift' or 'swiftly-passing' or 'fleeting', as in *les heures rapides*. What is *répondre* if not 'to answer'? Sometimes 'to reply', sometimes 'to respond'. A word with an even greater vogue in France than in England is *vague*, which may mean 'dim', 'cloudy', 'indeterminate', etc., besides 'vague.' Of course *vêtu* is 'clothed', but that is not what we always call it, even in prose; 'attired', 'arrayed', 'clad', 'dressed' are not unknown to the average schoolboy. How, then, should he translate *vêtu* in *un gamin* vêtu *d'une blouse bleue*? By none of these words. Simply by 'wearing'. And if by suggesting one variant after another and then saying that none will do, we seem to be merely teasing the youthful learner, we must remind him that hard is the way of translators, and make amends by asking one more question—and answering it in English: *Vous sera-t-il* utile *d'avoir lu ce paragraphe?* Yes, it will be *useful.* In the next examination it may even prove to have been—*advantageous*!

§ 26. ON AVOIDING STILTED LANGUAGE

Philologers tell us that the French language is not *derived from* Latin, but *is* Latin. It is a direct descendant of Vulgar Latin. It contains other elements as well, but is in the main the Latin spoken by Cæsar's soldiers, Roman settlers, early Christian missionaries, etc., which was orally transmitted from them to generation after generation of Frenchmen, and underwent, naturally, considerable changes on the way. This original stock has been at all times copiously augmented by direct borrowings from Classical Latin, for the French have always looked upon themselves as inheritors of the Roman tradition and have taken kindly to Latin words, even long ones which to us look rather learned or even pedantic. We too have borrowed from Latin almost as extensively, but the Germanic element still remains the chief one in English and gives us many of our homeliest, most expressive words.

These facts have an important bearing upon translation. The word 'home' has no more sacred associations in our hearts than *la patrie*, = one's native land, has in French hearts. For a Frenchman the word *habitation* is a simpler term than 'habitation', and in some contexts we should find a more exact equivalent for it in the Germanic half of our vocabulary, for instance 'dwelling-place'. In French descriptive writing *con-*

templer le paysage is a phrase bound to occur sooner or later. We too 'contemplate' a scene, sometimes even scenery. But to 'gaze at' is usually all that the French writer means when he says *contempler*.

When people in Paris try to board a tramcar without waiting till other passengers have alighted and the conductor, very naturally, says *Laissez descendre, s'il vous plaît!* it would be as unfair to translate his *descendre* by 'descend' as it would be to translate his *laissez* by 'permit' or his *s'il vous plaît* by 'prithee'! To him *descendre du tramway* is nothing more nor less than what 'to get off the car' is to us; *descendre de cheval* is 'to get off a horse' or, at the very most, 'to dismount'. Let us therefore not forget in translation to be simple, and when we come across *se préparer, monotone, des rochers stériles, succomber,* before writing down 'to prepare oneself', 'monotonous', 'sterile rocks', 'succumb', let us think of 'get ready', 'dreary', 'barren rocks', 'yield'. Often, though not always, the simpler English word is the more effective. In like manner *apercevoir* means, besides 'perceive', to 'see', 'notice', 'spy', 'catch sight of'; *continuez* is 'go on'; *le soleil déclinait* just says that the sun 'was sinking' or 'going down'; *rendre* means, besides 'render', 'to make': *vous rendre heureux*, 'to make you happy'. It would be *singulier*, i.e. 'odd', 'strange', to talk about a school friend or chum as a 'school comrade', but in a French boy's use of *camarade d'école* there is nothing 'singular'.

§ 27. SOME DIFFICULT WORDS

The following words usually give the translator considerable trouble:

âpre: 'rough', 'rugged'; 'harsh', 'bitter': *l'âpre paysage*, 'the inhospitable scene'.

un astre: any heavenly body, sun, moon or stars; often = stars: *le cours des astres, consulter les astres.*

attendrissement (m.): 'emotion', 'tender emotion'.

disputer: Ney, *disputant sa montre à trois Cosaques,* was '*fighting them for* his watch'. *Ces deux élèves se disputent la première place,* 'These two boys are fighting (striving eagerly) for the first place'; *Ces objets se disputaient mon attention,* 'vied with each other (contended) for my attention'.

s'emparer de: 'to lay hold of', 'seize upon'.

ennui (m.): 'boredom', 'weariness', 'world-weariness'.

épreuve (f.): 'trial', 'ordeal'.

épris de: 'enamoured of'.

frisson (m.): a 'shiver' or 'shudder' or 'quiver'; it may be either of cold or of fear or of delight.

jeune: *jeune fille,* 'girl'; *jeunes gens,* 'young people', often 'young men' as opposed to *jeunes filles,* but we must reserve liberty to translate it otherwise, e.g. *les enfants et les jeunes gens* is not 'children and young men' ('young folks', 'young people'); it is 'children and older boys and girls'.

là-bas: 'away', 'yonder'.

percer: 'to show through': *Dans la bonhomie* perçait *le dédain,* 'Under the hail-fellow-well-met manner disdain *showed through*'; 'to peep through': *Des fleurs* perçaient *sous la neige,* 'Flowers *peeped through* the snow'; cp. *perce-neige,* a snowdrop'.

§ 28. SOME PREPOSITIONAL AND OTHER PHRASES

au besoin: 'if need be', 'at need'.

au bout d'une heure: 'in an hour'.

du côté de: 'in the direction of': *Le loup s'en alla* du côté du *village,* 'The wolf went off *in the direction of* the village'; *Je regardais à l'horizon* du côté du *bois ensoleillé,* 'I looked towards the horizon *in the direction of* the sun-lit wood'.

à l'écart: 'apart', 'aside', 'aloof', 'by oneself'.

au fond du jardin: 'at the end of the garden': au fond du *salon*, 'at the end furthest from the door'; au fond de *son âme*, 'in his inmost heart'.

à force de: 'by dint of'—which is a useful expression, but not always suitable; sometimes 'through' is a better translation, sometimes the construction should be altered, e.g. à force de *pleurer* ils..., 'they wept so bitterly that...'.

grâce à: 'thanks to', but the phrase has often a French flavour: grâce à *lui* may be 'through him', 'because of him'; grâce à *son intelligence*, 'because of his cleverness'.

au loin: 'afar', 'far and wide'.

de loin: 'at a distance', 'from afar': *Je l'ai entendu* de loin; *Il vient* de loin.

au beau milieu de: 'in the very middle of'.

par là: 'thereby'.

en pareil cas: 'in such a case'.

en plein air: 'in the open air'; *en* pleins *champs*, 'in the *open* fields'.

quoi qu'il en soit: 'be that as it may'.

Ce n'étaient que in enumerations, e.g. *Ce n'étaient que parfums et concerts infinis* somewhat like *Il n'y avait que*.

quel qu'il soit: 'whatever he (it) be'. In this phrase *quel* of course agrees with the noun or pronoun and the verb is in the Present or Past Subjunctive according to the verb in the main clause.

For *quelque* in *quelque grand qu'il soit*, see p. 85.

avoir de quoi vivre: literally 'to have the wherewithal to live', i.e. 'to have enough to live upon'.

il s'agit de: 'it is a question of'. But a more natural phrase can often be found: *Nos frères ont fait la République*. Il s'agit *pour nous* de *la sauver*, 'Our brethren made the Republic. What we have to do (Our part) is to save it'.

comme il arrive (parenthetical): 'as is apt to happen', 'as happens'.

avoir beau: 'in vain': J'avais beau *regarder de tous les côtés. Personne.* 'In vain I looked on every side. No one'. But it is impossible to treat every case of *avoir beau* in this way; the translation must vary according to the circumstances: Vous avez beau *essayer, vous n'y réussirez jamais,* 'Try as you like, you will never succeed'; Vous avez beau *dire,* 'It's no use saying', 'You can say what you like'; Vous aurez beau *faire, vous n'arriverez pas à temps,* 'In spite of all your efforts (For all you can do), you will not arrive in time'.

on dirait que: 'one would *think* (*not* say) that'.

§ 29. THE CONSTRUCTION OF THE SENTENCE

Much more important than the meaning of any given word is the meaning of the sentence as a whole. This depends on the construction. When the construction is not understood, translation is a hopeless task. The sentence, or even the entire passage, will remain unintelligible. Once a wrong assumption has been made, there is a tendency to make the other words suit it. Thus the initial error leads to many more.

The prepositions require particular care, especially when a phrase intervenes between them and the word which governs them. This sentence has been found to defy examination candidates: *Les délégués du peuple se flattaient de parler au nom de la patrie et, puisant leurs pensées dans la Bible, d'être, eux aussi, inspirés de Dieu.* It is quite simple if attention is paid to the construction of *de* in *d'être.* Then this *de* is seen to depend on *se flattaient* and the sense becomes clear.

Here is another instance, showing how deceptive prepositions may be: *L'Apennin central avec tout son bric-à-brac pêle-mêle: ses tabourets, ses tables, ses pupitres et ses* chaises de marbre... *la plus médiocre des chaînes de montagnes*... *les parents pauvres de l'Alpe.* In a recently published translation, excellent as a whole though not always exact in detail, this is rendered: 'The Central Apennines with all their bric-à-brac huddled together, stools, tables, desks and marble chairs...the most common-place of the mountain ranges...the poor relatives of the Alps'. The reader who knew no French but had an inquiring turn of mind might perhaps ask what 'poor relatives' are. They seem to be only translator's English for 'poor relations'. But if he were anxious also to know what the 'stools, tables and desks' were made of, he would receive no enlightenment from the English, which states that the chairs were of marble and about the rest says nothing at all. The French is more communicative. It tells us that *all* the objects enumerated were made of marble, since *de marbre* clearly goes with *tables*, etc., as well as with *chaises*, which happens to be the last mentioned.

The agreement of participles and adjectives is apt to be overlooked, yet it is essential to the sense.

The gender of a pronoun often leaves no possible doubt in French as to what noun it stands for in a preceding sentence. But the English rendering may be obscure or ambiguous or erroneous because our 'it' does not show gender.

The pronoun may give the key to the whole sentence. Do not begin to translate until you are quite sure that you understand the construction and can point out with certainty the noun for which the personal pronoun stands.

§ 30. THE CONSTRUCTION OF THE VERB

The construction of the verb is naturally a vital point. With *faire* we must always bear in mind that an active infinitive dependent on it may be equivalent to an English passive: *se faire nommer*, 'to get oneself appointed'; that when it governs two objects one of them is a dative: *Napoléon* lui [i.e. à son cheval] fit *flairer* la fumée *de l'obus*, 'Napoleon made his horse sniff at the shell'.

The instance of *flairer* in the preceding sentence recalls the fact that the English equivalents of some French verbs require a preposition. Such are *attendre* = to wait *for*, *chercher* = to look *for*, *écouter* = to listen *to*, *regarder* = to look *at*, etc. The fact is elementary, but it is often neglected, with the result that the construction of the sentence is misunderstood. A striking example will be found on p. 98.

The absolute construction as in *Les yeux sur ses enfants* is sometimes not recognized or, when recognized, is not accompanied by the necessary 'with': '*With* her eyes fixed on her children'.

The case of *devenir* requires care. *Il ne savait pas ce qu'ils étaient devenus* is not 'what they had become' but 'what *had become of them*'. Hence *Le pauvre écolier devenait ce qu'il pouvait* is a French way of saying that he was left to his own devices. Cp. *Il ne sait que devenir*, 'He does not know what to do with himself'.

§ 31. ON ALTERING THE FRENCH CONSTRUCTION

The constructions used in the rendering must of course be English. Foreign syntax cannot be carried over without danger. Where the French construction is un-English it should be altered without hesitation. Here, as always, we must follow Nature's rule and speak naturally. 'Do you wish that I should accompany you?' is a stilted phrase. It is not for that reason debarred from ever appearing in any translation. It might suit some circumstances very well. But it is almost certain to be unsuitable when its use is merely due to laziness on the part of a translator unwilling to think of anything better for *Voulez-vous que je vous accompagne?* In nine cases out of ten the English should be simply 'Do you want me to go with you?' or 'Shall I come with you?' *J'aime mieux que vous ne restiez pas*, 'I prefer you not to stay', or 'I'd rather you didn't stay'; *Je voudrais être là,* I wish I were there'. In oral work a boy who says, 'Do you wish that I should accompany you?' can be taken off his high horse without much effort and made to talk like an ordinary person. In written work he must make the effort himself and be natural.

§ 32. ON PRESERVING THE FRENCH ORDER OF WORDS

The order of the French words should be preserved so far as possible. It is seldom haphazard. It was selected by the author as the best for the expression of his ideas in French, and the chances are that it will be the best in English. The safe rule is: **Never make a change in the order of the French unless you can show**

that you gain by it. The common tendency to change for the sake of change is quite unjustifiable. But the order of words in a good translation must be that in which an English writer would *naturally* place them.

Departure from the French order is necessary when English idiom demands it: *sans boire ni manger* is obviously *not* 'without drinking or eating'. The almost regular inversion of subject and verb in a Relative Clause is not customary in English and need not be reproduced. Adverbs of time and place which generally begin a French sentence come more naturally into the body of the sentence in English: Alors *Charles fut amené à Whitehall,* 'Charles was *now* brought to Whitehall'.

We need not reproduce the French habit of throwing forward the subject as in Il *part, le grand* navire, 'The great ship gets under weigh'. In parentheses French inverts subject and verb regularly, but English inverts only now and again: '*Hélas,*' *dites-vous,* '"Alas," you say', '*Oui,*' *ajouta-t-il,* '"Yes," he added'. In some cases retention of the original order would create ambiguity or worse: e.g. Anatole France in *Le Jongleur de Notre-Dame*: '*Hélas!*' *soupirait-il en se promenant seul dans le petit jardin* sans ombre du couvent, '"Alas!" he sighed, as he walked to and fro all alone in the *unshaded* little garden of the monastery'.

Occasionally the French subject becomes the object in English, and vice-versa: Vous *nous manquerez beaucoup,* 'We shall miss you very much'; L'enfant *lui plut,* 'He took a liking to the child'; Il *plaît à tout le monde,* 'Everybody likes him'.

More liberty is of course necessary in translating poetry, where one of the main difficulties is the constant inversion, against which the translator must always be on his guard.

GRAMMATICAL HINTS

§ 33. THE INDEFINITE ARTICLE

Un (*une*) is not always 'a' ('an').

It is often 'some': *comme un chant triste*, 'like some sad song'.

When opposed to some other number *un* is not the Indefinite Article, but the Numeral 'one': *Je donnerais* deux étés *pour* un *automne*, 'I would give *two* summers for *one* autumn'. This point is not always so apparent as in the above case, and is generally missed by the hasty translator.

A phrase like *un son de flûte* really means 'a flute-sound', but the shade of meaning can seldom be exactly rendered in English, which says either '*the* sound of a flute' or else 'a sound *as* of a flute'; *comme un cœur d'enfant* may be rendered 'as a child's heart' or 'as the heart of a child'.

In phrases of the type *une femme* d'une *rare beauté* the article can be retained in English, but it is usually better to drop it: 'a woman of rare beauty'.

The article, omitted in *Vous êtes prisonnier*, must be supplied: 'You are *a* prisoner'. Similarly, in apposition, *Il est franc*, qualité rare, 'He is outspoken—an uncommon quality', or 'He is outspoken—which is an uncommon quality'.

§ 34. THE DEFINITE ARTICLE

The definite article, used with abstract nouns in French and omitted in English, must be retained when there is a further qualification; *la politesse* is 'politeness' but *L'exactitude est la politesse des rois* is 'Punctuality is *the* politeness of kings'. It is to be omitted, e.g. in *Après* le *souper on ira* au *lit*, 'After supper we shall go to bed', and also in sentences like *M. Daudet a* le *charme*, where the sense is 'M. Daudet has what is called "charm"', the abstract quality 'charm', as opposed to *M. Daudet a* du *charme*, where *du charme* means 'some charm' and the sense is merely that 'M. Daudet is not devoid of charm'.

In the plural the definite article makes the sense general; for instances, *les grandes pensées*, 'great thoughts', i.e. 'all great thoughts'; *Les* belles plumes font *les* beaux oiseaux, 'Fine feathers make fine birds'.

Care must be taken not to overlook the difference between *les* and *des*, which may be used in the same sentence to bring out some necessary distinction, e.g. *Les enfants sèment devant la porte* des *grains et* les *miettes du repas*, 'The children scatter in front of the door grain and *the* crumbs left over from the meal'. The point may not always seem very important, but the French author was at some trouble to make it and his intention should be respected. The number of marks lost per annum by mere inattention in mistaking *les* for *des*, and vice-versa, must be considerable.

§ 35. THE ADJECTIVE

A French adjective is very readily converted into a noun: *un pauvre* = a poor man, *un blessé* = a wounded man, *une vieille* = an old woman, *le petit* = the child, the boy, *la petite* = the girl; *le haut d'un arbre* = the top of a tree, *au haut de l'escalier* = at the top of the staircase.

The following adjectives require caution, as they are used in various senses.

AUTRE: *les autres*, 'the rest'; *d'autres*, 'others', 'some others'; *des autres*, 'of (from) the others'; *nous* (*vous*) *autres*, 'we (you) folks', or simply emphasising 'we (you)', e.g. *nous autres Français*, 'we Frenchmen', *vous autres Anglais*, 'you English people'. Like 'other', *autre* often means 'different' and, by a restriction of sense, 'differing for the better', 'greater': *Les exemples vivants sont d'un* autre *pouvoir*, 'Living examples are of much greater force' or 'have much more force'. For the similar use of *autrement* see p. 64, § 51.

SEUL: *une seule fenêtre*, 'a single window'; *au seul récit de ses malheurs*, 'at the mere recital of his misfortunes'; *les seuls échos*, 'the echoes alone'.

TEL: *une telle terreur*: 'such terror' or 'such a terror'; *de tels hommes*, 'such men'.

TOUT: *Tout homme qui pense*, 'Every thinking man'.

§ 36. THE PLURAL OF NOUNS

The plural may have a different sense from the singular: *la clarté* = light, *des clartés* = gleams of light, patches of brightness; also, intelligence, enlightenment; *lumière* = light, *lumières* = enlightened judgment (advice); *le fer* = iron, i.e. the sword, *les fers* = irons, chains; *le genou* = the knee, *sur les genoux* = on one's lap. The plural of words like *le blé* denotes growing or standing corn as opposed to *du blé*, corn in the form of grain: *les blés* = the cornfields; *l'orge* = barley, *les orges* = the barley-fields; *le seigle* = rye, *les seigles* = rye-fields. Somewhat similarly *le chaume* = stubble (also thatch), *les chaumes* = stubble-fields.

The plural of an abstract noun means 'acts of', 'cases of'. This use is easily understood when we remember that in French as in English the singular too may indicate an act, e.g. *Je croyais lui faire une politesse*, 'I thought I was doing him a politeness'. French goes much further than English in this respect, e.g. *les vengeances* = acts of vengeance, *les petites trahisons* = cases of petty treachery. Where Anatole France says in *Abeille*: *On n'aime sûrement que ceux qu'on aime jusque dans leurs* faiblesses *et leurs* pauvretés, we can say 'weaknesses', but not so easily 'pettinesses' as 'acts of pettiness' or 'petty actions'.

§ 37. THE RELATIVE PRONOUN

The relative pronoun is more readily used in French than in English. It sometimes stands alone=*celui qui*, 'anyone who, whoever'; *Qui dort dîne*; and often appears where we should certainly put a participle: *Je le vois qui vient*, 'I see him coming'; *la table, que recouvre une nappe*, 'the table, covered with a cloth'. An excessive number of 'who's' in an English passage suggests a bad translation from French. The fault may be remedied by expanding 'who' into 'and he' (e.g., in Model Lesson I A, p. 84), or occasionally using a participle, or by employing the ordinary English 'but' for *qui* used negatively in sentences like *Il n'est point de jour* qui *ne doive finir*: 'There is no day *but* must come to an end'.

When *que* appears idiomatically in a sentence like *Quelle belle chose* qu'*une forêt par un beau soir d'été!* it may usually be represented by 'is': 'What a beautiful thing a forest is on a fine summer evening!' In the idiomatic *C'est se tromper* que *de croire que*, etc., the *que* is simply dropped: 'It is a mistake to think that', etc.

The objective *que* is frequently mistaken for a nominative because of the French habit of inverting subject and verb in Relative Clauses. But there is a world of difference between *Pierre,* qu'*a frappé Paul* and *Pierre,* qui *a frappé Paul*!

It is absolutely necessary to remember that *qu'* always stands for *que*, never for *qui*, and that *que* relative must be the object, not the subject of the subordinate clause. The danger of forgetting this is increased by the fact that frequently the wrong translation makes sense—of a kind: *ce terrain inculte que domine un monument*, 'that uncultivated ground which a monument overlooks (over which a monument towers)'; *dans son regard noir, qu'éteint un sombre ennui*, 'in his gloomy glance, dimmed by dull listlessness'.

§ 38. THE RELATIVE ADVERB *OÙ*

The relative adverb *où* is in much more common use than 'where' or 'whither'. It is frequently to be rendered by 'at which', 'in which', 'on which', 'to which', etc. *C'était l'heure où* may be 'It was the time when' or 'at which'; *Au moment où je l'ai vu* need not be fully rendered 'At the moment when I saw him'; we usually say 'The moment I saw him'. The possibility of using 'with' should be kept in mind: *Les Nains portaient des capuchons* où *des feuilles de fougère étaient piquées*, 'The Dwarfs wore hoods *with* fern-leaves stuck in them'; *des rochers* où pendaient *de longues algues*, 'rocks *with* long drooping sea-weed'.

§ 39. THE PERSONAL PRONOUN

At school *il* is rashly assumed to be always 'he' or else 'it', referring to some noun. But *il* is often quite impersonal. Thus *il est* simply = *il y a*, in *Il est, au fond des mers, une île où...*, 'There is, in the far seas, an island where...'; *il était* = *il y avait*; *Il était une bergère*, 'There was once a shepherd girl'.

The impersonal *il* often prepares the way for the subject when there is Inversion: *Il se fit un grand silence*, 'There was a deep silence'. In such cases the French order of words should be preserved unless the effect in English would be too odd: *Il s'élevait des cris* is best rendered by 'Shouts arose'; so, *Il ne s'est rien fait de mal*, 'Nothing wrong has been done'; *L'on nous lançait des pierres. Il en tomba une devant moi.* 'They threw stones at us. One fell in front of me'.

The accented form *lui*, used to mark some contrast, occasionally perplexes the translator. It is 'he' emphasized or italicized: *Lui est là, sa femme n'est pas venue*, '*He* is here, his wife has not come'. Similarly, *eux*, e.g. *Je m'arrêtai, timide, désirant encore les entendre.* Eux *me virent*, 'I stopped, feeling shy, and wishing to hear them further. *They* caught sight of me'.

In the special use of the Dative of the Personal Pronoun known as the 'Ethic Dative', the pronoun is not as a general rule translated by the corresponding English form: *Fermez-moi ce livre*, 'Just close that book'; *Allez me jeter cette lettre à la poste*, 'Please go and post this letter'.

§ 40. *EN* AND *Y*

In many sentences it is unnecessary to translate *en* meaning 'of them'; *en* is in fact often redundant, as in *De tous ces livres il* en *est un que je garderai soigneusement*, where *en* is the same thing as *de tous ces livres.* But *en* is often essential to the meaning: *Il n'*en *est que plus heureux*, 'He is all the happier for that' ('on that account'); *La petite fille aura demain les paupières* *gonflées et sa beauté* en *sera moindre*, '...her beauty will be thereby less'.

It is well to be familiar with the idiomatic uses of *en* illustrated in e.g. *Il* en *est de l'histoire comme des vastes paysages: on ne les découvre que quand on a gravi le sommet*, 'It is with history as with vast landscapes...'; *Il* en *est ainsi de la plupart des hommes*, 'It is so with most men'.

Nor is *y* always to be explicitly rendered: *Il se connaît en musique, moi je ne m'*y *connais pas*, 'He is a judge of music, I am not'; *Tu n'*y *vois pas.—Mais si, j'*y *vois très bien*, 'You don't see.—Yes I do, I see very well'. But the presence of *y* in the sentence must never be overlooked, and translation of it is often essential: *Les grenadiers sentirent la leçon terrible qu'il leur donnait. Moi, j'*y *sentis*, etc. '...I felt *in it*', etc.

Remember that *en* and *y* are two of the most common, most idiomatic and most expressive words in the French language. Never treat them in an offhand way, for they will of a certainty have their revenge.

§ 41. *ON*

There is of course no harm in using 'one' in English, but as it is not nearly so common as *on* is in French it can be easily overdone and may sound odd. It is a marked feature of the language apparently spoken in that quaint world which some translators inhabit, no longer France nor yet quite England, the world where 'one descends' from 'one's apartment', 'seats oneself' in a 'public garden' and 'contemplates spectacles' of which some are 'intriguing' and others 'give to think'. 'One' can do these things in English if 'one' is so disposed, but not with such unfailing regularity. 'One's'

English suffers and, instead of always writing down 'one', 'one' should consider the other methods of translating *on*, namely:

1. By 'we', 'you', 'they', etc.; see Model Lesson II A, p. 117; or by 'people': *On nous dit souvent*, 'People often say'.

2. By the Passive: *Ici on parle anglais*, 'English spoken'.

3. By a different turn of phrase: *On répondit quelque chose*, 'There was some answer'.

§ 42. THE POSSESSIVE ADJECTIVE

It should be remarked that *son* (*sa*, *ses*) is often insufficiently rendered by 'his', 'her', 'its', and requires the addition of 'own': *un garçon de mon âge*, 'a boy of my own age'.

When *son* is more fully emphasized, the pronoun with *à* is added: *son passé à lui*, 'his own past', and this usage must be noted in translation.

In many cases French uses the Definite Article where we use the Possessive Adjective, e.g. *Il baissa les yeux*, 'He dropped *his* gaze (lowered his eyes)': *Il me tourna le dos*, 'He turned *his* back on me'. Similarly, *Il me prit la main*, 'He seized my hand'.

Avoid translating *son, sa, ses*, by 'his' in such a sentence as: *Il faut aimer* son *prochain comme soi-même*, 'One should love *one's* neighbour as oneself'.

§ 43. THE VERB: MOOD

The rules for the use of the Subjunctive, which are so important in French Composition, require no detailed treatment here. It is enough for the purposes of translation into English to exercise care in recognizing the

Subjunctive; e.g. we must not confuse *répondit* and *répondît*, *fut* and *fût*, and especially *eut* and *eût*, or neglect the sense of constructions like: *Que chacun se retire*, 'Let everyone withdraw' (and with omission of *que*: *Plût à Dieu* and *A Dieu ne plaise*, 'Might it please God', 'May it not please God', i.e. 'God forbid!') and *Faisons que le travail soit une joie*, 'Let us act so that (Let us see to it that) work is a delight'; *Non certes que les écoliers* soient *de petits saints*, 'Not indeed that schoolboys are plaster saints'.

§ 44. THE VERB: TENSE

Of all the possible errors in translation, an error in tense is perhaps the worst, partly because it could so easily have been avoided, but chiefly because it conveys an entirely wrong impression of the facts described. The translator knows perfectly well what the tense is—it is not very difficult to distinguish *est* from *s'est*, *voulut* from *voulait*, *pourra* from *pourrait*—but he does not reflect on the matter at all. He just writes down the English tense which first occurs to him. It may not make nonsense, but it will mean something quite different from the French. Relationship in time is always very carefully indicated in French and to translate tenses loosely opens the door to grievous error. For *Le soleil* s'est voilé...*l'horizon s'obscurcit*, to say 'The sun is veiled...the horizon is getting dark' is not true; *s'est voilé* is not in the same tense as *s'obscurcit*. Nor is it the same thing as *est voilé*. The sentence means that the sun *has* become veiled and that consequently the horizon is getting dark. In *Une grande nappe blanche* s'est étendue *en silence sur la campagne* the writer did not say *est étendue* because he meant '*has spread*'. Examine carefully as typical the following forms: *elle s'assit,* or *elle s'est assise,* 'she sat down' (*act*); *elle s'asseyait,* 'she used to sit (down)' or 'she was sitting down' (*act*); *elle est assise,* 'she is sitting' (*state*); *elle s'était assise,* 'she had sat down' (*act*); *elle était assise,* 'she was sitting' (*state*). Perhaps the most gratuitous error, and one of the commonest, is to translate a Future in the Past as if it were a Future, or vice-versa.

The Past Historic should be carefully watched, because its use often indicates a special shade of meaning, so marked that something must be added to the English verb, or a different verb be used: *Elle comprit,* 'She (then) understood—She realized'; *Elle sut,* 'Then she knew—She learned'; *Elle crut mourir de joie,* 'She nearly died of joy'; *Elle* voulut *me faire partager son souper. Je répondis que je* voulais *attendre un peu,* 'She *insisted* on my sharing her supper. I replied that I *would rather* wait a little'.

Of course when idiom comes into play, alteration of the French tense may be necessary, e.g. *Voilà plus d'une heure que je vous* attends, 'I *have been* waiting for you more than an hour'; *J'*étais *là depuis longtemps,* 'I *had been* there for a long time'; *Il y avait des mois qu'il était là,* 'He *had been* there for months'.

The force of the Imperfect must be noted, but it is not always to be rendered by the form in '-ing' or by 'used to'; frequently 'would' makes a better equivalent: *Mon grand-père disait souvent...,* 'Grandfather would often say...'.

When the translator, who for the French Imperfect has overdone the use of '-ing', comes to the Present, he tends to forget '-ing' altogether. *J'habite Londres maintenant,* 'I *am living* in London now; *Qui parle?* 'Who is speaking?'

In several idiomatic constructions the Future is translated by a Present, and the Future in the Past is translated by a simple Past tense: e.g. *Dès que vous* serez *fatigué, nous nous reposerons,* 'As soon as you *are* tired we shall take a rest'; *Quand vous* serez *vieux,* 'When you *are* old'; *Il se promit d'avertir son ami quand l'occasion* s'en offrirait, 'He promised himself (resolved) to warn his friend when the chance to do so *occurred*'; *Il avait décidé qu'il partirait au moment où le roi* rendrait *son dernier soupir,* '. . . when the King *breathed* his last'; *Quand cela serait vrai, quel mal y aurait-il?* 'Even though that were true, where would be the harm?' *Il l'aurait dit qu'on ne l'aurait pas cru,* 'Even if he had said it, no one would have believed him'.

§ 45. THE PARTICIPLES

The Present Participle has often the force of 'while', 'though'; e.g. Corneille, *Le Cid*:

Et poursuivre le crime aimant *le criminel,*

where Chimène demands vengeance for the offence, *though* loving the offender.

The Past Participle is more freely employed than in English: *arrivés à* = arriving at; *rentrés de l'école* = home from school. It sometimes requires to be expanded into a Relative Clause: *Son cheval, tenu près de lui, broutait l'herbe,* 'His horse, *which was being* held near him, was munching the grass'.

The Accusative Absolute construction is more common than the corresponding English Nominative Absolute and often requires to be expanded into a clause: *La lettre terminée, il la relut,* 'When the letter was finished he re-read it'.

§ 46. THE GERUND

The remark made in § 45 about the Present Participle applies also to the Gerund. *Il a glissé en descendant l'escalier*, 'He slipped *while* coming downstairs'; *Je me distrais de mes malheurs en songeant aux divers événements de la journée*, 'I get away from my present afflictions *by* thinking of the divers events of the day'; *Il a fait fortune en travaillant dur*, 'He made his fortune *by* working hard'; *En ouvrant la porte*, '*On* opening the door'.

When *tout* is added it makes the phrase concessive, meaning 'though', 'even while', or 'despite the fact': *Tout en admettant que vous avez raison*, 'Although admitting (Despite the fact that I admit) you are right'.

After *après*, *sans*, etc., the French regularly use *avoir* where we generally do without 'having': *après avoir* parlé, 'after speaking'.

§ 47. *DEVOIR, POUVOIR, SAVOIR, VOULOIR*

The meaning of these verbs depends peculiarly on their tense:

DEVOIR:

Je dois y aller, 'I have to go'.
J'ai dû y aller, 'I have had to go'.
Je devais y aller, 'I was to go', 'I should have gone'.
Ils durent s'arrêter, 'They had to stop'.
Vous devriez aller, 'You should go'.

The distinction between *nous devons y aller* and *nous devrions y aller* is that the first is necessity, the second, moral obligation.

J'aurais dû y aller, 'I ought to have gone'.

POUVOIR:

Je peux vous le dire, 'I can tell you'.

Je pourrai y aller demain, 'I can (= shall be able to) go to-morrow'.

J'aurais pu y aller, 'I could have gone'.

Note: *Il se peut que* (Subjunctive), 'It may be that'.

Il aurait pu, il aurait dû être heureux, et il ne l'était pas, 'He could have been, he should have been happy and he was not'.

SAVOIR:

The Future in the Past has the sense of a modified Present in: *Je ne saurais vous le dire*, 'I cannot tell you', i.e. 'I should be unable to (even if I tried)'.

VOULOIR:

Je veux savoir, 'I want to know'.

J'aurais voulu en parler plus longuement, 'I should have liked to speak about it more fully'.

Venez quand vous voudrez, 'Come when you like'.

§ 48. THE CONSTRUCTION AFTER VERBS

Some verbs have a different sense according as they are construed with a preposition or stand alone:

Abuser = to deceive; *abuser de* = to abuse; *user* = to wear out; *user de* = to use: *Mon fils a usé ses souliers*; Usez de *patience. Il les* traitait d'*enfants*, 'He called them children' [cp. *Ces îles peuvent être* qualifiées de *rochers*, 'These islands may be termed rocks']; *Il les traitait trop* en *enfants*, 'He treated them too much like children'. *Servir* = to serve; *servir à* = to serve for, do duty for, to help: *Cela* sert à *prouver que*, 'That helps to prove that'; *servir de* = to serve as: *Cette pièce nous* sert de *petit salon*, 'We use this room as a parlour'.

The construction after *croire* is clear enough, but the sense is somewhat subtle: *Cet acteur joue si bien qu'il fait* croire aux *personnages qu'il représente,* 'This actor plays so well that he makes us believe in the existence of the characters whom he represents', i.e. makes his characters live; cp. Musset, *Sur une Morte*:

Elle pensait, si le vain bruit
D'une voix douce et cadencée,
Comme le ruisseau qui gémit,
Peut faire croire à la pensée,

i.e. can make us believe that thought is there (and not mere sound), can give an impression of thought; *On* se croirait *au milieu de l'hiver,* 'You *would think* we were in the midst of winter'; *Je* vous croyais *plus de courage,* 'I gave you credit for more courage', 'I thought you were more courageous'; *Un endroit qu'on* croit *reconnaître,* 'A place one seems to recognize'.

When the Infinitive depending on *faire* (also on *entendre, laisser, voir*) has a direct object, a Noun or Pronoun governed by these verbs is put in the Dative: *J'ai entendu dire à des connaisseurs que ce tableau est son chef-d'œuvre,* 'I have heard connoisseurs say that this picture is his masterpiece'.

The passive sense of the Infinitive after *laisser*, etc., must be noted: *Ils se sont laissé prendre,* 'They have allowed themselves to be caught', familiarly 'They have got caught'.

§ 49. REFLEXIVES

The root idea of the reflexive form is 'self'. In translation this should always be noted: *Il faut s'être dit,* 'One must have said to oneself'. But it need not always be stated; *se laver* is of course 'to wash oneself', but 'to wash' is quite enough. The sense has often to be given by using a different word: *dormir* = to sleep, *s'endormir* = to fall asleep; *plaindre* = to pity, *se plaindre* = to complain; *se tenir dans la chambre* = to stay in the room. The difference between the verb with *se* and without *se* is sometimes slight: *jouer* = to play, *se jouer* = to play about, to sport, to frolic.

By an extension of scope, the reflexive becomes equivalent to a passive and must often be so rendered in English: *Cela ne se dit pas*, 'That is not said'; *Cela ne peut pas se faire*, 'That cannot be done'.

By a further extension the reflexive comes to mean 'each other'. This need not be the actual translation used every time, but it is a sense which is very often overlooked in translation: *Il vaut mieux ne pas* nous revoir *car nous pourrions* nous *disputer*, 'It is better we should not meet again, for we might squabble'.

The following require special notice:

douter de: 'to doubt', 'to mistrust', 'to lose faith in'.
se douter de: 'to suspect'.
passer: 'to pass', 'to spend', etc. (see p. 29, §18).
se passer de: 'to do without': *Cela se passe de commentaire*, 'That requires no comment' (to be carefully distinguished from *se passer* without *de*: *Ce n'est pas ainsi que les choses se passent*, 'That is not how things are done').
se plaire: 'to like to be', 'to be happy', etc.: *Je me plais ici*, 'I like this place'.
se plaire à: 'to take delight in': *Je me plais à me rappeler*, 'I take delight in recalling'.

§ 50. CONJUNCTIONS

Even the simple task of translating the co-ordinating Conjunctions *et* and *mais* is not always as simple as it looks. The words which *et* connects may not in English admit of being connected by 'and'. In some cases *et* should not be translated at all. *Une seule et mauvaise lampe* is not 'a single and poor lamp' but 'a single lamp and a poor one at that', or just 'one poor lamp'. Similarly, *mais* is not always to be translated by 'but' (see p. 151). It is not to be translated at all in phrases like *Ah* mais *tu m'ennuies*, 'What a tiresome person you are'; *aussi* may mean (1) 'also' or (2, usually with Inversion) 'and so', 'therefore', 'consequently'; *ni* after *sans* is 'or'; *sans boire ni manger*, 'without eating or drinking'; *soit...soit* may be noted here; it means 'whether...or', when it introduces an alternative reason, but often the more natural English for it is 'either...or'.

Of the subordinating Conjunctions the following require special attention in translating:

À MESURE QUE: properly 'in proportion as', although 'as' alone is often a sufficient translation.

SI: in *à peine si* the *si* can usually be neglected: *A peine si la cloche avertit la contrée*, 'Hardly did the bell warn the countryside'.

si...ne usually means 'unless', 'except', rather than 'if...not': *Si le bon Dieu ne le protège*, 'Unless God protects him'.

Phrases like *Si* (or *Quelque*) *grand qu'il soit* are to be translated as 'However great he is' or 'Great though he is'.

QUE: may be equivalent to almost any conjunction in English, as it may stand for almost any in French: *Que l'occasion fût grande ou petite*, 'Whether the occasion was great or small'; *Peu importe que ce soit vous ou lui*, 'It matters little whether it is you or he'; Qu'*un héros inédit fasse le bien modestement, est-ce que l'histoire le reconnaîtra?*, 'Suppose' or 'If'...

When *que* is used to avoid repetition of *quand*, etc., the English conjunction need not, as a rule, be repeated: *Quand l'horizon s'empourpre et* que *le soleil va paraître,* 'When the horizon reddens *and* the sun is about to appear'; *Puisque je ne sais où il est et* qu'*il ne sait où me trouver,* 'Since I do not know where he is and he does not know where to find me'.

After *comme* and *tant* the order of words is different from that in English: *Comme il parle clairement,* 'How distinctly he speaks'; *Tant ils vous sont familiers,* 'So familiar are they to you'.

§ 51. ADVERBS

Several adverbs which have more than one meaning must be rather narrowly scanned, lest their sense be missed.

D'ABORD: (1) 'firstly', 'at first', as opposed to *ensuite,* 'next', or 'secondly', and to *enfin,* 'lastly'; (2) 'first of all': *Lisez d'abord le passage,* 'Read the passage first of all'.

AUTREMENT: (1) 'otherwise': *Lisez d'abord le passage. Autrement vous ferez sûrement des fautes,* '... Otherwise you will certainly make mistakes'. (2) 'far more' (cp. *autre,* p. 50, § 35): *Il est autrement intelligent que son frère,* 'He is far cleverer than his brother'.

BIEN: (1) 'very', 'very much': *J'en suis bien content,* 'I am very much pleased with it'. (2) 'quite': *Il n'est pas bien jour,* 'It is not quite day'; *Est-ce bien sûr?* 'Is it quite certain?'

N.B. (1) *Vous sentez* bien *que vous avez tort?* 'You *do* feel you are wrong?' (2) *bien de* + Definite Article = *beaucoup de*: *Il fallait* bien du *courage,* bien de la *patience,* bien des *efforts*: 'It required much courage, much patience, many efforts'.

CEPENDANT: (1) 'however'; (2) 'meantime': *Cependant l'ouvrage se faisait*, 'Meantime work was proceeding'.

COMME: (1) 'as if', 'as it were': *On voyait, lorsqu'on suivait les étroits sentiers, comme des lacs*, 'We could see, as we followed the narrow paths, as it were lakes (what seemed like lakes)'. (2) 'as...as': *naïf comme un savant*, 'as simple-minded as a scholar'. (3) 'such as':

...L'air
N'a caressé que des créatures divines,
Comme *les feuilles, l'eau, les herbes et les fleurs.*

SI: (1) 'so': *un si grand prix*, 'so great a price'. (2) 'such': *une si terrible chute*, 'such a terrible fall'.

TOUJOURS: (1) 'always'; (2) 'still': *Il pleut toujours* could have either meaning, according to the context: (1) *Il pleut* toujours *quand je prends mon parapluie*; (2) *La pluie a-t-elle cessé? Non, il pleut* toujours.

TOUT: (1) 'just': *tout comme moi*. (2) 'right': *tout en haut*, 'right at the top', 'at the very top'.

§ 52. NEGATIVES

After *craindre*, etc., *ne* alone is not to be translated, but *ne...pas* is: *Je crains qu'il ne vienne*, 'I am afraid he will come'; *Je crains qu'il ne vienne pas*, 'I am afraid he will *not* come'. On the other hand, a negative must be supplied in English after *se garder*: *Gardez-vous de l'écouter*, 'Take care *not* to listen to him', because *se garder de* really means 'to keep oneself from'.

If *ne...que* is translated by 'only', the word 'only' should come at the same place in the English as *que* in the French: *Il n'est ici que depuis deux jours*, 'He has been here *only* two days'; *Je ne l'ai vu que deux fois*,

'I have seen him *only* twice'; *ne...que* is not always to be rendered by 'only': *Je ne pourrai vous le dire que demain*, 'I cannot tell you *till* to-morrow'. When the word modified by *ne...que* is a verb, *faire* is added; it is not to be translated: *Je ne* fis *qu'entrevoir son visage*, 'I only caught a glimpse of his face'.

The negative is not translated in such cases as: *Il y a si longtemps que nous* n'*avons causé ensemble*, 'It's such a long time since we had a chat'; *Vous devez beaucoup plus que vous* ne *croyez*, 'You owe much more than you think'; *Elle ne peut douter que je* n'*en sois instruit*, 'She can't doubt that I know all about it'.

§ 53. *PLUS*

The sense of *plus* as a negative is 'no longer': *Le roi ne voulait plus gouverner par la force*, 'The King would no longer govern by force'. It is often to be translated by *now*: *Je n'habite plus Londres*, 'I do not live in London now'; *Il n'en reste plus que trois*, 'There are only three now', or 'There are only three left'. *Plus...plus* is 'the more...the more'; *plus* alone is 'no more': *Plus d'amour, partant plus de joie*, 'No more love, therefore no more joy'.

N.B. *Plus d'un*, 'more than one', often 'many a'; *de plus*, 'in addition'; *ni moi non plus*, 'nor I either'.

§ 54. ON TRANSLATING PREPOSITIONS

Of all the parts of speech prepositions give the linguist most trouble when he is using the foreign language for himself. When he is translating it, they are less troublesome, for their meaning can generally be deduced from the context. This is very fortunate for us because in the use of prepositions French and English differ strangely. French writers seem almost to delight in confronting us with the most unexpected prepositions. Thus Anatole France in *Abeille*:

— *Georges ! Georges ! où est mon frère Georges ? criait-elle en sanglotant.*
Les Nains ne le lui dirent pas, par *la raison qu'ils l'ignoraient.*

If we ourselves had had to express in French 'The Dwarfs did not tell her, for the reason that they did not know' it would probably never have occurred to us to say *par la raison.* But when Anatole France says it we have no difficulty in seeing what it means.

This example will serve as a general hint. It is most unwise to connect any English preposition in our minds with any French one, and assume for instance that *à* is 'to' and *de* is 'from'. Such a fixed idea is a constant source of error—often of utter error. In some contexts the French preposition may mean exactly the opposite of what we assume and we may very easily find ourselves talking nonsense. That was the fate which befell many in a Higher School Certificate Examination in 1927 when the deceptive little preposition *à* lay in wait for them in an easy-looking line in which Victor Hugo, telling how man changes and Nature changes not, says:

le fleuve des campagnes
Prendra sans cesse aux monts les flots qu'il donne aux mers.

Many were those who gaily wrote down 'The river of the countrysides shall take without cease *to* the mountains the water that it gives to the seas'. They thought that *à* means 'to', that *prendre aux monts* means 'shall take *to* the mountains'—and they made the river run uphill into the mountains. What they failed to realize —besides other matters into which we need not enter here—was that when *à* is used with *prendre* it means not 'to' but 'from': *J'ai pris le couteau* au *petit garçon*, 'I took the knife *from* the little boy'. With other verbs, such as *cacher*, *emprunter*, *enlever*, *ôter*, *à* shows the same peculiarity.

We must, then, learn not to attach fixed meanings to French prepositions, but be prepared to supply the English preposition suitable to the context. Any given French preposition may thus have many and various English equivalents, in addition to that which we are apt to bear too constantly in mind.

§ 55. THE PREPOSITIONS *À* AND *DE*

À

'by': *à la lumière de la raison*, 'by the light of reason'; *un à un*, 'one by one'; *à vous seul*, 'by yourself'; *reconnaître à*, 'to recognize by', e.g. *À leurs tabliers de cuir et à leurs marteaux on les reconnaissait pour des ouvriers travaillant les métaüx*, 'By their leather aprons and their hammers they could be recognized as metal-workers'; similarly, *Dans les provinces perdues on sentait bien, à un frémissement continuel, que la pensée était ailleurs*, 'In the lost provinces one did feel, *by* a continual unrest, that thought was elsewhere'.

'from': see above, § 54.

'in': *personne au monde*, 'nobody in the world'; *à l'armée*, 'in the army'; *à voix très basse*, 'in a very low voice'.

'with': *l'homme à la barbe blanche*, 'the man with the white beard'; *la dame au chapeau vert*, 'the lady with the green hat'.

'away': *à quelques pas*, 'some paces away'.

In idioms *à* is to be translated idiomatically:

C'est à vous de jouer, 'It is your turn to play'; *Ce n'était pas à moi de le dire*, 'It was not for me (It was not my place) to say it'.

The preposition *de* has a great variety of meanings which are comparatively seldom rendered by 'of'. In particular the possessive ''s' must be kept persistently in view. There is nothing more irritating in a translation from French than the Ollendorffian 'of': 'The hat of the gardener is on the head of John'. This is an extreme case, but there are cases of much more insidious danger, where 'of' wrongly used for the possessive makes a sentence faintly un-English. No rule can be given. The translator must in every case ask himself whether 'of' or ''s' is the better, and rely on instinct to give him the right answer. The opposite fault must also be avoided. But it is much less common; for instance, *Le Tombeau du Soldat inconnu* would not readily be mistranslated as 'The Unknown Warrior's Tomb'. This is a matter for tact. There are sentences in which *le tombeau de Napoléon* is clearly 'Napoleon's tomb'. There are others in which it is just as clearly 'the Tomb of Napoleon'. Other translations of *de* are:

DE

'by': *frappé de la ressemblance*, 'struck by the resemblance'.

'for': *Je vous remercie de votre lettre*, 'I thank you for your letter'; *Il a été puni de ses fautes*, 'He was punished for his faults'.

'from': *à dix milles de Londres*, 'ten miles from London'.

'in': *compagnons d'infortune*, 'companions in misfortune'; cp. *frères de douleur*, 'fellow-sufferers'; *riche d'espérance*, 'rich in hope'; *d'une voix amicale*, 'in a friendly voice'; *d'un ton plus ferme*, 'in a firmer tone'; *jamais de ma vie*, 'never in my life'; *de mémoire d'homme*, 'in the memory of man'.

'on': *vivre de*: *Je vis de bonne soupe et non de beau langage*, as Chrysale says in *Les Femmes savantes*.

'with': *remplir un verre de vin*, 'to fill a glass with wine'.

The idiomatic *de* in e.g. *Ce sera toujours un repas de fait* is not translatable: 'It will be always a meal to the good'.

§ 56. OTHER PREPOSITIONS

CHEZ

'at the house of', etc.: *chez nous*, 'at our house', 'at home'; *chez la Dauphine*, 'in the Dauphiness's apartments'; *chez Martin*, 'at Martin's' (house, shop, office, etc.); *chez Racine*, 'in the works of Racine'; see also p. 29, § 18.

CONTRE

'for': *échanger une chose contre une autre*, 'to exchange one thing for another'.

'with': *se fâcher (s'irriter) contre quelqu'un*, 'to become angry (irritated) with someone'.

DANS

'from': *prendre un revolver dans un tiroir*, 'to take a revolver from a drawer'; *puisant leurs exemples dans la Bible*, 'drawing their examples from the Bible', or 'drawing on the Bible for their examples'.

EN

'in the character of', 'in the guise of', 'as': *des soldats travestis en paysans*, 'soldiers disguised as peasants'; *Il a agi en honnête homme*, 'He acted as a gentleman'; *répondre en Normand*, 'to answer like a Norman', i.e. cautiously; *celle que je sers en esclave*, 'she whom I serve as a slave'.

JUSQU'À

'even', 'very': *J'aimais jusqu'à ses défauts*, 'I loved even her faults (her very faults)'.

PAR

'in', 'on': *par le grand soleil*, 'in the full sunshine'; *par un beau jour d'été*, 'on a fine summer day'.

'out of': *jeter quelque chose par la fenêtre*, 'to throw something out of the window'; *Il l'a fait par fierté, par charité*, etc., 'He did it out of pride, out of charity', etc.

SANS

'but for': *Francœur aurait été beau* sans *ses cheveux gris et son nez rouge*, Anatole France, *Abeille.*

'-less': *sans abri*, 'homeless'; *sans pitié*, 'pitiless', 'ruthless'; *sans le sou*, 'penniless'; *sans tache*, 'spotless'; *sans voix*, 'voiceless', 'inarticulate.'

'un-': *sans bornes*, 'unbounded'; *sans lecture*, 'unread'; *sans travail*, 'unemployed'.

SOUS

'in': *sous les bois*, 'in the woods'; *sous une forme différente*, 'in a different form'; *sous la neige* (*la pluie*), 'in the snow (rain)'; *sous le règne de Louis XIV*, 'in the reign of Louis XIV'.

'on': *sous aucun prétexte*, 'on no pretext', 'on no account'.

SUR

'in': *Je l'ai vu sur le journal*, 'I saw it in the newspaper'; *La clef est sur la porte*, 'The key is in the door'.

'off': *Elle balayait* sur *la table les perdrix et les jetait dans son tablier tendu*, 'She swept the partridges off the table into her outstretched apron'.

'out of': *neuf fois sur dix*, 'nine times out of ten'.

§ 57. ON OMITTING PREPOSITIONS

As is shown above, the essential thing in translating prepositions is to keep absolute liberty, treat each case on its own merits, and decide from the context what is the proper English preposition. Furthermore, we must reserve the right to omit a preposition altogether.

In many cases English requires none. Thus, *J'ai donné un cadeau* à *mon neveu*, 'I gave my nephew a present'. It is just as good English, of course, to say, 'I gave a present to my nephew', but the use of 'to' will often give a sentence a slightly foreign appearance which in translation it is better to avoid. When should we use the preposition and when should we drop it? There is no definite rule. We must bear both courses in mind and trust to instinct to keep us right. Should we say for *Il est plus grand que moi de deux pouces*, 'He is taller than I by two inches'? There is no reason why we should not. But if we remembered the other way of expressing the fact, 'He is two inches taller than I am', we should probably prefer it and so make our translation look a little less like a translation.

In *Versailles est* à 19 *kilomètres de Paris*, or *Il remonte* sur *son cheval*, or *Nous sommes entrés* dans *le bois*, the preposition is necessary in French, but in English it would be odd. In other cases, to use a preposition in English would be a positive error: thus in *l'épithète* de *séduisant s'applique aux Cyclades*, 'the epithet "attractive" is applicable to the Cyclades', the *de* is a purely French idiom, which allows of the phrase being printed without inverted commas, *l'épithète de séduisant* being exactly the same thing as *l'épithète* '*séduisant*'; cp. also *les initiales* de *E. R.*, 'the initials "E. R."' Similarly, *faire* de *chaque citoyen un soldat* is 'to make every citizen a soldier'.

§ 58. STYLE

The sins which translators commit in the name of Style are as the sands of the sea. The name is so often invoked to excuse ignorance, inaccuracy and slipshod methods that the less said about 'Style' here will perhaps be the better. If translators would only *translate*, honestly and accurately, what they have before them, the result would usually be excellent English. If for the French words and phrases they have really chosen the best English equivalents, then they have practically solved the problem of style and in nine cases out of ten should leave well alone.

'The best English equivalent' is, of course, that which is most suitable not only as regards meaning, but also as regards tone. It is obvious that English words and phrases appropriate in translating a conversational passage from a modern French novelist are inappropriate in translating Corneille and Racine. They are *not* 'the best English equivalents'. These are more likely to be found in Shakespeare than in our modern speech.

Since the language of serious prose is not the language of everyday life in English any more than it is in French, we must, in translating it, avoid dropping into conversational style and using phrases which would not be used in similar English books. Reading of good English authors is a necessary condition of writing good English prose. But there is of course danger in aiming too high and the translator should keep well within his powers. For a descriptive passage the tone of, say, Scott or Stevenson may be adopted. A French essayist may be translated in the style of Hazlitt or De Quincey, a modern historian in that of Macaulay. For Rousseau, older writers like Addison or Goldsmith should set the example.

In translating lighter prose, the pompous and the free-and-easy are alike to be avoided. On the one hand, little fishes must not be made to talk like whales. On the other hand, familiarity must not descend to vulgarity. In this matter any of the better contemporary English novelists will serve as a guide.

In modern drama, where the language is conversational and idiomatic, more liberty is allowable. The French characters should be made to speak naturally like English people belonging to the same stratum of society. The translator may allow himself more latitude here and freely imitate the cultivated conversation of, for instance, the dialogues in the novels of Anthony Hope or the plays of Mr Bernard Shaw.

§ 59. ON TRANSLATING VERSE

In translating poetry it must not be forgotten that English, partly because of the double element it contains, Latin and Germanic (see p. 39, § 26), has a fuller poetical vocabulary than French, which is peculiarly dependent for its poetical effects on the artistic use of ordinary material. The words used in French poetry are those used in French prose, with the exception of a few like *le trépas* meaning 'death', *onde* (f.) meaning properly 'wave', but in verse meaning 'water', and *la bise* which is properly 'the North Wind', but is used in verse for any cold inhospitable blast. English, on the other hand, possesses a large number of words of which the use is confined to verse or poetic prose, and naturally these must be employed in translating French verse into English prose. As a general rule English words of Latin origin should be avoided, where possible. They are usually more prosaic and colourless in English than in French. Thus *les monts éternels* are not 'the eternal mountains' but 'the everlasting hills'. Commonplace trivial expressions must of course be shunned.

The English should be dignified and, if not rhythmical, at least harmonious. What is most valuable in this respect is to know by heart as much English poetry as possible. Distant reminiscences are very effective, although trite quotations are apt to jar.

Much of the beauty of poetry lies in the imagery, which we must therefore keep intact so far as we can. Especially must we be careful not to read an English metaphor into a French one. Thus in *Pauvre fleur moissonnée par la tempête* we might think first of 'harvested', since *la moisson* means 'harvest'. But further reflection shows that this cannot be the sense intended. The tempest does not 'harvest' flowers. It destroys them, breaks them, or cuts them down; it does not gather them in. Like death, the tempest is a reaper rather than a harvester. The error we made was to read into *moissonner* or into *moisson* an English sense (which in French is expressed by *récolter* or *la récolte*).

It is as a rule better to keep to poetic prose than to venture on a rendering in verse. That French poetry necessarily loses much of its beauty when translated into English prose is self-evident. It is not at all certain, however, that it loses less when translated into English verse. Though the use of verse might well be expected to convey the spirit better than prose, it seldom does, because too much has been conceded to the exigencies of metre. The delicate shades are given too roughly, or else lost altogether. Practice in this art is a valuable and pleasant exercise, but one which seems out of place in the examination room. Many candidates are tempted by a congenial piece to employ the medium of verse and some perform their self-imposed task with distinction, as in the example quoted on p. 99. But as a rule their rendering is so free that it is useless as evidence that exact shades of meaning have been perceived or difficult constructions really understood.

As an example of the points missed, inevitably perhaps, in a verse rendering, we take a few lines from two of the best modern translations of La Fontaine:

Dans un chemin montant, sablonneux, malaisé,
Et de tous les côtés au soleil exposé,
Six forts chevaux tiraient un coche.
Femmes, moine, vieillard, tout était descendu;
L'attelage suait, soufflait, était rendu.
Une Mouche survient, et des chevaux s'approche...
'Le Coche et la Mouche,' *Fables*, VII, 9.

One translator begins:

On the road up a steep sandy hill in the sun,
With no shade from beginning to end of the run,
Six strong horses are dragging a coach.

La Fontaine is so difficult to translate that to criticize this severely would be unfair. But it is open to an obvious objection. The French lines are often quoted as a striking example of La Fontaine's skill in reproducing in verse the actual sound of what he describes —here, the extremely laborious and slow ascent of the coach, despite the efforts of *Six forts chevaux*. Because of the rollicking metre selected, the translator makes the coach take the hill at the gallop, in fine style, after the manner of young Lochinvar:

O, young Lochinvar is come out of the west,
Through all the wide Border his steed was the best!

Our second translator continues, in a different metre:

They sweat, they pant, they're almost at a stand;
Women—old men—a curate—all get out
To ease the load. Behold a fly approach
And round the horses buzz about
To prick them to a further bout.

This raises objections of another sort. The phrase 'to a further bout' is perhaps rather too obviously brought in for the rime; 'curate' somehow suggests a light-weight, while *moine* evokes a portly presence, and greater reluctance to budge from a comfortable seat on a warm day. The translator's curate would have got out first. La Fontaine's monk would have been among the last to leave the coach and take to the dusty road.

Translation of seventeenth-century drama is a somewhat thankless task (see Model Lesson IV, p. 173), but an instructive one. It is also an excellent test for examination purposes. The presence of such passages in examination papers encourages the reading of Classical Tragedy and provides an invaluable exercise in literary taste—and in logic, because the constructions require to be thought out very carefully and inversions are very frequent and deceptive. The language itself is comparatively simple, but the sense of many words differs from that which they have in present-day French. Of these words some of the most common are:

clartés, 'ideas', 'enlightened notions', somewhat like the modern 'culture'.
encore un coup = *encore une fois*: 'once again'.
courage, 'heart'.
effet, 'result'.
ennui, 'grief'.
estomac, 'chest', 'breast'.
étonné, 'thunderstruck', 'astounded'.
feu, *flamme*, 'love'.
gêne, 'torment'.
gêné, 'tortured'.
gloire, 'reputation', 'honour'.
honnête homme, 'gentleman'.
honnêtes gens, 'gentlefolks'.
longueur = *lenteur*, 'slowness', 'tardiness'.

neveux, 'descendants' (Latin *nepōtes*).
succès, 'outcome', 'result (good or bad)'.

The English used may well be somewhat archaic. Use of 'thou' or 'ye' instead of 'you' adds greatly to the effect. But care must be taken not to confuse the forms by dropping occasionally into 'you' or following up 'thou' with 'your'. In translating Classical Drama much help may be obtained from the Bible and from Shakespeare, particularly plays like *Julius Cæsar*, and from any of the standard translations of Greek plays, such as those by Mr Way or by Professor Gilbert Murray.

§ 60. PRACTICAL HINTS IN THE EXAMINATION ROOM

1. Before beginning to translate, read through the whole passage carefully with a view to forming a general impression of its meaning. Try to obtain a clear picture of the circumstances. When time is short, as it too often is, do not hurry over this part of the process and so miss the sense of the French. There are other and less dangerous ways of saving time. Not only the words but the logical sequence must be clearly understood before translation becomes possible.

2. If time permits, write a rough copy. Make up your mind where the difficulties lie and concentrate upon them. Otherwise confine the rough copy to the most difficult sentences.

3. Study carefully the construction of any sentence, the sense of which is not apparent to you at first sight. Endeavour to supply from the context the meaning of words which are wholly or partly unknown.

4. Remember that the French passage has a definite meaning and that your version must at least make sense. See that the whole translation, every sentence and every word of it, at least means something. Those parts of it which mean nothing, or are self-contradictory, are certainly wrong.

5. Remember that you are translating ideas, not words. Do not allow yourself to become hypnotized by the French text. Staring at French will not produce English. Rather take your eyes off the examination paper, make a mental picture of the circumstances, and think how they would naturally be described in English.

6. Revise your rough copy, improving the order of the words and examining the words themselves in the light of your knowledge of English synonyms (see p. 37, § 35). Be suspicious of any word or phrase which, when you read it to yourself, does not sound right or does not look right. Then ask yourself honestly whether you would really say such a thing, were you not translating from French. If you would, it is probably correct. If you would not, it is wrong, but can, after a little reflection, be corrected from your own instinctive knowledge of English or your reminiscences of English authors. Avoid unpleasant repetitions of the same word at too close intervals.

7. Do not add or subtract or 'embellish.' Remember that you are, for the time being, acting only as an interpreter. The French author may have omitted something interesting, or said something unnecessary, or expressed himself less well than he might have done. But that is no fault of yours. Keep the metaphor, wherever possible. Do not, for instance, translate one derived from sound by one derived from sight.

8. Try to hand in a finished version, legible and neat, not disfigured by numerous alterations and erasures. Do not give variants and expect the examiner to choose between them. Selection is your business, not his, and he will be quite entitled to count one of the variants as an error. Do not leave blanks which could have been filled by thinking out the sense. An approximate rendering is better than none. Half a loaf is better than no bread—and half a mark is more helpful than none.

9. Be sparing of annotations, especially those which cast doubt on the examiner's intelligence. Your translation should be clear enough to explain itself. Annotations may reveal ignorance. Remember the case of the candidate who translated *le sénat équitable* as 'the equitable senate' (quite correctly, though 'fair-minded' would have been better) but added in a footnote 'This means consisting of Roman *equites*.'

10. Ability to keep one's head is useful in everyday life, e.g. in cycling. Remember that it is as useful in examinations.

PASSAGES FOR TRANSLATION

SECTION I

MODEL LESSON I A

Dans la rue

1. Alors, sans attendre la réponse de la vieille, je poussai la petite charrette devant moi. 2. Elle ne fit aucune résistance; elle me remercia simplement, et se mit à marcher à mes côtés. 3. J'appris qu'elle venait d'acheter aux halles une provision qu'elle devait revendre. 4. Quels que fussent la saison et le temps, elle continuait à parcourir Paris jusqu'à ce qu'elle eût tout placé. 5. Depuis trente années, elle vivait de ce commerce, qui lui avait fourni les moyens d'élever trois fils.

6. "Mais quand je les ai eus grands et forts, on me les a pris, me dit la pauvre femme: deux sont morts à l'armée, et le dernier est prisonnier sur les pontons.

7. — De sorte, m'écriai-je, que vous voilà seule, sans autre ressource que votre courage!

8. — Et le protecteur de ceux qui n'en ont pas d'autre, ajouta-t-elle. 9. Faut bien que le bon Dieu ait quelque chose à faire dans son paradis; et à quoi passerait-il son temps, si ce n'était à prendre soin des créatures comme moi? 10. Allez, allez, on a beau être vieille et misérable, l'idée que le Roi de tout vous regarde, qu'il vous juge et vous tient compte, ça vous soutient." Émile Souvestre, *Confessions d'un Ouvrier*.

This is a simple passage of ordinary colloquial French relating a little street incident and a conversation with a poor old coster-woman. What we have to do is to turn the passage into ordinary colloquial English, describe the incident as clearly and simply as it is described in French and make the old woman talk as she would probably have talked had she spoken English instead of French. Any attempt at high-flown language, any striving after literary effect, would here be quite out of place. The simpler our English is, the more faithfully will it render the French.

To ascertain the exact meaning of the French must always be our first task. In this instance it is also our main task. Once we have a clear idea of all that was said and done, we can surely express it in our mother-tongue as well as the humble folk in this passage expressed it in theirs.

The general sense can be grasped at the first reading. The person relating the incident is a working-man, as we see from the title of the book. He has offered to lend an old coster-woman a friendly hand and wheel her barrow for her. They talk as they go, and from her conversation he learns that she has had a hard life, that the three sons for whom she laboured have been taken from her, but that, in spite of all, she has not lost her trust in God.

With this general sense in mind, we proceed to fill in the details, sentence by sentence:

1. *Alors, sans attendre la réponse de la vieille, je poussai la petite charrette devant moi.*

sans attendre la réponse: 'without waiting for the reply'; *attendre* is often intransitive, meaning 'to wait', e.g. *J'ai* attendu *à la gare*, 'I waited at the station'; when transitive it is translated 'to wait *for*'; so *chercher quelque chose*, 'to look *for*', see p. 45, § 30.

la vieille = *la vieille femme*, but use of the adjective alone is generally contemptuous or patronizing. Thus *le vieux* is 'the old fellow', 'the old 'un', whereas the noun *le vieillard* is 'the aged man'.

je poussai la petite charrette devant moi: literally, 'I pushed the little cart before me'. But this is not translation. It is merely putting one English word for each French word and saying nothing, or next to nothing, that is intelligible. Yet the French words, when taken all together, do say something. And what they say is quite intelligible, for they describe a definite action. An old coster-woman does not usually have a 'little cart' but a 'hand-cart' or 'barrow'. She does not usually 'push' it, she 'wheels' it along. The action described in the French is: 'I wheeled the little hand-cart along in front of me'.

'Then, without waiting for the old woman's reply, I wheeled the hand-cart along in front of me.'

2. *Elle ne fit aucune résistance; elle me remercia, et se mit à marcher à mes côtés.*

Elle ne fit aucune résistance is 'She made no resistance' or 'She offered no resistance' or 'She did not make any resistance'. There is not much difference between these phrases. But perhaps the last is the best here, because the most conversational.

elle me remercia simplement is 'she thanked me simply' (or 'in a simple way') rather than 'she simply thanked me', which would suggest 'merely' and for which the French would be *Elle* ne fit que *me remercier*.

à mes côtés: the French in their phrase rather strangely use the plural; we use the singular: 'at my side'.

'She did not make any resistance; she thanked me in a simple way and began walking alongside of me.'

3. *J'appris qu'elle venait d'acheter aux halles une provision qu'elle devait revendre.*

elle venait d'acheter: 'she had just bought'. Originally the words meant 'she *came from* buying', but they have become the regular French way of expressing what we express by the use of 'just.' *Elle* vient *d'acheter* is thus 'She *has* just bought' and the past of this is *Elle* venait *d'acheter*, 'She *had* just bought'.

aux halles: 'at the market-hall'. In Paris *les Halles* are the great central market, corresponding in London to Covent Garden. There is always some doubt how to deal with such proper names in translation. If we boldly say 'Covent Garden', then we must alter 'Paris' to 'London' and make any other similar changes which may be required. Perhaps translation is unnecessary, for most English people have heard of *les Halles*. If the word is to be translated, it will be 'the wholesale market', or 'the Market' with a capital M, or 'the Market Hall'.

une provision: is of course, in a way, 'a provision'. But would any old English coster-woman say that she had just been buying 'a provision'? Certainly not. What *would* she say? Perhaps 'a stock', as in *Notre* provision *de bois est presque épuisée*, 'Our *stock* of wood is almost exhausted'.

qu'elle devait revendre: *devait* has many shades of meaning, 'was to', 'had to', etc.; here 'had to', or 'was going to', will give the sense; *revendre* is 'to sell again', 'to re-sell', i.e. here 'to retail'.

The first draft of our rendering would thus be: 'I learned that she had just bought, at the Market Hall, a stock which she was going to retail'.

This, however, is peculiar English. It could be improved by altering the order of the words, substituting for 'bought' the fuller term 'bought in' and expanding 'which' to 'and...it'.

'I learned that she had just bought in a stock at the Market Hall and was going to retail it.'

4. *Quels que fussent la saison et le temps, elle continuait à parcourir Paris jusqu'à ce qu'elle eût tout placé.*

Quels que fussent la saison et le temps: the construction *quel que* is a very common one and must be learned. *Quel* agrees with the noun it qualifies, and the order of the words is different from that usual in English. Quelles que soient *les conséquences* is '*Whatever* the consequences *may be*'. The past form of this is Quelles que fussent *les conséquences*, '*Whatever* the consequences *might* be'. Frequently *le temps* is 'time', but not always. In this instance it is 'weather'. If 'time' were meant, the French would be *l'heure*.

elle continuait: this Imperfect denotes custom as if meaning 'she used to continue', but in English 'continued' alone, or 'went on', is sufficient.

parcourir: is composed of *par* (Latin *per*), 'through', and *courir* 'to run', and therefore means properly 'to run through'. But it comes to have a much less definite sense; e.g. 'Le roi *parcourait* sans cesse son vaste empire' does not of course mean that the King continually ran, any more than the present phrase means that the old woman with the barrow went through the streets of Paris at the double. She only 'trudged about' the streets.

jusqu'à ce qu'elle eût tout placé: the order of the last two words is that which is customary in French, e.g. *J'ai tout vu,* 'I have seen everything'. If only we bear in mind the general circumstances, we shall not translate *placé* unintelligibly (and unintelligently) by 'placed', even though hitherto unaware that it has a specialized sense; *placer ses marchandises* is 'to dispose of one's wares', i.e. by finding customers for them. The conjunction *jusqu'à ce que* takes the subjunctive; hence *eût,* which is not 'should have', but merely 'had'.

'Whatever the season and the weather, she went on trudging about Paris till she had disposed of the whole.'

5. *Depuis trente années, elle vivait de ce commerce, qui lui avait fourni les moyens d'élever trois fils.*

Depuis trente années, etc.: 'For thirty years she had been living'; see p. 44, § 57; for *vivre de*, 'to live by', see p. 70, § 55.

qui lui avait fourni les moyens: *qui* goes with *commerce* and in the English sentence we must be careful to make 'trade' the last word of the preceding phrase; thus 'She had made her living by the *trade which*', etc. But we should have a better sentence if we turned *qui* by 'and it'. French says *fournir quelque chose à quelqu'un*, whereas English says 'to furnish (provide) someone with something'. Hence the French phrase, literally 'had furnished to her the means', is in English 'had furnished her with the means', i.e. 'had enabled her'.

'For thirty years she had been making her living by that trade, and it had enabled her to bring up three sons.'

6. "*Mais quand je les ai eus grands et forts, on me les a pris, me dit la pauvre femme: deux sont morts à l'armée, et le dernier est prisonnier sur les pontons.*

Quand je les ai eus grands et forts: 'When I had them big and strong' is not very clear English; 'When I had got them big and strong' would be clearer, but it is perhaps better to say 'When they had grown big and strong'.

on me les a pris: 'they took them from me'; *me* is the dative used with a verb of taking away; see p. 68, § 54. The passive rendering 'they were taken away from me' gives the most natural English. But it is not quite so exact as 'they took them from me', because *on* is a more or less direct allusion to certain *persons*, viz. the military authorities.

dit la pauvre femme: for the Inversion, unnecessary in English, see p. 47, § 32.

sont morts: not 'are dead'; it is the past tense of *mourir*, 'died'.

à l'armée: 'in the army'; see p. 68, § 55.

est prisonnier: 'is a prisoner'; see p. 48, § 33.

les pontons. The English word 'pontoon', coming from the French, gives some clue to the meaning. A 'pontoon bridge' was originally a floating bridge made of 'pontoons' or flat-bottomed boats. *Les pontons* are what we call 'the hulks', the old dismantled ships used as prisons at various times, e.g. in England for prisoners of war and in France for political prisoners, etc.

'"But when they had grown up big and strong, they took them away from me," said the poor old woman; "two died in the Army and the last is a prisoner on the hulks."'

7. *De sorte, m'écriai-je, que vous voilà seule, sans autre ressource que votre courage!*

De sorte que: 'So that', 'With the result that'.

m'écriai-je: the Inversion is not required in English: we say 'I exclaimed'.

vous voilà seule: literally 'there you are alone'. But we shall have, as often, to add something to make the phrase English.

The literal translation is: "So that," I exclaimed, "you are left alone without other resource than your courage". The effect of this is not English. Why not? Firstly, the parenthesis comes in very awkwardly after 'So that'. Then, we generally say '*all* alone', or 'alone in the world', in a case like this. Also, 'without *any* other resource' or 'with no other resource' is the natural phrase. Lastly, 'your courage' does not convey the force of *votre courage*, which is really (see p. 55, § 42) 'your *own* courage'. With a few slight alterations, we arrive at a better rendering:

'"So that you are left all alone," I exclaimed, "with no other resource than your own courage (or pluck)."'

8. *Et le protecteur de ceux qui n'en ont pas d'autre, ajouta-t-elle.*

qui n'en ont pas d'autre. What noun does *en* stand for? For *ressource*, no doubt, although it might just possibly stand for *protecteur.*

ajouta-t-elle: the Inversion, customary in French in a parenthesis, is not required in English.

'"And the Defender of those who have no other," she added.'

9. *Faut bien que le bon Dieu ait quelque chose à faire dans son paradis; et à quoi passerait-il son temps, si ce n'était à prendre soin des créatures comme moi?*

Faut bien: popular or conversational for *Il faut bien.*

le bon Dieu. In French the phrase is in common use where English employs the noun alone (see p. 36, § 24).

à quoi: the construction of *passer* with *à* must be noted here, e.g. "*À quoi passez-vous votre temps? — Je passe mon temps* à *lire*".

si ce n'était: 'if it were not', i.e. 'except' or 'unless'.

des créatures comme moi: 'creatures like me' or as an English coster-woman might say, 'the likes of me'.

'God must have something to do in His Paradise; and what would He spend His time on, unless looking after the likes of me?'

10. *Allez, allez, on a beau être vieille et misérable, l'idée que le Roi de tout vous regarde, qu'il vous juge et vous tient compte, ça vous soutient.*"

Allez, allez: a mere interjection, 'Come, come' or 'Well, well'.

on a beau être, etc.: for the phrase *avoir beau* see p. 43, § 28. The sense is 'old and wretched though I be' or 'miserable old woman as I am'.

vous regarde: not quite 'is looking at you', but rather 'is watching you'; *vous*, in this general sense, is used as if it were the objective case of *on*.

vous tient compte: literally 'keeps count to you', i.e. 'gives you credit for (what you suffer)'.

ça vous soutient: 'that (*l'idée*, etc.) keeps you up'.

'"Well, well, miserable old woman as I am, the thought that the King of all is watching you, judging you and giving you credit,—that helps you to bear up."'

Suggested Rendering

Then, without waiting for the old woman's reply, I wheeled the hand-cart along in front of me. She did not make any resistance; she thanked me in a simple way and began walking alongside of me. I learned that she had just bought in a stock at the Market Hall and was going to retail it. Whatever the season and the weather, she went on trudging about Paris till she had disposed of the whole. For thirty years she had been making her living by that trade, and it had enabled her to bring up three sons.

"But when they had grown up big and strong, they took them away from me," said the poor old woman; "two died in the Army and the last is a prisoner on the hulks."

"So that you are left all alone," I exclaimed, "with no other resource than your own courage."

"And the Defender of those who have no other," she added. "God must have something to do in His Paradise; and what would He spend His time on, unless looking after the likes of me? Well, well, miserable old woman as I am, the thought that the King of all is watching you, judging you and giving you credit,—that helps you to bear up."

The best way to translate such a passage, which has no literary pretensions, is, as the phrase goes, to 'put it into your own words'. For examination purposes the phrase is not to be taken too literally and, in any case, one's 'own words' are apt, under examination conditions, to become somewhat stilted. The version might not be in the King's English, but if the words really were one's own, they would at least show very clearly if the incident described in the French had or had not really been *seen*. As an example of real visualizing, we give the following free rendering, or transposition, by an (imaginary) Aberdeen policeman who *has* seen what he describes, and reports it orally—'in his own words':

Suggested Rendering in Aberdeen Dialect

A didna wite for ony answer fae the auld wifie, A jeist ca'd the hurley ben the road. She didna mak' nae objekshun, she jeist thankit me, simple-like, an' started traivellin' alangsides o' me. A ascertained she'd jeist been doon at the Market Ha', laying in a stock, like, an' wiz for re-tailin' it. At a' sizzins o' the 'ear, in a' kin' o' wither, she wiz aye stravaigin' the streets o' Aiberdeen wi' a hurley till she hid it a' selt. For therty 'ear, she'd been livin' on't, and makin' eneuch be't tae bring up three sins.

"Aye, but fan I'd gotten them big and forcy-like"—It's the wifie speakin' noo—"they nippit them awa' fae me. There's twa o' them deid, aye wi' the Gordons, like, and the yingest laddie's a prisoner in Germany."

"That wye o't,"—it's me that's speakin' noo—"y'ere a' yer lain sel' in the warld, an' nae help for ye but yer ain stoot he'rt?"

"Aye, an' Him that protects them that hinna ither! There maun be something for Goad to dee, hine awa' up in's Paradise. Fat wye wid He spen's time, gin it wisna wi' notticin' craturs like me? Awa' wi' ye, man! It disna maitter a ba'bee foo auld an' disjaskit a wifie is, the thocht that the Keeng o' a' the warld is aye takin' a keek at ye, jidgin' ye, like, and pittin' it a' doon tae yer credit—that's fat keeps up the likes o' hiz."

MODEL LESSON I B

Le Cimetière au bord de la Mer.

Loin du monde et du temps, sous la garde des cieux,
C'est là que du hameau reposent les aïeux.
Là, sous l'épais gazon d'une terre inégale,
D'où l'on voit d'humbles croix sortir par intervalle,
Ils viennent, déposant leur fatigue et leurs maux,
De la longue journée oublier les travaux.
Ceux-ci, rameurs du port, dès la première étoile,
Pour jeter leurs filets, arrondissaient la voile;
Celui-là conduisait les chèvres au vallon;
Cet autre dans la plaine allongeait le sillon,
Et chaque soir, du ciel observant les nuages,
Y cherchait pour ses blés de rassurants présages;
Cependant qu'avec eux, et plus près de la croix,
Au milieu du troupeau qu'il guidait autrefois,
Leur pasteur dort lui-même, et, comme aux jours de fête,
Pour les conduire au ciel reste encore à leur tête.

Scottish Education Department: Leaving Certificate Examination, 1927.

Anyone with even a slight knowledge of French who reads over the passage will have little doubt as to its general meaning. It is evidently a meditative poem on a churchyard. The poet first recalls the quiet spot with its mounds and crosses, then muses on what those who lie buried there were in their lifetime. Some were fishermen. Some herded goats. Some ploughed the fields. One, who lies a little apart, was the pastor of the flock. In death he remains at their head, that on the Day of Judgment he may lead them to heaven.

Anyone with even a slight knowledge of English literature will scarcely read the French without being reminded of Gray's 'Elegy in a Country Churchyard'. Reminiscences of that poem will not only help to clear up difficulties of meaning in the French original, but suggest words or phrases to translate it.

The meaning of the title *Le Cimetière au bord de la Mer* is not very obscure. Yet to find suitable words to translate it was apparently beyond the powers of many boys and girls of sixteen or seventeen in the Scottish Leaving Certificate Examination of 1927. Some omitted it, thinking perhaps that it was given not for translation, but merely as additional help supplied by a kind examiner. But if his intention had been only to help, he would probably have given the title in English. When the title is given in French, it should be translated, unless there are printed instructions to the contrary. Of those who did translate it, it is strange how many said 'The Cemetery at the Seaside'. 'Cemetery' was very generally misspelled. But even with the correct spelling it is unsuitable here. It is a word of Greek origin. Etymologically it means 'sleeping-place', and ought therefore to be suitable enough. But in English, though not in French, it remains slightly technical. It is chiefly used of the large burying-grounds in our cities and towns. One could hardly imagine Gray selecting for his poem the title 'Elegy in a Country Cemetery'. The present poem was written a century ago when the custom in France was to bury the dead round the church; cp. Renan, in *French Prose from Calvin to Anatole France* (Dent), p. 271: '*une église de hameau, entourée, selon l'usage, du* cimetière'. The phrase 'at the seaside' is equally out of place. It calls up pleasing memories of summer holidays, a beach, pierrots, donkeys, and such cheerful ditties as

I love to be beside
The seaside!

A more appropriate phrase occurs in another and more old-fashioned song, 'The Cottage *by the Sea*'.

Loin du monde et du temps, sous la garde des cieux,
C'est là que du hameau reposent les aïeux.

The idea contained in this first couplet is that the churchyard lies in a quiet sequestered spot; *le monde* means the busy world of men; *le temps* means the changes and chances of time. An equivalent of *Loin du monde et du temps* would thus be 'Far from the madding crowd'. But the quotation is too hackneyed and 'Far from the world and changing time' will give the sense.

des cieux: not 'of the skies' but 'of heaven', as in *le royaume des cieux.*

C'est là, etc.: We must carefully note the order of the words, and remember that in French poetry inversion is a constant snare to the unwary translator. For *du hameau reposent les aïeux* one feels a strong temptation to borrow a whole quotation and say 'the rude forefathers of the hamlet sleep'. But it is better to resist it. There is nothing about 'rude' in the French, and the use of familiar quotations may easily be overdone. Moreover, the word *reposent* need not be translated by 'sleep'; 'rest' is the normal rendering, the two regular formulas on tombstones in France being *Ci-gît*, 'Here lies', and *Ici repose*, 'Here rests'. The first couplet might be translated:

'There, far from the world and changing time, in Heaven's keeping, lie the forefathers of the hamlet.'

Là, sous l'épais gazon d'une terre inégale,
D'où l'on voit d'humbles croix sortir par intervalle,
Ils viennent, déposant leur fatigue et leurs maux,
De la longue journée oublier les travaux.

l'épais gazon d'une terre inégale. This was usually translated 'under the thick turf of an unequal earth'. For an explanation of such strange English we must look to the French. Although *épais* is often to be rendered by 'thick' and *gazon* by 'turf', it by no means follows that *l'épais gazon* is necessarily 'the thick turf'. Among other reasons, *gazon* may be 'sod' as well as 'turf' and it is often used where we use 'grass', as in the notice in public parks, *Défense de marcher sur le gazon*, 'Keep off the grass'. Hence 'thick grass' or 'rich grass' or 'grassy turf' or 'grassy sod' may be closer to the idea. Why is *la terre* said to be *inégale*? Because it is 'uneven', 'irregular' in a country churchyard 'where heaves the turf in many a mouldering heap'; *d'une terre inégale* thus means 'of uneven' or 'irregular' or, more poetically, 'mounded' earth.

D'où l'on voit: *D'où* goes with *sortir*, not with *l'on voit.*

sortir: not 'coming out' but, as often, 'rising'; here the actual word 'rising' might perhaps suggest too much the action of springing up; 'one sees', 'we see', 'are seen', etc., can scarcely be worked into the English sentence without a clumsy effect, but something of the force of *l'on voit sortir* can be given by saying 'standing *forth*'.

par intervalle: 'at intervals', i.e. 'here and there' or, though perhaps too freely, 'straggling'.

déposant: a beautiful metaphor referring to the laying down of their burden by the weary and the heavy-laden.

leur fatigue et leurs maux: *maux*, the plural of *mal*, means 'ills', not 'evils' as many candidates wrote. The literal translation is thus 'their fatigue and their ills'. It would no doubt pass in an examination paper. But it is wooden and un-English. Why not say 'weariness' since the Bible speaks of 'the weary'? Once we have said 'weariness' the English love of alliteration prompts 'woes', which, however, had better be made singular, 'woe'.

De la longue journée, etc. The inversion must be carefully noted; 'the labours of the long day'.

'There, under the thick grass turfing over earthy mounds, whence lowly crosses stand forth here and there, they come, laying down their weariness and woe, to forget the labours of life's long day.'

Ceux-ci, rameurs du port, dès la première étoile,
Pour jeter leurs filets, arrondissaient la voile.

rameurs du port: *une rame* is 'an oar', *ramer* is 'to row', *un rameur* is thus 'an oarsman' or 'rower' or 'boatman'; *du* means sometimes 'of the', sometimes 'belonging to', sometimes 'from the'; *un port* is 'a port' or 'harbour' or 'haven'. These facts, or most of them, were within the knowledge of the average candidate. But he did not utilize them to much purpose in his translation, for no one could say that 'rowers of the harbour' is a very expressive phrase. Does it convey *any* meaning? Where did they row to? Where did they row from? What was their connection with the harbour? Did they row round the harbour? Or did they sometimes venture outside? If they spent their lives in rowing, whether round the harbour or out and in, were they paid for it? Had they any other occupation? The candidate does not tell us. He only says that some of those buried in this churchyard were in their lifetime 'rowers of the harbour'. We can make nothing of this, and must turn to the French. Presumably it means something. Otherwise the poem would not be a poem, and, if it were nonsense verse, it would scarcely have been selected for translation. We take it that these *rameurs du port* were rowers *belonging to* the harbour, that they rowed out to fish, and were simply what an English poet would call 'fishers from the haven'. Kingsley says, 'Three *fishers* went sailing', etc. Tennyson adds, '*To their haven* under the hill'. The French poet describes them as 'rowers' perhaps because he wishes to emphasize the laborious nature of their calling, but Heredia calls men somewhat similarly engaged *pêcheurs*: *Que de hardis* pêcheurs *qui ne reviendront pas!*

dès la première étoile: *dès* is literally 'just from', 'as soon as', and the phrase means 'as soon as the first star came out'. Many candidates oddly translated it 'at dawn'. But it is when the sun goes down that the stars come out and the fishers sail into the west—in Kingsley's poem, and in others, e.g. J. Elroy Flecker, *The Dying Patriot*:

Evening on the golden, the golden sea of Wales
When *the first star* shivers and the last wave pales.

arrondissaient la voile. When one does not know a word like *arrondissaient*—and even when one does—it is useful to break it up into its component parts and think of their exact meaning. The last part of this word will not give us much trouble. It is the verbal ending *-issaient.* The remainder divides itself into the prefix *ar-* (Lat. *ad*) and the stem *rond*; *ar-rond-issaient* must thus mean 'were making *round*'. What were the fishermen making round? *la voile*, 'the sail'—singular because each boat is represented as having one sail.

How then were the fishermen 'making the sail round'? By hoisting it in the wind, of course, so that it 'bellied' or 'swelled'. *Ceux-ci, rameurs du port,...arrondissaient* is a clear enough construction in French, but in English 'These, fishers of the haven', would not be clear, even though the commas after 'These' and 'haven' were converted into dashes. We may therefore supply 'were', and say:

'These were fishers of the haven; soon as the first star shewed, they would, to cast their nets, hoist the swelling sail.'

Celui-là conduisait les chèvres au vallon;
Cet autre dans la plaine allongeait le sillon,
Et chaque soir, du ciel observant les nuages,
Y cherchait pour ses blés de rassurants présages.

Celui-là conduisait les chèvres: *les chèvres* are 'the goats', not 'the hares' as some said. Even if *les chèvres* did look in print something like *les lièvres*, common-sense might have told them that 'hares' can have had little to do with the earthly occupations of '*Celui-là*'. In a French village there is usually only one goat-herd, who 'collects' all the goats before starting for the pastures, upland or lowland. To collect and conduct to the valley a flock of *hares* would require the services of more than one man, however nimble he might be!

allongeait. Applying the same method as in the case of *arrondissaient,* we find that the word divides itself thus, *al-long(e)-ait.* The main part is *long,* and this idea of length must be preserved in translating. But 'lengthened the furrow' will not do. The duty of a ploughman is to make long furrows, not merely to lengthen furrows already begun.

du ciel observant les nuages: note the inversion.

Y = *dans les nuages.*

chercher means to look *for*; it is transitive and governs a direct object, here *présages.*

blés: 'standing corn', 'corn-fields' (see p. 50, § 36), as opposed to the singular, which means the reaped corn or 'grain'.

présages. Provided that the construction of the sentence is kept clearly in mind, the meaning of *présages* can almost be deduced from the context. In the evening the farmer scans the clouds. He *searches* in them *for* something reassuring as regards his standing wheat. What is this something? Presumably it is connected with the weather: 'forecasts' or 'omens'. If, on the other hand, constructions are neglected, e.g. if *cherchait* and *pour* are slumped together as if the equivalent of 'look for', even those who do know the meaning of *présages* will make nothing of the sentence.

'This one led the goats to the valley; that other drew, in the plain, the long furrow, and would every evening scan the clouds of heaven for favourable omens for his crops.'

Cependant qu'avec eux, et plus près de la croix,
Au milieu du troupeau qu'il guidait autrefois,
Leur pasteur dort lui-même, et, comme aux jours de fête,
Pour les conduire au ciel reste encore à leur tête.

la croix: no doubt the large cross or crucifix which stands near the gate of many churchyards, somewhat as the Cross of Remembrance in the British military cemeteries in France.

troupeau. . .*pasteur*. These two words give the key to the meaning of the last two lines. The village priest, the *curé*, is the *pastor* of his *flock*. It should be noted here how unsuitable 'herd' would be.

aux jours de fête: 'on feast-days' (when there were religious processions, headed by the priest).

à leur tête: although the poet's intention is evident, the relative position of the pastor's grave and the graves of his flock is not made clear. He is said to be buried *avec eux* and yet *à leur tête, plus près de la croix* and yet *au milieu du troupeau.* But all these expressions need not be taken quite literally.

'While, with them and nearer to the cross, amid the flock he guided of old, sleeps their pastor himself, and, as on feast-days, that he may lead them heavenwards he still remains at their head.'

Suggested Rendering

There, far from the world and changing time, in Heaven's keeping, lie the forefathers of the hamlet. There, under the thick grass turfing over earthy mounds, whence lowly crosses stand forth here and there, they come, laying down their weariness and woe, to forget the labours of life's long day. These were fishers of the haven; soon as the first star shewed, they would, to cast their nets, hoist the swelling sail. This one led the goats to the valley; that other drew, in the plain, the long furrow, and would every evening scan the clouds of heaven for favourable omens for his crops; while, with them and nearer to the cross, amid the flock he guided of old, sleeps their pastor himself, and, as on feast-days, that he may lead them heavenwards he still remains at their head.

As evidence of the standard which can be reached by well-trained candidates, we give below a verse rendering by a fifth-year pupil, aged 17, at a Scottish High School for Girls. It is printed from the copy which she handed her teacher on leaving the Examination Hall:

The Churchyard by the Sea

Far from the stormy world, beneath the skies
The fathers of the hamlet take their rest.

There, where the thick green turf uneven grows
Rise, now and then, rude emblems of the cross.
Hither they come, their weariness and woe
Laid down, to seek forgetfulness from toil.
These sturdy rowers who were wont to sail
With the first star and swelling canvas spread,
To cast their nets, now quietly lie at rest.
There sleeps the herdsman of the valley-goats,
That other ploughed his furrow in the plain,
And every night, scanning the cloudy sky,
Looked there for promises of plenteous crops;
While close beside them, nearer to the cross,
Amid the flock in former days he led,
Their shepherd sleeps, and, as at festivals,
To guide them heavenward, at their head still leads.

1. *LA VEILLÉE*

VOCABULARY

toucher à, to be near, to approach.
veiller, to be awake, watch; to spend the evening.
le foyer, the hearth, fireside.
le noyer, walnut (tree *or* wood of tree).
s'assied, 3rd sing. pres. indic. of *s'asseoir*, to sit down.
le feuillet, leaf (of book).
le châtaignier, chestnut (tree *or* wood of tree).
rêveur, *rêveuse*, dreamy, dreaming.
le sort, fate, lot, destiny.
la chimère, fond dream.
époux, husband; *épouse*, wife.

Mais plus tard, lorsqu'on touche aux soirs gris de septembre,
En cercle réunis[1] dans la plus grande chambre,
C'est alors qu'il est doux de veiller au foyer!
On roule[2] près du feu la table de noyer,
On s'assied; chacun prend son cahier, son volume;
Grand silence! on n'entend que le bruit de la plume,
Le feuillet qui se tourne, ou le châtaignier vert
Qui craque, et l'on se croit au milieu de l'hiver.
Les yeux sur ses enfants, et rêveuse, la mère
Sur leur sort à venir invente une chimère[3],
Songe à l'époux absent depuis la fin du jour,
Et prend garde que rien ne manque à son retour[4].

BRIZEUX.

NOTES

1 Prose order: *réunis en cercle.* 2 Do we use 'roll' in such a context? 3 Note the inversion. 4 'against his return'.

2. *LA PORTE FERMÉE*

VOCABULARY

résoudre, to solve.
la question, question, problem.
être de retour, to be back *or* to be home again.
la marche, step.
l'escalier (n.m.), staircase.
le lieu, place; *au lieu de*, in place of.
effaré, scared, excited-looking.
le chuchotement, whispering.
partager, to share.
la veuve, widow.
de sitôt, so soon; *here* for a while.

Un soir d'hiver, mon maître m'avait gardé plus tard pour résoudre des questions; je ne revins chez nous qu'à la nuit close[1]. En arrivant, je trouvai la porte fermée! c'était l'heure où mon père était habituellement de retour, et où ma mère préparait le souper. Je ne pouvais comprendre ce qu'ils étaient devenus tous deux; je m'assis sur les marches de l'escalier pour les attendre.

J'étais[2] là depuis quelque temps, lorsque Rose descendit et m'aperçut. Je lui demandai si elle savait pourquoi notre porte était fermée; mais au lieu de me répondre, elle remonta tout effarée, et je l'entendis crier en rentrant chez elle: Pierre est là....On[3] répondit quelque chose, puis il y eut des chuchotements précipités[4]; enfin la mère Cauville parut au haut de l'escalier, et m'invita d'une voix très amicale à monter. Elle allait se mettre à table avec ses enfants, et elle voulut[5] me faire partager leur souper. Je répondis que je voulais[5] attendre ma mère.

"Elle est sortie...pour une affaire[6], dit la veuve, qui avait l'air d'hésiter; peut-être bien[7] qu'elle ne rentrera pas de sitôt; mange et bois, mon pauvre Pierre; ce sera toujours un repas de fait[8]." ÉMILE SOUVESTRE.

NOTES

1 *à la nuit close*, lit. 'when night had closed in.' Can you find a more familiar expression? 2 Tense. See p. 57, § 44. 3 See p. 55, § 41. 4 'a hurried whispered consultation'. 5 See p. 57, § 44. 6 'on business'. 7 = conversational 'may be'. 8 'to the good'.

3. *LES OISEAUX EN HIVER*

VOCABULARY

hélas! alas!
le sol, ground.
se rassurer, to reassure oneself.
peureux, timid, full of fear.
la racine, root.
creux, hollow.
un abri, shelter.
se serrer, to press *or* crowd together.
blotti, cowering, hiding.
un asile, shelter.
la bise, north wind, icy blast.
le frisson, shivering, *here* cold breath.

Hélas! dis-tu, la froide neige
Recouvre le sol et les eaux;
Si le bon Dieu ne les protège[1],
Le printemps n'aura plus d'oiseaux;

Rassure-toi, tendre peureuse;
Les doux chanteurs n'ont point péri;
Sous plus d'une[2] racine creuse
Ils ont un chaud et sûr abri.

Là se serrant l'un contre l'autre,
Et blottis dans l'asile obscur,
Pleins d'un espoir pareil au nôtre,
Ils attendent l'avril futur;

Et malgré la bise qui passe
Et leur jette en vain ses frissons,
Ils répètent à voix très basse
Leurs plus amoureuses chansons.

Cambridge Senior, December 1910.

NOTES

1 See p. 63, § 50, SI. 2 See p. 66, § 53, PLUS.

4. *EN GRÈCE*

VOCABULARY

de mauvaise mine, villainous-looking.
le détour, turn, bend.
le canon, cannon; (gun-) barrel.
braquer, to level, aim, point.
par-dessus, over and above.
le marché, the bargain.

Nous n'emportions[1] pas d'armes. J'aurais bien voulu prendre mon fusil: on m'en dissuada énergiquement.

"Que voulez-vous en faire? me dit-on; chasser? vous n'aurez pas le temps. Quand vous aurez été[2] dix heures à cheval dans votre journée, vous ne songerez qu'à souper et à dormir. Si vous voulez vous armer contre les brigands, vous avez doublement tort. D'abord, vous n'en rencontrerez pas. Si quelque homme de mauvaise mine vous arrête au détour d'un chemin, ce sera un gendarme qui vous demandera l'heure qu'il est et une poignée de tabac. Mais je suppose[3] que vous rencontriez des brigands; votre fusil ne servirait qu'à vous faire tuer[4]. Les brigands de ce pays-ci ne sont pas des héros de théâtre[5], qui aiment le danger et qui jouent avec la mort; ils se mettent prudemment dix contre un et vous vous apercevrez de leur présence quand vous aurez trente canons de fusil braqués sur vous. En pareil cas, la seule chose à faire, c'est de descendre de cheval et de donner consciencieusement tout ce qu'on a; ne vous exposez pas à perdre votre fusil par-dessus le marché." Je me laissai convaincre par ce raisonnement.

Scottish Leaving Certificate Examination, Lower Grade 1925.

NOTES

1 See p. 18, § 13. 2 See p. 58, § 44, QUAND. 3 *je suppose* = 'Suppose'. 4 *vous faire tuer*, 'to get you killed'. 5 *des héros de théâtre*, 'stage heroes', 'heroes of melodrama'.

5. *PERDUS DANS LA FORÊT*

VOCABULARY

la cime, top (of tree *or* mountain). *à plusieurs reprises*, several times.

Il monta au haut d'un grand arbre pour découvrir[1] au moins la montagne des Trois Pitons[2]; mais il n'aperçut autour de lui que les cimes des arbres. Cependant[3] l'ombre des montagnes couvrait déjà les forêts dans les vallées; le vent se calmait, comme il[4] arrive au coucher du soleil; un profond silence régnait dans ces solitudes. Paul, dans l'espoir que quelque chasseur pourrait l'entendre, cria alors de toute sa force: "Venez, venez au secours de Virginie!" Mais les seuls[5] échos de la forêt répondirent à sa voix et répétèrent à plusieurs reprises: "Virginie!...Virginie!"

BERNARDIN DE SAINT-PIERRE.

NOTES

1 See p. 18, § 13, *découvrir*. 2 *piton*, a local word for 'peak'. 3 'meanwhile' *or* 'however'? 4 Does this *il* refer to *le vent*, or is it impersonal? See p. 53, § 39, and p. 42, § 28. 5 See p. 50, § 35, SEUL.

6. *LA MORT DES OISEAUX*

VOCABULARY

le squelette, skeleton. *le gazon*, turf, grass.

Le soir, au coin du feu, j'ai pensé bien des fois
A la mort d'un oiseau, quelque part dans les bois.
Pendant les tristes[1] jours de l'hiver monotone[2],
Les pauvres nids déserts[3], les nids qu'on abandonne,
Se balancent[4] au vent sur le ciel gris de fer.
Oh! comme les oiseaux doivent mourir l'hiver!
Pourtant, lorsque viendra[5] le temps des violettes
Nous ne trouverons pas leurs délicats squelettes
Dans le gazon d'avril, où nous irons[5] courir.
Est-ce que les oiseaux se cachent pour mourir?

FRANÇOIS COPPÉE.

NOTES

1 See p. 30, § 18, *triste*. 2 Could you find a better word than 'monotonous'? 3 See p. 38, § 25. 4 See p. 61, § 49. 5 See p. 58, § 44.

7. *LA CHATTE*

VOCABULARY

la course, race, chase.
affolé, frantic, distracted.
échapper, to escape.
se sauver, to run off.
dans tous les sens, in every direction.
la jupe, skirt.
atteindre, to reach.
formidable, tremendous.
s'accrocher, to cling (*lit.* hook oneself).

Sœur Marie n'aimait pas la chatte. Elle resta un moment immobile, puis, elle courut prendre[1] un bâton et se lança après la bête. Ce fut[2] une course épouvantable: la chatte affolée sautait de tous côtés, échappant au bâton qui ne frappait que les bancs et les murs. Toutes les petites filles, prises de peur, se sauvaient vers la porte. Sœur Marie les arrêta d'un[3] mot: Que personne ne sorte! Puis la poursuite continua. Sœur Marie, le bâton haut[4], courait en silence; ses lèvres s'étaient ouvertes[5] et on voyait ses petites dents pointues; elle courait dans tous les sens, sautant les bancs en relevant[6] rapidement ses jupes; au moment où elle allait l'atteindre, la chatte fit un bond formidable et s'accrocha après[7] un rideau, tout[8] en haut d'une fenêtre.

S. C. 1923.

NOTES

1 See p. 33, § 21. 2 Tense? See p. 57, § 44. 3 Preposition? See p. 69, § 55, DE. 4 See p. 45, § 30. 5 Tense? See p. 56, § 44. 6 For *en* here, see p. 59, § 46. 7 *après* means other things besides 'after'. What must it mean here? 8 See p. 65, § 51, TOUT.

8. *LE PERROQUET ET LA CHATTE*

VOCABULARY

fébrile, feverish.
hérisser, to ruffle.
secouer, to shake.
repasser, to whet (strop, iron).
la mangeoire, manger, seed-box.
sensiblement, sensibly, visibly.
l'échine (n.f.), spine.
se délecter, to delight; *here* lick one's lips.
un arc, bow.
épouvanter, to terrify.
la fanfare, fanfare, flourish.

Le perroquet suivait les mouvements de la chatte avec une inquiétude fébrile: il hérissait ses plumes, secouant sa chaîne, levait une de ses pattes en agitant les doigts, et repassait son bec sur le bord de la mangeoire. Quant aux yeux de la chatte, fixés sur l'oiseau avec une intensité fascinatrice[1], ils disaient, dans un langage que le perroquet entendait fort bien et qui n'avait rien d'ambigu: "Quoique vert, ce poulet doit être bon à manger."

Nous suivions cette scène avec intérêt, prêts à intervenir quand besoin serait[2]. La chatte s'était sensiblement rapprochée; son nez rose frémissait, elle fermait à demi les yeux, sortait[3] et rentrait[3] ses griffes. De petits frissons lui couraient sur l'échine; elle se délectait à l'idée du repas succulent et rare qu'elle allait faire. Tout à coup, son dos s'arrondit comme un arc qu'on tend, et un bond d'une vigueur élastique la fit tomber juste sur le perchoir. Le perroquet, voyant le péril, d'une voix grave et profonde, cria soudain, "As-tu bien déjeuné, Jacquot?"

Cette phrase épouvanta la chatte, qui[4] fit un saut en arrière. Une fanfare de trompette, une pile de vaisselle se brisant par terre[5], un coup de pistolet tiré à ses oreilles n'eussent pas causé à l'animal félin une plus violente frayeur. THÉOPHILE GAUTIER.

NOTES

1 The idea is the same as in the English phrase: 'the serpent *fascinates* its prey'. Often *fasciné* = spell-bound. 2 See p. 58, § 44. 3 A good example of the transitive use of these verbs. 4 The Relative need not always be used in English. See p. 51, § 37. 5 Expand.

9. *LE DÉPART*

VOCABULARY

d'ailleurs, besides, moreover.
mince, thin, small, slender.
le linge, linen.
la lieue, league ($2\frac{1}{2}$ miles).
la pointe du jour, daybreak, dawn

La comtesse essaya d'interroger son fils sur ses projets d'avenir: mais elle comprit[1] qu'ils étaient si incertains et si vagues qu'il fallait avoir confiance en lui, et ne pas trop insister pour savoir ce que peut-être il ne pouvait pas lui dire. D'ailleurs, le plus pressé[2] maintenant c'était de procéder aux préparatifs du départ. Lucien ne voulait point perdre de temps. Il fit un mince paquet de ce qu'il croyait utile d'emporter, un peu de linge et quelques vêtements, et, le soir venu[3], quand tout le monde fut endormi au château, après avoir embrassé sa mère, il jeta son bagage sur les épaules du jardinier, qui, comme la plupart des gens de la maison, lui était entièrement dévoué, et prit un sentier à travers champs pour s'en aller à cinq lieues de là, gagner la station du chemin de fer, où passait[4] à la pointe du jour le train montant vers Paris.

Cambridge Senior, 1918.

NOTES

1 What is the full sense of the Past Historic here? See p. 57, § 44. 2 *le plus pressé*, 'the most urgent thing'. 3 Expand: see p. 37, § 24. 4 See p. 29, § 18.

10. *LA MAISON CHAMPÊTRE*

VOCABULARY

le sentier, path.
la façade, front.
le volet, (outside) shutter.
le parterre, flower-bed.
le jet d'eau, fountain.
le verger, orchard.
l'aube (n.f.), dawn; *dès —*, from early dawn.
ailé, winged.
le buisson, bush, shrub.
retentir, to ring, echo.
le tilleul, lime (tree).
couché, *here* brooding.
charmé, spell-bound.
la haie, hedge.
la fauvette, warbler.
le saule, willow.
le lierre, ivy.
gazouiller, to twitter.
ravir, to plunder, steal.
la nichée, brood, nestlings.
semer, to scatter.
la miette, crumb.
le rossignol, the nightingale.
l'avancée (n.f.), jutting out, projection.
l'ardoise (n.f.), slate.

Je sais une maison champêtre, à mi-pente du vallon[1]. Le sentier des prés conduit à la porte rustique: la façade blanche aux volets verts se cache derrière les grands arbres. Point[2] de parterre brillant, ni jet d'eau, ni fleurs rares; mais jardin et verger, au printemps, sont pleins de nids et de chansons d'oiseaux. Dès l'aube et tout le jour, c'est un concert de petites voix ailées; chaque arbre, chaque buisson retentit. Le soleil baissé[3], tous se taisent pour laisser au soir son silence. Seulement, par les nuits claires, le merle du tilleul fait entendre sa voix forte et pénétrante comme un son de flûte[4]; la femelle, couchée sur ses œufs, écoute charmée, à moitié endormie.

Merles dans le tilleul, rouges-gorges dans la haie, fauvettes par les saules, moineaux sous le lierre du vieux mur, gazouillez gaiement, dormez tranquilles!

Les enfants de la maison blanche ne raviront pas vos nichées. Ils chérissent leurs petits amis; tous les jours, ils sèment pour eux devant la porte des[5] grains de blé et les[5] miettes du repas. Chaque avril, on attend le rossignol. Que la gentille hirondelle vienne[6] maçonner[7] sa chambrette au bord du toit, sous l'avancée de l'ardoise, elle sera la bienvenue! CHARLES DELON.

NOTES

1 'half-way up the slope of the valley', i.e. on the hill-side. 2 Though *point* is stronger than *pas*, it is sometimes difficult to show the difference in translation. 3 *le soleil baissé*, accus. absolute; change the construction; see p. 37, § 24. 4 See p. 48, § 33. 5 See p. 49, § 34. 6 Lit. 'Let the swallow come', etc. In English we should rather say, 'If the swallow comes'. 7 Since *maçon* means 'mason', what must *maçonner* mean?

11. *MORT DE LOUIS XV*

VOCABULARY

l'écurie (n.f.), stable.
convenu, agreed.
la bougie, candle.
les gardes du corps, the body-guard, life-guards.
l'écuyer (n.m.), equerry.

Enfin, le 10 mai, 1774, se termina la longue carrière de Louis XV. — Le dauphin avait décidé qu'il partirait de Versailles au moment où le roi rendrait[1] son dernier soupir. Les chefs des écuries étaient donc convenus[2] avec les gens dans la chambre du roi que ceux-ci placeraient une bougie allumée auprès d'une fenêtre, et qu'à l'instant où le mourant cesserait[1] de vivre, un d'eux l'éteindrait. —

Cette bougie fut éteinte; à ce signal les gardes du corps, les pages et les écuyers montèrent à cheval; tout fut prêt pour le départ.

Le dauphin était chez la dauphine[3] quand un bruit terrible, semblable à celui[4] du tonnerre, se fit entendre[5]: c'était la foule des courtisans qui désertaient l'antichambre du souverain expiré pour venir saluer la nouvelle puissance de Louis XVI. A ce bruit étrange, ce dernier et son épouse reconnurent qu'ils allaient régner, et, par un mouvement spontané qui remplit d'attendrissement ceux qui les entouraient, tous deux se jetèrent à genoux et, versant des larmes, ils s'écrièrent: "Mon Dieu, guidez-nous, protégez-nous; nous régnons trop jeunes." Cambridge Senior, 1919.

NOTES

1 Tense? See p. 58, § 44. 2 *étaient convenus*, 'had arranged'. 3 See p. 70, § 56, CHEZ. 4 See p. 36, § 24. 5 *se fit entendre*, 'made itself be heard', i.e. 'was heard'.

12. *LA POLITESSE*

VOCABULARY

remettre, see p. 19, § 13.
exquis, exquisite, delightful.
l'enseignement (n.m.), teaching, instruction; *sometimes as here* lesson.
ajouter, to add.
l'aumône (n.f.), alms.
l'inconscience (n.f.), unconsciousness; *here almost* 'innocence.'
le droit, right; *avoir le — de faire*, to be justified in doing.

Un petit garçon de cinq ans rencontre un pauvre, très vieux et très infirme. Sa mère donne un sou à l'enfant, qui le porte au vieux pauvre; mais, en le lui remettant, il ôte d'abord devant lui sa petite casquette et le salue. N'est-ce pas exquis? Quel enseignement profond! Comme[1] ce petit enfant, qui se découvre devant la pauvreté, et qui ajoute l'aumône du cœur à l'aumône de la main, nous montre tout à coup la politesse sous[2] une forme nouvelle! Comme[1] il nous dit, sans le savoir, le cher petit! et son inconscience ajoute à la force de sa leçon; comme il nous dit clairement d'honorer dans tout être humain une créature de Dieu[3] et un frère de douleur[4]! Grâce à lui, nous avons le droit de compléter la phrase de Vauvenargues en disant: "La politesse est comme les grandes pensées: elle vient du cœur!" E. LEGOUVÉ.

NOTES

1 See p. 47, § 32, and p. 64, § 50; the second *comme il nous dit* simply repeats the first, the intervening part being a parenthesis. 2 See p. 71, § 56, SOUS. 3 Is this 'a creature of God' or 'one of God's creatures'? 4 *frère de douleur*, 'fellow-sufferer'. See p. 69, § 55.

13. *UNE LEÇON TERRIBLE*

VOCABULARY

un obus, shell.
un mouvement, movement; impulse.
la honte, shame; *avoir* —, to be ashamed, feel shame.
flairer, to sniff, sniff at.
se tut, 3rd sing. past hist. of *se taire*, to be *or* become silent.
éclater, to burst.
atteindre, to reach; hit.
un abandon, desertion.
serrer, to clasp, shake.
tacite, tacit, silent.
le siècle, century, generation, age.

L'Empereur me[1] tourna le dos et remonta sur son cheval, tenu[2] à quelques pas. En ce moment, notre tête de colonne[3] avait attaqué et l'on nous lançait[4] des obus. Il en tomba un[5] devant le front de ma compagnie, et quelques hommes se jetèrent en arrière[6], par un premier mouvement dont ils eurent honte. Bonaparte s'avança seul sur l'obus qui brûlait et fumait devant son cheval, et lui fit flairer cette fumée. Tout se tut et resta sans mouvement; l'obus éclata et n'atteignit personne[7]. Les grenadiers sentirent la leçon terrible qu'il leur donnait; moi, j'y sentis de plus quelque chose qui tenait du désespoir[8]. La France lui manquait, et il avait douté[9] un instant de ses vieux braves. Je me trouvai[10] trop vengé et lui trop puni de ses fautes par un si grand[11] abandon. Je me levai avec effort et, m'approchant de lui, je pris et serrai la main qu'il tendait à plusieurs d'entre nous. Il ne me reconnut point, mais ce fut pour moi une réconciliation tacite entre le plus obscur et le plus illustre des hommes de notre siècle.

ALFRED DE VIGNY.

NOTES

1 Do we say in English 'he turned his back *to* me'? 2 Expand; see p. 58, § 45. 3 *nôtre tête de colonne*, lit. 'our column-head', i.e. 'the head of our column'. 4 See p. 25, § 16, LANCER. 5 See p. 53, § 39. 6 Lit. 'threw themselves to the rear', i.e. 'started back'. 7 Turn by a passive construction. 8 'which bordered on despair', 'akin to despair'. 9 *douter de*, 'to doubt', 'mistrust'; here 'lose faith in'. 10 See p. 57, § 44, 'Past Historic'. 11 *si grand*, 'such'; see p. 65, § 51.

14. *LA MAISON DU PÈRE LORET*

VOCABULARY

la croisée, window.
le rebord, ledge.
la jacinthe, hyacinth.
étaler, to display.
les conserves (n.f. plur.), preserves, tinned meat.
la giroflée, wallflower.
la soupière, soup-tureen.
ébréché, chipped.

La maison dans laquelle le père Loret occupait un logement au cinquième étage était à deux pas de là; précédé de Maurice, il en[1] gravit lentement les cent vingt marches et, après avoir ouvert[2] la fenêtre de sa chambre, fit signe à celui-ci d'approcher. Séparée[3] de lui par une cour très étroite, Maurice aperçut alors une autre croisée dont le rebord était élargi par une planche et sur cette planche se trouvaient rangées les fleurs du pauvre infirme dans les vases[4] les plus divers: de belles jacinthes commençaient à s'ouvrir dans de vieux pots à moutarde; primevères et violettes étalant leurs boutons et leurs feuilles vert tendre[5] avaient pour domaine d'anciennes boîtes à conserves, et au beau milieu[6], se dressant fièrement, la giroflée double plongeait ses racines jusqu'au fond de la terre que[7] contenait une petite soupière ébréchée. S. C. 1921.

NOTES

1 What noun does *en* refer to? 2 Tense? 3 Construction? 4 Were these 'vases'? 5 Compare '*des yeux* bleu clair', '*des cheveux* brun foncé'. 6 See p. 42, § 28. 7 Construction? See p. 51, § 37.

15. *MAISON À VENDRE*

VOCABULARY

contourner, to go round, come round.
le fond, the bottom, the inmost part; *here* au fond de = at the head of.
la grève, the beach, strand.
le faîte, the top, summit.
le genêt, broom.
tressaillir, to start, thrill.
séduire, to charm.
un écriteau, notice, ticket.

Je contournai un petit promontoire et j'aperçus au fond d'une plage étroite et ronde, une maison blanche, bâtie sur trois terrasses[1] qui descendaient jusqu'à la grève, comme des marches géantes. Et chacune portait, ainsi qu'une couronne d'or, sur son faîte, un long bouquet de genêts en fleur!

Pourquoi la vue de cette maison me fit-elle tressaillir de joie? Le sais-je? On trouve parfois, en voyageant ainsi, des coins de pays qu'on croit[2] connaître depuis longtemps, tant[3] ils vous sont familiers, tant ils plaisent[4] à votre cœur. Est-il possible qu'on ne les ait jamais vus? qu'on n'ait point vécu là autrefois? Tout vous séduit, vous enchante, la ligne douce de l'horizon, la disposition des arbres, la couleur du sable!

Je m'arrêtai, saisi d'amour pour cette demeure. Comme j'eusse aimé la posséder, y vivre, toujours! Je m'approchai de la porte, le cœur battant d'envie, et j'aperçus, sur un des piliers de la barrière, un grand écriteau: "*A vendre.*" MAUPASSANT.

NOTES

1 The position of the house is somewhat difficult to visualize. In such cases it is unwise to make the translation too definite.
2 See p. 61, § 48. 3 See p. 64, § 50. 4 See p. 47, § 32, PLAIRE À

16. *L'ORIGINE DU SYSTÈME FÉODAL*

VOCABULARY

le poids, weight, burden. *la trêve*, truce, respite.
le seigneur, liege-lord (*feudal*).

Les générations modernes ne savent plus ce que c'est que le danger. Elles ne savent plus ce que c'est que de trembler chaque jour pour sa moisson, pour son pain de l'année, pour sa chaumière, pour sa vie, pour sa femme et ses enfants. Elles ne savent plus ce que devient l'âme sous le poids d'une telle terreur, et[1] quand cette terreur dure quatre-vingts ans sans trêve ni merci. Elles ne savent plus ce que c'est que le besoin d'être sauvé.

On donna tout aux seigneurs. On oublia tout pour eux. On ne pensa ni à des rois qu'on ne voyait pas, ni à des libertés dont on n'aurait su que faire[2]. On obéit à ceux par qui l'on était défendu. On donna la sujétion en échange de la sécurité. Des milliers et des millions de contrats se formèrent entre chaque champ et le guerrier qui combattait pour lui, entre chaque existence humaine et le guerrier à qui l'on devait de vivre.

FUSTEL DE COULANGES.

NOTES

1 This *et* has almost the sense of *surtout*. 2 There is an implied supposition—'if they had possessed such (liberties)'. Translate carefully.

17. *LA MALADIE CHEZ LES PAYSANS*

VOCABULARY

entraver, lit. to hobble; to hinder, impede.
les bestiaux (n.m.), the cattle.
s'inquiéter, to be anxious, to worry.
la ménagère, housewife.
pesamment, heavily.
la meule, millstone.
grincer, see p. 5, § 3.
beugler, to bellow.
un abri, shelter.
accoter, to prop up.
le revers, the side, slope.
réclamer, to claim, call for.

C'est une chose singulière que[1] la maladie dans ces intérieurs de paysans. Elle n'entrave rien, n'arrête rien. Les bestiaux entrent, sortent aux heures ordinaires. Si l'homme est malade, la femme le remplace à l'ouvrage, ne prend pas même le temps de lui tenir compagnie, de s'inquiéter, de se désoler. La terre n'attend pas, ni les bêtes non plus. La ménagère travaille tout le long du jour; le soir, elle tombe de fatigue[2] et s'endort pesamment. Le malheureux couché à l'étage supérieur, au-dessus de la chambre où la meule grince, de l'étable où beuglent les bœufs, c'est le blessé tombé pendant le combat. On ne s'occupe pas de lui. On se contente de le mettre à l'abri dans un coin, de l'accoter à un arbre ou au revers d'un fossé, pendant que la bataille qui réclame tous les bras continue.

ALPHONSE DAUDET.

NOTES

1 See p. 51, § 37. 2 Render by some idiomatic English expression.

18. *L'AUTOMNE*

VOCABULARY

la bourrasque, squall.
le soupir, sigh.
jauni, (turned) yellow.
tourbillonner, to whirl.
le sentier, footpath.
détrempé, soaking.
la flaque, pool, puddle.
certes, certainly.
follement, madly, wildly, extravagantly.
la flambée, blaze, bright blazing fire.
la guêtre, gaiter, legging.
lécher, to lick.
la ferraille, (old) iron.
la grange, barn.
hurler, to howl.
rugir, to roar.
le croassement, cawing.
lugubre, dismal.

Connaissez-vous l'automne, l'automne en pleins[1] champs, avec ses bourrasques, ses longs soupirs, ses feuilles jaunies qui tourbillonnent au loin[2], ses sentiers détrempés, ses beaux couchers de soleil, pâles comme[3] le sourire d'un malade, ses flaques d'eau dans les chemins?...Connaissez-vous tout cela?

Si vous avez vu toutes ces choses, vous n'y[4] êtes certes pas restés indifférents: on les déteste ou on les aime follement.

Je suis au nombre de ceux[5] qui les aiment et je donnerais deux étés pour un automne. J'adore les grandes flambées: j'aime à me réfugier dans le fond de la cheminée[6], ayant[7] mon chien entre mes guêtres humides. J'aime à regarder les hautes flammes qui lèchent la vieille ferraille aux dents pointues et illuminent les noires profondeurs. On entend le vent siffler dans la grange, la grande porte craquer, le chien tirer sur sa chaîne en hurlant, et malgré le bruit de la forêt, qui tout près de là rugit en courbant le dos, on distingue les croassements lugubres d'une bande de corbeaux qui luttent contre la tempête. La pluie bat les petites vitres; on songe à ceux qui sont dehors, en allongeant ses jambes vers le feu. GUSTAVE DROZ.

NOTES

1 See p. 42, § 28. 2 See p. 42, § 28. 3 See p. 65, § 51. 4 To what noun does *y* refer? 5 'one of those'. 6 In France the great fireplaces of old-fashioned country houses have seats at each side of the fire. 7 See p. 33, § 21.

19. *POUR LA POSTÉRITÉ*

VOCABULARY

lier, to bind.
un associé, associate, partner.
témoigner, to show.
commode, convenient, comfortable.
livrer, to hand on, pass on.
un devancier, one who goes before, predecessor.

Il n'y a pas aujourd'hui un homme intelligent qui ne se sente[1] lié par des fils[2] invisibles à tous les hommes passés, présents et futurs. Nous sommes les héritiers de tous ceux qui sont morts, les associés de tous ceux qui vivent, la providence[3] de tous ceux qui naîtront. Pour témoigner notre reconnaissance aux mille générations qui nous ont fait graduellement ce que nous sommes, il faut perfectionner la nature humaine en nous et autour de nous. Pour remercier dignement les travailleurs innombrables qui ont rendu notre habitation[4] si belle et si commode, il faut la livrer plus belle et plus commode encore aux générations futures. Nous sommes meilleurs et plus heureux que nos devanciers; faisons[5] que notre postérité soit meilleure et plus heureuse que nous. E. ABOUT.

NOTES

1 Which part of the verb *sentir* is this? On the translation of *qui*, see p. 51, § 37. 2 Does this mean 'sons'? See p. 9, § 7. 3 The abstract *la providence* is awkward, coming after *les héritiers* and *les associés*: 'the Providence of' means 'those who make provision for', 'who provide for'. 4 i.e. 'this world', 'the earth'. 5 See p. 56, § 43.

20. *NAPOLÉON*

VOCABULARY

la trahison, treason.
hors de lui, beside himself.
la raillerie, raillery, jesting, jeering.

On ne peut pas dire précisément que l'empereur manquât de cœur, ni de tout sentiment du bien et du beau. Loin d'être incapable d'amitié, il se montrait souvent bon camarade, et c'était là justement ce qui le rendait[1] cruel; il voulait être aimé et admiré pour lui-même, et s'irritait contre[2] ceux qui n'avaient pas envers lui ces sentiments. Sa nature était jalouse, susceptible, et les petites trahisons[3] le mettaient hors de lui. Presque toutes ses vengeances[3] s'exerçaient sur des personnes qu'il avait admises dans son cercle intime, mais qui abusèrent de la familiarité qu'il encourageait pour le percer de leurs railleries.

Cambridge Senior, 1916.

NOTES

1 See p. 40, § 26. 2 See p. 70, § 56, CONTRE. 3 See p. 51, § 36.

SECTION II

MODEL LESSON II A

1. Si l'on compare les couvents où s'élevaient les filles nobles il y a cent ans, aux couvents qui reçoivent aujourd'hui les petites demoiselles riches, on est frappé du changement des mœurs. 2. On enseignait aux héritières des premières maisons de France les soins domestiques. 3. Elles apprenaient à serrer le linge, à balayer les chambres, à servir à table, à faire la cuisine. 4. Cet enseignement valait bien celui de la minéralogie, dont nous tirons aujourd'hui beaucoup d'orgueil. 5. Il instruisait les riches à ne point mépriser les pauvres; il les gardait de croire que le travail des mains avilit ceux qui s'y livrent et qu'il est noble de ne rien faire. 6. Il leur montrait le but de la vie, qui est de servir, et non point par occasion, mais tous les jours, à toute heure, humblement et avec simplicité. 7. Nous voyons fort bien les préjugés de la vieille aristocratie; ils étaient cruels, j'en conviens. 8. Mais il ne faut pas prêter à la société d'autrefois ceux que nous avons et qu'elle n'avait point. 9. Nous avons inventé l'aristocratie des mains blanches, et maintenant les petites filles de nos

gros industriels ne comprennent pas que Peau d'Ane fît des gâteaux, puisqu'elle était fille de roi.

ANATOLE FRANCE.

Scottish Universities Entrance Board Preliminary Examinations, September 1927.

1. *Si l'on compare les couvents où s'élevaient les filles nobles il y a cent ans, aux couvents qui reçoivent aujourd'hui les petites demoiselles riches, on est frappé du changement des mœurs.*

Si l'on: *l'* is regularly used between *si* and *on* for euphony, to prevent a hiatus which the French feel to be unpleasant. It adds nothing to the meaning. Of the possible translations of *on* (see p. 55, § 41) those suitable here are 'one', 'we' and 'you'. 'They' is out of the question. The passive form will not do for *on est frappé* further on in the sentence, and a single translation of *on* to suit both phrases is evidently necessary.

les couvents, etc.: not 'convents', but '*the* convents'. This is not a case of *les* used in a general sense as in *J'aime les poires* (see p. 49, § 34), where *les poires* includes all pears; it is a case of *les* with a noun qualified by a relative clause, as in *J'aime* les *poires que vous m'avez données*, where the pears are specified. There is often some doubt as to whether we should or should not use 'the' in English. But when, as here, the relative clause which follows *specifies*, 'the' is clearly required.

où: 'where' is possible; 'at which' seems no better (see p. 52, § 38).

s'élevaient: not quite 'were brought up', but 'were educated'. The reflexive may perhaps have also some slight notion of *self*-education, but this shade of meaning can scarcely be shown in English.

les filles nobles: 'girls of noble descent', i.e. 'the daughters of the nobility', not 'noble girls' as it was generally translated. The point is not their character, but their social rank.

il y a cent ans. This was usually taken to go with *couvents,* as if meaning 'the convents of a hundred years ago'. But surely it goes with *s'élevaient.*

les petites demoiselles riches: *les demoiselles* are 'young ladies' as contrasted with *les filles nobles* who are called 'girls' without more ado, although of higher degree; *demoiselle* is therefore a little ironical here, as it often is, and suggests the 'uppishness' of *nouveaux riches.* The epithet *petites* defines the age more closely; *une demoiselle* might be an unmarried lady of uncertain age; *une vieille demoiselle* is 'an old maid', *une petite demoiselle* is a schoolgirl, in one of the lower forms; *les petites demoiselles riches* are, in familiar style, 'rich young things', but here 'young ladies of the wealthy classes' will suffice.

on est frappé: 'one is (we, you are) struck (surprised)'. Whichever of these forms we have selected for translating *Si l'on compare* above must of course be used again here.

mœurs: a word with various senses: sometimes it means 'mode of life', sometimes 'manners and customs', 'ways'. Here it refers to changing educational ideas.

'If we compare the convents at which the daughters of the nobility received their education a hundred years ago with the convents which nowadays take the young ladies of the wealthy classes, we are struck by the changed conditions.'

2. *On enseignait aux héritières des premières maisons de France les soins domestiques.*

On: *On* cannot refer to the same person as the *on* of the first sentence, since this *on* lived a hundred years ago. It must be translated by the indefinite 'They' or, better, by the passive construction.

des premières maisons de France: *premières* means

'first' (as when we talk of the Queen as 'the first lady in the land'), or 'foremost' or 'greatest'; *maison*, like 'house', is used of illustrious families, e.g. *la maison des Stuart*; *de* depending on a superlative is generally 'in', e.g. *la plus grande ville* du *monde*, 'the greatest city *in* the world'.

les soins domestiques: not 'domestic cares' of course, but 'household tasks', 'household duties', 'house-keeping', what is, when taught in our modern schools, called 'Housewifery' or 'Domestic Science'.

'The heiresses of the greatest houses in France were taught house-keeping.'

3. *Elles apprenaient à serrer le linge, à balayer les chambres, à servir à table, à faire la cuisine.*

serrer le linge: literally 'to put away the linen', but implying the whole preliminary operations, sorting, examining and mending the things that had come from the wash.

balayer les chambres. Nearly all the candidates said 'to sweep the rooms'—just as they would have said 'to sweep the chimneys'. But is not the proper phrase 'to sweep *out* the rooms'? It must be constantly borne in mind that while a French verb is enough by itself, the sense of an English verb often requires to be eked out with an adverb; see p. 20, § 14. Thus *Le vent* balaie *les nuages* is not 'The wind *sweeps* the clouds'. That would give quite a wrong notion of what the French verb describes. It is 'The wind *sweeps away* the clouds'.

faire la cuisine: this is not 'to do the kitchen' nor even 'to do *out* the kitchen', though it is perfectly reasonable to imagine such to be the meaning; it is 'to do the cooking', 'to cook'. Advertisements drawing attention to the 'excellent cuisine', etc., of English hotels are so numerous in English newspapers that most readers, whether they know French or not, must know perfectly well what *cuisine* means in this connection. Even those who have learned French at school must have a shrewd suspicion that the attraction advertised is not that of inspecting the kitchen. It is a pity that they so seldom apply their knowledge of the world to examination papers.

'They learned to look after the linen, sweep out the rooms, serve at table, and cook.'

4. *Cet enseignement valait bien celui de la minéralogie, dont nous tirons aujourd'hui beaucoup d'orgueil.*

This sentence proved to be the undoing of most candidates. The difficulty was mainly due to ignorance of the meaning of the words *valait bien*; they mean 'was worth quite as much as', 'was every bit as good as'. Also it was not realized that *celui* stands for *l'enseignement.* Although the meaning of *tirer*, 'to draw', and *orgueil*, 'pride', were generally known, the sense of the phrase was missed. It is, literally, 'from which we draw to-day much pride', i.e. 'which we are now very proud of', or 'on which we now plume ourselves'.

'Such teaching was quite as valuable as the teaching of mineralogy, on which we now plume ourselves.'

5. *Il instruisait les riches à ne point mépriser les pauvres; il les gardait de croire que le travail des mains avilit ceux qui s'y livrent et qu'il est noble de ne rien faire.*

The foolish, who in this examination were unusually numerous, translated *Il* by 'He'. Who 'he' was, or what 'he' was doing here, they did not explain. Since a pronoun stands for a noun, what noun does *Il* stand for? Clearly *enseignement.*

à ne point mépriser: 'not to despise'. Many candidates who knew that *point* is rather stronger than *pas* said 'not to despise at all' (or 'in the least'), but this is awkward. The difference which the French make between *pas* and *point* is often left in English to be shewn by the tone of the voice.

il les gardait de croire. This usually became woeful nonsense. To translate it requires some knowledge of French, but also the exercise of some common-sense; *garder* does sometimes mean 'to guard', but must we really translate it so every time and all the time? *Gardez vos rangs, Gardez vos pardessus, Gardez la monnaie pour vous-même,* and innumerable other examples, have nothing to do with 'guarding', only with 'keeping'. The sense of *il les gardait de croire* is simply 'it kept (prevented) them from thinking'. Similarly, *Gardez-vous de le dire,* though meaning 'Beware of saying so' or 'Take care not to say so', is literally 'Keep yourself from saying so'.

le travail des mains: 'manual work' is not far from the sense, but 'manual labour' would suggest very heavy work indeed, such as that of a navvy; 'the work of the hands' is unnecessarily Biblical.

avilit is in the same tense as *est* in *il est noble,* which it balances. There is no need to say 'was' in English; 'is' is quite correct. Manual work *is* not yet degrading; neither is idleness a mark of nobility.

ceux qui s'y livrent: *se livrer à quelque chose* is to give oneself up to something, to engage in something; *y* = *au travail des mains.*

qu'il est noble, etc. This depends, like *que le travail,* etc., on *croire*: 'and [prevented them from thinking] that it is aristocratic ('noble' would not be very clear, since it would imply nobility of character rather than noble descent) to do nothing'.

'It taught the rich not to despise the poor; it kept them from thinking that manual work degrades those who engage in it, and that it is aristocratic to do nothing.'

6. *Il leur montrait le but de la vie, qui est de servir, et non point par occasion, mais tous les jours, à toute heure, humblement et avec simplicité.*

le but: 'the goal', 'the aim', 'the purpose', 'the object'.

servir: 'service' as in 'social service', etc., is the ordinary present-day term, but the verb, 'serve', goes better with what follows and has besides very good credentials; notably it is implied in the Prince of Wales's motto *Ich dien* = I serve, and Milton says 'They also *serve* who only stand and wait'.

et: 'and that' is clearer than 'and' alone.

par occasion: we say '*on* occasion'.

tous les jours: 'every day', not 'always', which is *toujours*.

à toute heure: 'at every hour' or, as we might say, more fully, 'at every hour of the day'.

avec simplicité: 'with simplicity' is probably sufficient; if not, 'simplicity of heart' would put the meaning beyond doubt.

'It showed them the object of life, which is to serve, and that not on occasion, but every day, at every hour of the day, humbly and with simplicity.'

7. *Nous voyons fort bien les préjugés de la vieille aristocratie; ils étaient cruels, j'en conviens.*

fort bien: is rather ironical: 'we see beautifully', 'we see splendidly', 'we see, most clearly', etc.

ils étaient cruels. We do not readily speak of 'cruel' prejudices; perhaps 'harsh' or 'unfeeling' or 'bitter' is more suitable.

j'en conviens: is a stock expression meaning 'I admit',

'I agree', in which *en* is not to be translated, any more than it is in *Je n*'en *sais rien*, 'I don't know'.

'We see, most clearly, the prejudices of the ancient aristocracy; they were bitter, I admit.'

8. *Mais il ne faut pas prêter à la société d'autrefois ceux que nous avons et qu'elle n'avait point.*

il ne faut pas prêter. This was often translated 'it is not necessary to lend' (better, 'attribute'), but that is not quite the sense. A sentence like *Il ne faut pas employer ce mot-là* is not nearly so mild as 'It is unnecessary to use that word'; it is equivalent to 'You *must not* use that word'.

ceux que. It was quite clear that here very few candidates took any thought. Most wrote down 'those *whom*' and, by so doing, destroyed the whole sense of the passage. The feeling that Anatole France probably had something sensible to say would, if accompanied by a little reflection, have suggested that *ceux* must stand for *les préjugés.*

qu'elle n'avait point. The force of *point* can be brought out by placing 'not' at the end of our sentence.

'But we must not attribute to the society of former times those which we have and (which) it had not.'

9. *Nous avons inventé l'aristocratie des mains blanches, et maintenant les petites filles de nos gros industriels ne comprennent pas que Peau d'Ane fît des gâteaux, puisqu'elle était fille de roi.*

les petites filles: 'the little daughters', to be distinguished from *les petites-filles*, 'the grand-daughters'.

nos gros industriels. The most common rendering, curiously, was 'our great industrial centres', which looks as if it came straight out of the evening paper, together with another very frequent translation, 'our bloated industrial magnates'. *Un gros industriel* is 'a large manufacturer', but neither the French expression nor the English alludes to his personal appearance.

ne comprennent pas que Peau d'Ane fît des gâteaux. This is a treacherous phrase, because the mood of *fît* is apt to pass unnoticed. It cannot mean 'do not understand that she made cakes'; it must mean 'do not understand that she *should* make cakes', i.e. 'cannot understand her making cakes'.

Peau d'Ane: the heroine of one of Perrault's less well-known Fairy Tales; literally 'Ass's Skin'. Our English version has 'Cat-skin'.

elle était fille de roi: not '*the* daughter of *a* king', nor '*the* king's daughter', but 'a king's daughter'; cp. *il est soldat,* 'he is *a* soldier'.

'We have invented the aristocracy of white hands and now the youthful daughters of our large manufacturers cannot understand Cat-skin making cakes, since she was a king's daughter.'

Suggested Rendering

If we compare the convents where the daughters of the nobility received their education a hundred years ago with the convents which nowadays take the young ladies of the wealthy classes, we are struck by the changed conditions. The heiresses of the greatest houses in France were taught house-keeping. They learned to look after the linen, sweep out the rooms, serve at table, and cook. Such teaching was quite as valuable as the teaching of mineralogy, on which we now plume ourselves. It taught the rich not to despise the poor; it kept them from thinking that manual work degrades those who engage in it, and that it is aristocratic to do nothing. It showed them the object of life, which is to serve, and that not on occasion, but every day, at every hour of the day, humbly and with simplicity. We see, most clearly, the prejudices of the ancient aristocracy; they were bitter, I admit. But we must not attribute to the society of former times those which we have and it had not. We have invented the aristocracy of white hands and now the youthful daughters of our large manufacturers cannot understand Cat-skin making cakes, since she was a king's daughter.

MODEL LESSON II B

La Mort d'un Lion

Étant un vieux chasseur altéré de grand air
Et du sang noir des bœufs, il avait l'habitude
De contempler de haut les plaines et la mer,
Et de rugir en paix, libre en sa solitude.

Aussi, comme un damné qui rôde dans l'enfer,
Pour l'inepte plaisir de cette multitude
Il allait et venait dans sa cage de fer,
Heurtant les deux cloisons avec sa tête rude.

L'horrible sort, enfin, ne devant plus changer,
Il cessa brusquement de boire et de manger;
Et la mort emporta son âme vagabonde.

O cœur toujours en proie à la rébellion,
Qui tournes, haletant, dans la cage du monde,
Lâche, que ne fais-tu comme a fait ce lion?

LECONTE DE LISLE.

Scottish Universities Entrance Board, September 1925.

After reading through the passage we can all, however little we may have understood it, add something to the information given in the title, *La Mort d'un Lion*. The lion was a caged lion and his death was due to that fact.

Even without reading it at all, by merely holding the examination paper before us at arm's length, we could tell something about the passage. It is printed as poetry; it comprises four sections; the first two sections are of equal length and contain four lines each; the last two are also of equal length and contain three lines each; total, fourteen; it is a sonnet. It is therefore not an extract, but an entire poem, treating a single theme. We could also notice that each section is ended by a full stop and must therefore be complete in itself. If we know anything about the author, Leconte de Lisle, or indeed about any other modern French sonneteer, we can be tolerably certain that each of the four sections will convey a definite meaning of its own, make its own independent contribution to the sense of the whole; furthermore, that not improbably the first two sections will be descriptive, in the third something will *happen*, and in the fourth we shall find the moral.

A closer reading brings out easily enough the four main ideas in the sonnet, section by section:

1. This lion was once free.
2. In his cage he would move furiously to and fro.
3. At last he pined and died.
4. Moral.

If we keep these main facts steadily before us, we shall be saved from many errors when for purposes of translation we enter into the detail.

1. *Étant un vieux chasseur altéré de grand air*
Et du sang noir des bœufs, il avait l'habitude
De contempler de haut les plaines et la mer,
Et de rugir en paix, libre en sa solitude.

This section evidently describes the lion in his wild state, when he fed upon the oxen which he slew, and roamed at large as king of the animals. The difficulties are the meaning of *altéré* and the translation of *contempler* and *rugir*.

Either we know *altéré* or we do not. In the latter case we could hardly guess its meaning. At least we could hardly guess it from *grand air*, 'open air'. But we see that *altéré* takes *de* and that not only *grand air*, but also *sang noir* depends upon it, and from the latter fact we might possibly conclude that *altéré de* means 'thirsting for'. We ought, however, to know *altéré*, for it is a common enough word. Its opposite (*se désaltérer*, 'to slake one's thirst') occurs in one of the best known of all La Fontaine's Fables, *Le Loup et l'Agneau*:

> *Un Agneau* se désaltérait
> *Dans le courant d'une onde pure.*

In fact, *être altéré* is a very frequent literary equivalent of *avoir soif*; *un tigre altéré de sang* is 'a tiger athirst for blood'.

The English for *contempler* is no doubt often 'to contemplate'. But *do* we say in English that a lion 'contemplates' the scenery when he goes, as is his custom, to a high place and looks down upon the surrounding country, monarch of all he—*surveys*? Similarly, *rugir* (see p. 5, § 3) is not 'to blush', which is *rougir*; *rugir* means 'to roar'. At first sight *rugir en paix* seems self-contradictory; it is a bold way of saying that the lion, when free, roared at will, to his heart's content. Without spending much time on problems of English style, it might be remarked here that 'from on high' or 'from above' would perhaps be better expressed by 'from a high place' and 'the plains and the sea' by 'plains and sea'. Then we should say:

'Being an old hunter athirst for open air and the black blood of oxen, he was wont to survey from a high place plains and sea, and roar at will, free in his solitude.'

2. *Aussi, comme un damné qui rôde dans l'enfer,*
Pour l'inepte plaisir de cette multitude
Il allait et venait dans sa cage de fer,
Heurtant les deux cloisons avec sa tête rude.

The general sense is that in captivity, before the spectators in a menagerie or at the 'Zoo', the lion would pace furiously to and fro and vainly run his head against the walls of the cage. What is the connection between this and what went before? The logical relationship between this section of four lines, or quatrain as it is called, and the preceding quatrain is indicated by *Aussi*. The word *aussi* means sometimes 'also', sometimes 'and so' or 'therefore'. When it has the latter meaning, subject and verb are often inverted, but not always. Which is the sense intended here? The *general* sense will keep us right. The first quatrain said that the lion had been used to liberty. Does the second say '*Moreover* he paced furiously up and down the cage'? Or does it say, '*Consequently* he paced', etc.? Of these two statements one is sensible and the other is not. The sensible one is what the poet meant.

If we have difficulty with the simile introduced by *comme*, in the first line, we may leave it alone for the time being and pass on to the next line, which goes with what follows—as is shown by, among other things, the absence of a comma at the end of the line. It was, then, for the 'inept', or 'silly' pleasure of *cette multitude* (*cette* being contemptuous: 'that rabble') that the lion 'came and went in his iron cage'. Where was his 'coming and going'? Between the front bars and the back of the cage? Probably not. He went from one side of the cage to the other. What stopped him on either side? Not *un mur*, 'an outside wall', but *une cloison*, 'a partition', a sense which intelligent guessing (see p. 10, § 8) would give us, or which we may already know from the phrase *une cloison étanche*, 'a water-tight compartment'.

What did the lion do to the two partitions *avec sa tête rude*? What *could* he do to them—unless strike or batter them? Why is *sa tête* called *rude*? Certainly not because it was 'unmannerly'. It was 'rough' or 'strong' or 'rugged' or 'shaggy'. There remains the simile *comme un damné qui rôde dans l'enfer*, in which the word *rôde* may at first have given us pause. It means 'to prowl', 'to roam', 'to move restlessly hither and thither'. The lion in his cage is compared with a lost soul roaming in hell; somewhat as in the well-known expression *errer comme une âme en peine*.

'Therefore, like a lost soul prowling in hell, he would for the stupid pleasure of the vulgar pace up and down his iron cage, battering the two sides with his shaggy head.'

3. *L'horrible sort, enfin, ne devant plus changer,*
Il cessa brusquement de boire et de manger;
Et la mort emporta son âme vagabonde.

The general sense of this, the first 'tercet' or section of three lines, is: at last it became clear that escape was impossible; then the lion lost hope, refused food and drink—and died.

In *L'horrible sort, sort* might just possibly mean 'the power which metes out fate', but it is more probably the 'fate' meted out. The chief difficulty is the Present Participle *devant*. The meaning is best made clear by substituting for the Present Participle the Past Tense, and supplying a conjunction. The phrase is evidently equal to *Puisque l'horrible sort ne devait plus changer*, where the force of *devait* is 'was to', 'was destined to', as in *Il quitta sa ville natale qu'il* ne devait *plus revoir*, 'He left his native city which he was destined never to see again'. It thus means: 'At last, since horrible (better, 'dreadful') fate was no more to alter', i.e. 'was not to be altered', or, more freely, 'At last, his dreadful fate leaving no hope of change'. The meaning at the root of *Son âme vagabonde* is that the lion's instincts demanded a wandering life; 'his roving spirit' conveys this.

'At last, since his dreadful fate was never more to alter, suddenly he ceased to eat and drink, and death bore away his roving spirit.'

4. *O cœur toujours en proie à la rebellion,*
Qui tournes, haletant, dans la cage du monde,
Lâche, que ne fais-tu comme a fait ce lion?

The second tercet points the moral or, rather, asks us to supply one. They that have rebellion in their hearts, they that in this world feel ill at ease, cribbed, cabined and confined—why do they not as did this lion?

The phrase *en proie à* means 'a prey to', 'given over as a prey'. Thus Hugo in *L'Expiation* says of Napoleon, about to fall a victim to fate at Waterloo:

L'empereur était là, debout, qui regardait.
Il était comme un arbre en proie à *la cognée.*

In *Qui tournes*, the person of the verb must not be overlooked—'Who dost turn'. The verb itself perhaps requires some expansion in English, as, for instance, in Matthew Arnold's poem *Requiescat*:

Her life was turning, turning
In mazes of heat and sound,

(where we find also a distant parallel to *son âme vagabonde* in 'Her cabined ample spirit').

For *haletant*, literally, 'panting', 'breathless'; a vaguer term like 'restless' would also be appropriate.

'O heart for ever in revolt, that dost turn feverishly in this world's cage, O coward heart, why doest thou not as did this lion?'

Suggested Rendering

Being an old hunter athirst for open air and the black blood of oxen, he was wont to survey from a high place plains and sea, and roar at will, free in his solitude. Therefore, like a lost soul prowling in hell, he would for the stupid pleasure of the vulgar pace up and down his iron cage, battering the two sides with his shaggy head. At last, since his dreadful fate was never more to alter, suddenly he ceased to eat and drink, and death bore away his roving spirit. O heart for ever in revolt, that dost turn feverishly in this world's cage, O coward heart, why doest thou not as did this lion?

21. *REMPLISSONS NOTRE TÂCHE*

VOCABULARY

la part, the part, lot.
échu, p.p. of *échoir*, to fall.
l'envie (n.f.), envy, jealousy.
un émule, rival, competitor.
le but, end, aim, goal.
le concours, competition.

Que chacun de vous se contente donc de la part qui lui sera échue. Quelle que soit sa carrière, elle lui donnera une mission, des devoirs, une certaine somme de bien à produire. Ce sera là sa tâche; qu'il la remplisse avec courage et énergie, honnêtement et fidèlement, et il aura fait dans sa position tout ce qu'il[1] est donné à l'homme de faire. Qu'il la remplisse aussi sans envie contre ses émules. Vous ne serez pas seuls dans votre chemin; vous y[2] marcherez avec d'autres appelés par la Providence à poursuivre le même but. Dans ce concours de la vie, ils pourront vous surpasser par le talent, ou devoir à la fortune un succès qui vous échappera. Ne leur en veuillez[3] pas et, si vous avez fait de votre mieux, ne vous en veuillez pas à vous-mêmes. Le succès n'est pas ce qui importe, c'est l'effort: car c'est là ce qui dépend de[4] l'homme, ce qui l'élève, ce qui le rend content de lui-même. JOUFFROY.

NOTES

1 Construction? Is this *il* personal or impersonal? See p. 53, § 39. 2 Exact meaning of *y*? 3 *en vouloir à quelqu'un*, to have

a grudge *or* spite against someone, to be annoyed or angry with someone. 4 Preposition?

22. *LE DRAPEAU*

VOCABULARY

sevré, separated, cut off.
une étape, a day's march.
le lambeau, shred, rag.
la soie, silk.
clapoter, to flap.
point de ralliement, rallying-point.
déchiré, torn.
le foyer, hearth, home.
bercer, to rock.
enfermé, enclosed, included, contained.

Voyez-vous, disait souvent le vieux capitaine Fougerel en frappant sur la table, vous ne savez pas, vous autres[1], ce que c'est que le drapeau. Il faut avoir été soldat; il faut avoir passé[2] la frontière et marché sur des chemins qui ne sont plus ceux de la France; il faut avoir été éloigné du pays, sevré de toute parole de la langue qu'on a parlée depuis l'enfance; il faut s'être dit[3], pendant les journées d'étapes et de fatigue, que tout ce qui reste de la patrie absente, c'est le lambeau de soie aux trois couleurs françaises qui clapote là-bas au centre du bataillon; il faut n'avoir eu, dans la fumée de la bataille, d'autre point de ralliement que ce morceau d'étoffe déchirée pour comprendre, pour sentir ce que[4] contient dans ses plis cette chose sacrée qu'on appelle le drapeau.

Le drapeau, mes pauvres amis, mais, sachez-le bien, c'est, contenu dans un seul mot, rendu palpable dans un seul objet, tout ce qui fut, tout ce qui est la vie de chacun de nous: le foyer où l'on naquit, le coin de terre où l'on grandit, le premier sourire d'enfant, la mère qui vous berce, les espoirs, les rêves, les souvenirs; c'est toutes ces joies à la fois, toutes enfermées dans un mot, le plus beau de tous, la patrie. JULES CLARETIE.

NOTES

1 For this use of *autres* see p. 50, § 35. 2 Is this = 'passed'? see p. 29, § 18. 3 Perfect Infinitive of the reflexive verb. 4 Construction?

23. *LA FRANCE*

VOCABULARY

complaisant, kindly.
épars, scattered here and there, random.
crédule, trusting, simple.
vaste, huge.
le cercle, coil.
une écaille, scale.
le sapin, fir.
la rive, bank, slope.
le pressoir, wine-press.
le coteau, hill.

France! ô belle contrée, ô terre généreuse
Que les dieux complaisants[1] formaient pour être heureuse,
Tu ne sens point du Nord les glaçantes horreurs[2];
Le Midi de ses feux t'épargne les fureurs[3].
Tes arbres innocents n'ont point d'ombres mortelles,
Ni des poisons épars dans tes herbes nouvelles
Ne trompent une main crédule; ni tes bois
Des tigres frémissants ne redoutent la voix[3];
Ni les vastes serpents ne traînent sur tes plantes
En longs cercles hideux leurs écailles sonnantes.
Les chênes, les sapins et les ormes épais
En utiles rameaux ombragent tes sommets,
Et de Beaune et d'Aï[4] les rives fortunées,
Et la riche Aquitaine, et les hauts Pyrénées
Sous leurs bruyants pressoirs font couler en ruisseaux
Des vins délicieux mûris sur tes coteaux.

ANDRÉ CHÉNIER.

NOTES

1 It is often impossible to reproduce in translation the full force given to the adjective by its position in French. Here the idea is: 'the gods, *when* in kindly mood, *when* in good humour'. 2 *horreur* has something of the original Latin meaning, 'bristling', 'rugged': perhaps 'terrors' will suffice here. 3 Consider the construction of the line before translating. 4 *Ay* in Champagne and *Beaune* in Burgundy are famous for their wines.

24. *PROMENADES SOLITAIRES*

VOCABULARY

la douleur, grief, pain.
l'attendrissement (n.m.), tender emotion.
volontiers, willingly, with pleasure.
l'amertume (n.f.), bitterness.
la gouvernante, housekeeper.
la biche, hind, deer.
inconcevable, inconceivable (whom we cannot represent to ourselves).

Quand mes douleurs me font tristement mesurer la longueur des nuits, et que[1] l'agitation de la fièvre m'empêche de goûter un seul instant de sommeil, souvent je me distrais[2] de mon état présent en songeant aux divers événements de ma vie, et les repentirs, les doux souvenirs, les regrets, l'attendrissement, se partagent[3] le soin de me faire oublier quelques moments mes souffrances. Quels temps croiriez-vous, monsieur, que je me rappelle le plus souvent et le plus volontiers dans mes rêves? Ce ne sont point les plaisirs de ma jeunesse; ils furent trop rares, trop mêlés d'amertume, et sont déjà trop loin de moi. Ce sont ceux[4] de ma retraite, ce sont mes promenades solitaires: ce sont ces jours rapides[5], mais délicieux, que j'ai passés tout entiers avec moi seul, avec ma bonne et simple gouvernante, avec mon chien bien-aimé, ma vieille chatte, avec les oiseaux de la campagne et les biches de la forêt, avec la nature entière et son inconcevable auteur.

J.-J. Rousseau.

NOTES

1 See p. 63, § 50, que. 2 *se distraire de*, to withdraw one's attention from, to try to forget, seek relief from. 3 See p. 62, § 49. 4 What noun does *ceux* stand for? 5 Is 'rapid' the best translation available? See p. 38, § 25.

25. *PROMENADES SOLITAIRES* (*suite*)

VOCABULARY

le souhait, wish, desire.
le soin, care, task.
remettre, to put off, delay.
importun, importunate, troublesome, annoying, boring.
ménager, to spare, arrange, contrive.
s'emparer de, to take possession of, seize, get hold of.
s'esquiver, to slip away.
doubler, to round.
le pétillement, sparkling; *here* flutter.

En me levant avant le soleil pour aller voir, contempler son lever dans mon jardin, quand je voyais commencer une belle journée, mon premier souhait était que ni lettres, ni visites n'en[1] vinssent troubler le charme. Après avoir donné la matinée à divers soins que je remplissais tous avec plaisir, parce que je pouvais les remettre à un autre temps, je me hâtais de dîner pour échapper aux importuns, et me ménager un plus long après-midi. Avant une heure, même les jours les plus ardents, je partais par le grand soleil avec le fidèle Achate[2], pressant le pas, dans la crainte que quelqu'un ne vînt s'emparer de moi avant que j'eusse pu m'esquiver; mais quand une fois j'avais pu doubler un certain coin, avec quel battement de cœur, avec quel pétillement de joie je commençais à respirer en me sentant sauvé, en me disant: Me voilà maître de moi pour le reste de ce jour! J'allais alors d'un pas plus tranquille chercher quelque lieu sauvage dans la forêt, quelque lieu désert[3] où rien, en me montrant la main des hommes, n'annonçât la servitude et la domination, quelque asile où je pusse croire avoir pénétré le premier, et où nul tiers importun ne vînt s'interposer entre la nature et moi.

J.-J. Rousseau.

NOTES

1 What does *en* refer to? 2 His 'trusty Achates' is his dog. 3 See p. 38, § 25.

26. *PROMENADES SOLITAIRES* (*suite*)

VOCABULARY

déployer, to display, unfold.
le genêt, broom.
la bruyère, heather, heath.
le luxe, luxury, splendour, magnificence.
un arbuste, shrub.
fouler, to tread, trample.

C'était là que la nature semblait déployer à mes yeux une magnificence toujours nouvelle. L'or des genêts et la pourpre des bruyères frappaient mes yeux d'un luxe qui touchait mon cœur; la majesté des arbres qui me couvraient de leur ombre, la délicatesse des arbustes qui m'environnaient, l'étonnante variété des herbes et des fleurs que je foulais sous mes pieds, tenaient mon esprit dans une alternative[1] continuelle d'observation et d'admiration: le concours de tant d'objets intéressants qui se disputaient[2] mon attention, m'attirant sans cesse de l'un à l'autre, favorisait mon humeur rêveuse et paresseuse, et me faisait souvent redire en moi-même: "Non, Salomon dans toute sa gloire ne fut jamais vêtu comme l'un d'eux." J.-J. ROUSSEAU.

NOTES

1 The nearest equivalent, 'alternation,' is rather clumsy and it would be more satisfactory to change the construction and use a verb to express the idea contained in this noun. 2 See p. 62, § 49.

27. *LE REPAS PRÉPARÉ*

VOCABULARY

la laine, wool.
le pli, fold.
étincelant, sparkling, bright.
la faïence, china.
une anse, handle
le cygne, swan.
la pêche, peach.
le velours, velvet, velvety bloom.
la corbeille, basket.
cuire, to be baking (hot).
embaumer, to embalm, perfume.
chargé, laden.

Ma fille, lève-toi; dépose là ta laine.
Le maître va rentrer; sur la table de chêne,
Que[1] recouvre la nappe aux plis étincelants,
Mets la faïence claire et les verres brillants.

Dans la coupe[2] arrondie, à l'anse en[3] col de cygne,
Pose les fruits choisis sur des feuilles de vigne:
Les pêches qu'un velours fragile couvre encor,
Et les lourds raisins bleus mêlés aux raisins d'or;
Que le pain bien coupé remplisse les corbeilles;
Et puis, ferme la porte et chasse les abeilles.
Dehors, le soleil brûle et la muraille cuit;
Rapprochons les volets; faisons presque la nuit,
Afin qu'ainsi la salle, aux[3] ténèbres plongée,
S'embaume toute aux[3] fruits dont la table est chargée

ALBERT SAMAIN.

NOTES

1 Case of the relative pronoun? 2 *la coupe* is a 'bowl' rather than a 'cup', although a silver 'cup' is often round. 3 Preposition?

28. *L'ENFANCE DU GÉNÉRAL DROUOT*

VOCABULARY

le collège, secondary school.
le client, customer.
subir, to undergo, suffer, put up with.
l'éclat (n.m.), splendour.
une occasion, opportunity, chance.
infidèle, false (i.e. no true friend).
le four, (baker's) oven.
Tite-Live, Livy.

Rentré[1] de l'école ou du collège, il lui fallait porter le pain chez les clients, se tenir dans la chambre publique avec tous les siens, et subir dans ses oreilles et son esprit les inconvénients d'une perpétuelle distraction. Le soir, on éteignait la lumière de bonne heure par économie, et le pauvre écolier devenait ce qu'il pouvait, heureux lorsque la lune favorisait par un éclat plus vif la prolongation de sa veillée. On le voyait profiter ardemment de ces rares occasions. Dès les deux heures du matin, quelquefois plus tôt, il était debout; c'était le temps où le travail domestique recommençait à la lueur d'une seule et mauvaise[2] lampe. Il reprenait aussi le sien[3]; mais la lampe infidèle, éteinte avant le jour, ne tardait point de lui manquer de nouveau; alors il s'approchait du four ouvert et enflammé, et continuait, à ce rude soleil, la lecture de Tite-Live ou de César.

Telle est cette enfance dont la mémoire poursuivait le général Drouot jusque dans les splendeurs des Tuileries.

LACORDAIRE.

NOTES

1 See p. 58, § 45. 2 Beware of literal translation; see p. 63, § 50. 3 In such a sentence as: *Prêtez-moi votre livre, j'ai perdu le mien, le mien = mon livre.* What does *le sien* stand for here?

29. *LE VALLON*

VOCABULARY

chauffer, to warm.
le frêne, ash.
un orme, elm.
se quereller, to wrangle, dispute with one another.
la fierté, pride.

J'ai fait en arrivant dans l'île[1] connaissance
Avec un frais vallon plein d'ombre et d'innocence,
Qui, comme moi, se plaît[2] au bord des flots profonds.
Au même rayon d'or tous deux nous nous chauffons;
J'ai tout de suite avec cette humble solitude
Pris une familière et charmante habitude.
Là deux arbres, un frêne, un orme à l'air vivant,
Se querellent et font des gestes dans le vent
Comme deux avocats qui parlent pour et contre;
J'y vais causer un peu tous les jours, j'y rencontre
Mon ami le lézard, mon ami le moineau;
Le roc m'offre sa chaise et la source son eau;
J'attends, quand je suis seul avec cette nature,
Mon âme qui lui dit tout bas son aventure[3];
Ces champs sont bonnes gens, et j'aime, en vérité,
Leur douceur, et je crois qu'ils aiment ma fierté.

VICTOR HUGO.

NOTES

1 In 1851 Hugo, exiled from France, found a refuge in Jersey, later in Guernsey. 2 See p. 62, § 49. 3 'what has happened to it', 'its experience'.

30. *LA TORCHE*

VOCABULARY

la manœuvre, operation.
en perdition, in sore straits, in desperate peril.
sinistre, weird, eerie.
accroché, hanging on.
se tordre, to twist, writhe.
une étincelle, spark.
le salut, safety.

Le vieillard avait ordonné à l'enfant d'allumer une de ses torches de résine, soit[1] pour éclairer un peu sa manœuvre dans les profondeurs de la mer, soit pour indiquer aux marins de Procida qu'une barque était en perdition dans le canal et pour leur demander, non leur secours, mais leurs prières. C'était un spectacle sublime et sinistre que[2] celui de ce pauvre enfant accroché d'une main au petit mât qui surmontait la proue, et, de l'autre, élevant au-dessus de sa tête cette torche de feu rouge, dont la flamme et la fumée se tordaient sous le vent et lui brûlaient les doigts et les cheveux. Cette étincelle flottante apparaissant au sommet des lames et disparaissant dans leur profondeur, toujours prête à s'éteindre et toujours rallumée, était comme[3] le symbole de ces quatre vies d'hommes[4] qui luttaient entre le salut et la mort dans les ombres et dans les angoisses[5] de cette nuit. LAMARTINE.

NOTES

1 See p. 63, § 50, *soit*. 2 See p. 51, § 37. 3 See p. 64, § 50. 4 = 'these four human lives', but this is impossible: why? Which noun does *qui* go with? 5 The corresponding English word has no plural; we may translate by 'terrors'.

31. *RECOMMANDATIONS DE CHANTECLER À SES POULES*

VOCABULARY

la sauge, sage.
la bourrache, borage.
le coquelicot, poppy.
la maille, stitch.
le tricot, knitting.
écraser, to crush.
pousser, to spring up, grow.
une ombelle, umbel (*botanical term*).
pointillé, speckled.
cueillir, collect, pick up.
la faulx = *faux*, scythe.

Quand vos crêtes de sang,
Apparaissant[1], disparaissant[1], reparaissant[1],
Auront, là-bas, parmi la sauge et la bourrache,
Un air[2] de coquelicots, jouant à la cache-cache,
Ne faites pas de mal aux vrais coquelicots!
Les bergères, comptant les mailles des tricots,
Marchent sur l'herbe, sans savoir qu'il est infâme
D'écraser une fleur même avec une femme[3]:
Vous, mes Poules, soyez pleines de soins touchants
Pour ces fleurs dont le crime est de pousser aux champs.
La carotte sauvage a le droit d'être belle.
Si sur la plate-forme exquise d'une ombelle
Marche un insecte rouge et pointillé de noir,
Cueillez le promeneur, mais non le promenoir!
Les fleurs d'un même champ sont des sœurs, il me semble,
Qui doivent sous la faulx tomber toutes ensemble.
Allez!

EDMOND ROSTAND.

NOTES

1 Be careful to show the force of the prefix. See p. 19, § 13.
2 *avoir un air de*, to be like.
3 This is a parody of 'il ne faut pas battre une femme même avec une fleur'.

32. *LE COLLÈGE*

VOCABULARY

le milieu, environment.
la salubrité, healthiness, wholesomeness.
rectifier, to correct, amend.
une épreuve, trial, test.
le contrôle, checking, observation.
la fabrique, factory.

Dans ce milieu, d'une salubrité vraiment rare, ni la fortune, ni les relations ne comptent pour rien. On n'y connaît ni les protections, ni les influences; l'émulation y est toujours en éveil, mais une émulation honnête et qui ne sort jamais du droit chemin. Non certes que les écoliers soient tous de petits saints: si je vous le disais, je perdrais votre confiance. Mais ils se rectifient les uns les autres, et ils ne pardonnent jamais une faute contre l'honneur. Voilà comment la camaraderie devient une longue épreuve qui nous permet de nous apprécier[1] les uns les autres, de nous améliorer au besoin[2] par un contrôle réciproque[3] et de choisir nos amis pour la vie. Vous le savez, les vieux amis sont meilleurs et plus solides que les neufs, et la grande fabrique des vieux amis, c'est le collège.

EDMOND ABOUT.

NOTES

1 *apprécier* is used in a wider sense than 'appreciate'. It means 'to appraise', 'estimate'. 2 See p. 41, § 28. 3 One schoolboy acts as a 'check' upon the other, e.g. by toning down eccentricities.

33. *ADIEU À MA SŒUR HÉLÈNE*

VOCABULARY

clore, to shut, end.
la demeure, dwelling.
épanoui, in full bloom.
embaumer, to embalm, perfume.

Il[1] n'est point ici-bas d'heure si fortunée
Qui ne doive finir et n'ait son lendemain[2];
C'est la loi de ce monde, et notre destinée
Ne veut[3] rien d'éternel dans le bonheur humain;

Notre plus longue joie est vite terminée;
Ce n'est qu'un chant d'oiseau dans l'arbre du chemin[4];
L'adieu, le triste adieu vient clore la journée,
Sans qu'on ait eu le temps de se prendre[5] la main.

Mais l'absence n'est rien quand l'amitié demeure,
Et sur les murs détruits de la frêle demeure
Où nous avons rêvé notre songe d'un jour,

La fleur du souvenir s'entr'ouvre épanouie[6],
Et son parfum divin embaume notre vie
De[7] l'instant du départ à celui du retour.

HENRI CHANTAVOINE.

NOTES

1 Personal or impersonal? See p. 53, § 39. 2 Lit. 'its morrow', i.e. 'its successor'. 3 *veut* has a stronger meaning than 'wish'. 4 Translate idiomatically. 5 *se* lit. 'to one another'. 6 Beware of nonsense; try to find some natural expression. 7 Cp. *du matin au soir.*

34. *JACQUES IER*

VOCABULARY

juste, accurate, right.
sain, sound.
les lettrés (n.m.), scholars.
un travers, eccentricity, shortcoming.
gaspiller, to squander, waste.
un député, deputy, member of Parliament.
percer, to show through.
puiser, to draw (as from a well, *un puits*).

Beaucoup des idées de Jacques Ier sont justes et saines; il a horreur de répandre le sang; il souhaite la paix; il a beaucoup lu; il protège les artistes et les lettrés, les secourt d'une manière autrement[1] efficace qu'Élisabeth; il a, en matière religieuse[2], des dispositions plus réellement tolérantes qu'aucun de ses prédécesseurs depuis cent ans. Mais ses qualités sont bien moins apparentes que ses travers, ses ridicules et ses défauts, et la partie la plus saine de la nation voit en lui un pédant frivole qui perd son temps à la chasse et gaspille les ressources de l'État en fêtes païennes que Dieu réprouve.

Plusieurs de ses discours au Parlement sont pleins

d'humour, de bonhomie paternelle et de sages conseils. Mais, dans cette sagesse et cette bonhomie mêmes, les députés qui, en d'autres temps, auraient été charmés d'un ton si familier, sentaient percer le dédain. Ce roi paternel les traitait trop en[3] enfants. Or les délégués du peuple se flattaient, tout comme le souverain lui-même, de parler au nom de la patrie, et, puisant leurs pensées dans[4] la Bible, d'être[5], eux aussi, inspirés de[4] Dieu.

J.-J. JUSSERAND.

NOTES

1 See p. 64, § 51. 2 Avoid literal translation. 3 Preposition? See p. 60, § 48. 4 Preposition? 5 See p. 43, § 29.

35. *MARÉE MONTANTE*

VOCABULARY

se voiler, to veil itself, become overcast.
s'obscurcir, to become dark.
un tourbillon, whirlwind, eddy.
la grève, the strand, beach.
le coursier, race-horse, steed.
la crinière, mane.
pressé, hurrying.
s'effacer, to be (become) blotted out.
le goéland, seagull.
le récif, reef.

Le soleil s'est voilé[1]; la mer, sous des cieux lourds,
Monte et frappe ses bords de coups rythmés et sourds;
L'horizon s'obscurcit; un souffle chaud soulève
En jaunes tourbillons les sables de la grève.
Comme de blancs coursiers laissant flotter au vent
Dans un libre galop leurs crinières d'argent,
Les flots pressés au loin se couronnent d'écume;
Des ombres de vaisseaux s'effacent dans la brume
Et les blancs goélands autour des noirs récifs
Dans la clameur des eaux jettent leurs cris plaintifs.

HENRY THÉDENAT.

NOTES

1 Tense? See p. 56, § 44.

36. *LE NOUVEAU*

VOCABULARY

la rentrée, beginning of a new session.
abordé, accosted.
la figure, face.
bombé, bulging.
volontaire, determined, strong-willed.
la mèche, wisp, tuft.
un gaillard, fellow, chap.
autrement, otherwise; *often* far more.
un condisciple, fellow-pupil.
une ouverture, overture.
le concurrent, rival, competitor.
avoir affaire à forte partie, to have a redoubtable adversary to deal with.
l'acharnement (n.m.), tenacity; *avec* —, obstinately.
le cadet, the youngest.
batailler, to battle, struggle.
ne...guère, scarcely ever.

C'était à la rentrée d'octobre 1844. Je fus abordé dans la rue par un gamin de mon[1] âge vêtu[2] d'une blouse bleue. Il avait une longue figure éclairée par deux yeux observateurs, un front bombé et volontaire, surmonté de cheveux blonds aux mèches rebelles. "Tu entres en sixième, n'est-ce pas? me dit-il. — Oui. — Moi aussi; si tu[3] veux, nous serons camarades." Il avait l'air d'un gaillard autrement intelligent que le reste de mes condisciples, et je fus flatté de cette ouverture.

Nous ne fûmes pas seulement camarades, nous devînmes deux rivaux. Jusque-là j'avais tenu facilement la tête de ma classe, n'ayant eu pour concurrents que des élèves paresseux ou faibles; mais, avec Laguerre, je m'apercus bien vite que j'allais avoir affaire à forte partie. Nous nous disputions[4] la première place avec acharnement, et celui de nous qui arrivait second rentrait chez lui l'oreille basse[5], car nos parents à tous deux accueillaient peu agréablement le vaincu. Laguerre était le cadet d'une famille de six enfants, et son père, comme le mien, prétendait[6] qu'il n'y avait qu'une bonne place: la première. Mais tout en bataillant[7] l'un contre l'autre chaque semaine, nous n'en étions pas moins bons amis et nous ne nous quittions guère.

S. C. 1925.

NOTES

1 See p. 55, § 42. 2 See p. 38, § 25. 3 The familiar *tu*: is it to be translated by 'thou'? 4 See p. 62, § 49. 5 We

do not say 'with drooping ears' but we have a very similar metaphorical expression. See p. 5, § 2. 6 See p. 26, § 16, PRÉTENDRE. 7 What is the force of *tout* in this construction? See p. 59, § 46.

37. *LA MORT DE LOUISE*

VOCABULARY

le cortège, company (of mourners).
le deuil, mourning; *suivre le —*, to be a mourner at a funeral.
le cercueil, coffin.
un enfant (*de chœur*), chorister, choir-boy.
une oraison, orison, prayer.
avertir, to warn, inform.
le taillis, copse.
le genêt, broom.
le convoi, the funeral procession.
éclore, to burst into bloom.
l'aubépine (n.f.), the hawthorn.
le bourgeon, bud.

Quand Louise mourut à[1] sa quinzième année,
Fleur des bois par la pluie et le vent moissonnée[2],
Un cortège nombreux ne suivit pas son deuil;
Un seul prêtre en priant conduisit le cercueil;
Puis venait un enfant qui, d'espace en espace,
Aux saintes oraisons répondait à voix basse;...
A peine si[3] la cloche avertit la contrée
Que sa plus douce vierge en[4] était retirée.
Elle mourut ainsi. — Par les taillis couverts,
Les vallons embaumés, les genêts, les blés verts,
Le convoi descendit au lever de l'aurore:
Avec toute sa pompe Avril venait d'éclore,
Et couvrait en passant[5] d'une neige de fleurs[6]
Ce cercueil virginal, et le baignait de pleurs;
L'aubépine avait pris sa robe rose et blanche;
Un bourgeon étoilé tremblait à chaque branche;
Ce n'étaient que[7] parfums et concerts infinis:
Tous les oiseaux chantaient sur le bord de leurs nids.

BRIZEUX.

NOTES

1 Preposition? 2 *la moisson*, properly the *reaping* of the harvest; do not translate by 'harvested'. See p. 75, § 59. 3 ''Twas all if'; 'Hardly did'. 4 What does *en* refer to? 5 *en passant*, rather incorrect for *à son passage*. 6 Can *fleurs* here be 'flowers'? See p. 24, § 16. 7 See p. 42, § 28.

38. *L'ESPOIR*

VOCABULARY

le tremble, aspen.
hausser, to raise.
sommeiller, to slumber.
le gouffre, the gulf, deep.
le soufre, sulphur.
gémir, to groan, moan.

Un hymne harmonieux sort des feuilles du tremble;
Les voyageurs craintifs, qui vont la nuit ensemble[1],
Haussent la voix dans l'ombre[2] où l'on doit se hâter.
Laissez tout ce qui tremble
Chanter!

Les marins fatigués sommeillent[3] sur le gouffre.
La mer bleue où Vésuve épand ses flots de soufre
Se tait dès qu'il s'éteint, et cesse de gémir[4].
Laissez tout ce qui souffre
Dormir!

Quand la vie est mauvaise on la rêve[5] meilleure.
Les yeux en pleurs au ciel se lèvent à toute heure;
L'espoir vers Dieu se tourne et Dieu l'entend crier.
Laissez tout ce qui pleure
Prier!

C'est pour renaître ailleurs qu'ici-bas on succombe.
Tout ce qui tourbillonne[6] appartient à la tombe.
Il faut dans le grand tout tôt ou tard s'absorber.
Laissez tout ce qui tombe
Tomber!

VICTOR HUGO.

NOTES

1 Order of words? 2 Is 'shadow' or even 'shade' the best translation? What would an English poet say? 3 Why not 'doze' or 'nod'? 4 Examine the construction of this sentence carefully. What does *il* refer to, and what is the subject of *cesse*? 5 Requires some amplification, unless we are content with, e.g., 'imagines'. 6 Probably Hugo is thinking of the 'mad swirl' of life, or of the dead leaves 'whirling' in the wind.

39. *LA DIVINITÉ DES EMPEREURS ROMAINS*

VOCABULARY

appartenir à, to belong to. *s'appuyer sur*, to rest on. *irréfléchi*, unreflecting.

Nous ne devons pas d'ailleurs confondre les pensées de ce temps-là avec la doctrine du droit divin des rois, qui n'a appartenu qu'à une autre époque. Il ne s'agit[1] pas ici d'une autorité établie par la volonté divine; c'était l'autorité elle-même qui était divine. Elle ne s'appuyait pas seulement sur la religion; elle était une religion. Le prince n'était pas un représentant de Dieu; il était un dieu. Ajoutons même que, s'il était dieu, ce n'était pas par l'effet de cet enthousiasme irréfléchi que certaines générations ont pour leurs grands hommes. Il pouvait être un homme fort médiocre, être même connu pour[2] tel, ne faire illusion à personne, et être pourtant honoré comme un être divin. Il n'était nullement nécessaire qu'il eût frappé les imaginations par de brillantes victoires ou touché les cœurs[3] par de grands bienfaits. Il n'était pas dieu en vertu de son mérite personnel: il était dieu parce qu'il était empereur. Bon ou mauvais, grand ou petit, c'était l'autorité publique qu'on adorait en sa personne.

FUSTEL DE COULANGES.

NOTES

1 See p. 42, § 28. 2 Preposition? 3 It is better to supply a word here.

40. *À L'AUBE*

VOCABULARY

s'argenter, to become silvery.
le don, the gift, present.
la rosée, dew.
la veille, the day before, the eve.
le souffle, breath.
les blés (n.m.), the wheat-fields.
le veilleur, watchman, watcher.

Les étoiles fuient une à une. Les coqs chantent[1].
Le jour n'est pas levé, mais les hauteurs s'argentent,
Et les choses sortent de l'ombre et du sommeil.

Voici l'heure où la terre, heureuse et reposée,
Reçoit le don mystérieux de la rosée,
Et tressaille en sentant approcher le soleil.

Le monde est vierge et neuf. L'air qui vient des collines
N'a caressé que des créatures divines,
Comme[2] les feuilles, l'eau, les herbes et les fleurs.

L'homme dormant encor[3], la vie est fraîche et bonne:
Il[4] ne s'est rien encor fait de mal, et personne
N'a souffert d'aujourd'hui l'éternelle douleur.

La paix revêt les champs. Mûris, depuis la veille,
Au souffle de la nuit d'été, les blés s'éveillent,
Et blanchissent comme la mer au demi-jour.

Et du haut des clochers qui, veilleurs en prière,
Avant les toits humains voient venir la lumière,
Au loin les angelus tintent[5] et, tour à tour,

Bénissent le matin qui réjouit la terre. LOUIS MERCIER.

NOTES

1 Does *chantent* here mean 'sing'? 2 See p. 65, § 51. 3 As a rule the accusative absolute construction is not to be carried over into English. 4 Notice that this is impersonal. The *il* is not = *l'homme*. If it were, the construction would be *Il n'a rien fait de mal* unless it meant 'Man has as yet done himself no harm', which is not the case here. 5 See p. 35, § 23.

SECTION III

MODEL LESSON III

Cromwell

1. Pourtant Cromwell mourut triste. Triste, non seulement de mourir, mais aussi, et surtout, de mourir sans avoir atteint son véritable et dernier but. 2. Quel que fût son égoïsme, il avait l'âme trop grande pour que la plus haute fortune, mais purement personnelle et éphémère, comme lui-même ici-bas, suffît à le satisfaire. 3. Las des ruines qu'il avait faites, il avait à cœur de rendre à son pays un gouvernement régulier et stable, le seul gouvernement qui lui convînt, la monarchie avec le Parlement. 4. Et en même temps ambitieux au delà du tombeau, par cette soif de la durée qui est le sceau de la grandeur, il aspirait à laisser son nom et sa race en possession de l'empire dans l'avenir. 5. Il échoua dans l'un et l'autre dessein: ses attentats lui avaient créé des obstacles que ni son prudent génie ni sa persévérante volonté ne purent surmonter; et comblé, pour son propre compte, de pouvoir et de gloire, il mourut déçu dans ses plus intimes espérances, ne laissant après lui pour lui succéder, que les deux ennemis qu'il avait ardemment combattus, l'anarchie et les Stuart.

GUIZOT, *Histoire de la Révolution d'Angleterre*

1. *Pourtant Cromwell mourut triste. Triste, non seulement de mourir, mais aussi, et surtout, de mourir sans avoir atteint son véritable et dernier but.*

The points to note here are:

1. 'Yet Cromwell died sad' is not quite how Macaulay would have put it, though he might perhaps have said: 'And yet Cromwell died a disappointed man'. *Pourtant* is perhaps 'And yet', rather than the abrupt 'Yet';

triste is certainly 'disappointed' here, but in the next sentence 'sad to die' seems the inevitable translation; cp. *content de mourir*, 'glad to die'.

2. For *surtout* there are other renderings than 'above all', 'especially'; such are 'most of all', 'mainly', 'chiefly', 'above all things'.

3. Although *non seulement...mais aussi et surtout* is of course 'not only...but also and especially', this is not a characteristically English phrase and must therefore be adapted, e.g. by omission of part of it, with repetition of 'sad'.

4. *sans avoir atteint* is normally in English 'without reaching (attaining)' (see p. 59, § 46), but we sometimes do say 'without *having* reached (attained)' and that appears to be the full sense here.

5. *dernier* is 'last', but sometimes 'ultimate' or 'final'.

'And yet Cromwell died a sad man—sad not only to die, but also, and chiefly, to die without having attained his true and final aim.'

2. *Quel que fût son égoïsme, il avait l'âme trop grande pour que la plus haute fortune, mais purement personnelle et éphémère, comme lui-même ici-bas, suffît à le satisfaire.*

Before beginning to translate, or at least before writing down the first English words which occur to us, it will be well to reflect on the sense of the French.

Quel que fût: 'Whatever was' may in such a case as this be well rendered by 'Despite' or 'For all': 'For all his egoism'. In deciding the exact force of *il avait l'âme trop grande* it should be remembered that *âme* is not necessarily 'soul'; it may be 'heart' or 'mind'. Is Cromwell here described as 'great-souled' or 'great-hearted', as 'high-minded' or 'magnanimous'? The last term is perhaps the nearest to Guizot's meaning. It was actually used of Cromwell by contemporaries, but its etymological sense has been affected by the passage of time, and 'high-minded' seems safer. In *suffît à le satisfaire*, what does *le* refer to? Certainly not to *âme*, which is feminine; probably not to *égoïsme* either; no doubt to *Cromwell*.

In *mais purement personnelle et éphémère* what is the force of *mais*? Why *mais*? This conjunction limits a statement just made. We are first told that Cromwell had attained *la plus haute fortune*, i.e. 'the highest destiny', 'the loftiest fortune' to which a man could aspire. Then we are told that, after all, this *fortune* was only *personnelle* (since he was unable to transmit it as he wished) and only *éphémère* (since it would come to an end as soon as he himself was dead). The word *éphémère*, 'ephemeral', is Greek and in this context, as often, English prefers the Latin equivalent: 'transitory'. For *ici-bas*, 'here below' is appropriate in hymns, but not in historical style.

We should best give the sense by altering the construction and saying:

'For all his egoism, he was too high-minded to be entirely satisfied with the loftiest rank, so long as it was merely personal and transitory, even as he himself was in this world.'

3. *Las des ruines qu'il avait faites, il avait à cœur de rendre à son pays un gouvernement régulier et stable, le seul gouvernement qui lui convînt, la monarchie avec le Parlement.*

Las des ruines qu'il avait faites. Why the plural form? French *ruine* means 'downfall' or 'coming down with a crash' rather than the débris resulting from the downfall. In English the plural 'ruins' suggests the latter; in French it need not do so. The exact meaning here is 'Weary of the *ruin* he had wrought (in Church and State)'. Various institutions—Law, Parliament and Church—lay in ruin as the result of Cromwell's destructive policy, awaiting the time when he would begin to re-build them. Whatever noun we may choose to translate *ruines* we must find a verb to suit it. The verb *faire*, in such phrases, is, as we have seen, p. 31, § 19, a blank cheque, to be filled in according to circumstances. We speak of 'the *ruin* a man has *wrought*' or 'the *destruction* he has *worked*' or 'the *destructive policy* he has *carried out*' or 'the drastic *changes* he has *made*', or 'the *ruins* he had *strewn around* him' (or '*laid about* him'). The real meaning, however, of Guizot's phrase is perhaps not so much 'Weary of the manifold ruin he had laid about him' as 'Weary of laying ruins about him'.

For *il avait à cœur de rendre* the exact phrase is 'his heart was set on restoring...'. But, in strict grammar, we could not say 'Weary...his heart, etc.', without suggesting that 'his heart' had caused the 'ruins'. We might, however, justifiably alter the tense and say 'he had set his heart on restoring'.

le seul gouvernement qui lui convînt: *lui* = not *à Cromwell*, of course, but *à son pays*; not 'which suited *him*', but 'which suited *it*'.

la monarchie avec le Parlement: the English phrase is 'a King and Parliament'.

'Weary of the manifold ruin he had wrought, he had set his heart on restoring to his country a regular and settled government, the only government that suited it, a King and Parliament.'

4. *Et en même temps ambitieux au delà du tombeau, par cette soif de la durée qui est le sceau de la grandeur,*

il aspirait à laisser son nom et sa race en possession de l'empire dans l'avenir.

For *ambitieux au delà du tombeau* some expansion is necessary, such as 'with ambitions reaching beyond the grave'.

To translate *cette soif de la durée* is difficult. The sense is that Cromwell ardently desired that his works should live after him, should be lasting. But there is no English noun corresponding to 'lasting', and neither 'duration' nor 'durability' nor 'endurance' nor 'permanence' quite suits.

le sceau de la grandeur: the 'seal', i.e. the 'stamp ('hall-mark' seems too trivial to be quite in the tone of this passage) of greatness' or, as we should perhaps more naturally say, 'of true greatness'.

sa race: 'his race', i.e. 'his lineage'.

l'empire: not 'empire' but 'the supreme power' or 'the throne'.

dans l'avenir: 'in the future' or 'for the future' makes a very lame ending. We might strengthen the sentence by saying 'in the time (or, as 'time' will be required at the beginning of the sentence, 'days') to come'.

'And at the same time, with ambitions reaching beyond the grave, with that thirsting after permanence which is the stamp of true greatness, he aspired to leaving his name and lineage in possession of the supreme power, in the days to come.'

5. *Il échoua dans l'un et l'autre dessein: ses attentats lui avaient créé des obstacles que ni son prudent génie ni sa persévérante volonté ne purent surmonter; et comblé, pour son propre compte, de pouvoir et de gloire, il mourut déçu dans ses plus intimes espérances, ne laissant après lui pour lui succéder, que les deux ennemis qu'il avait ardemment combattus, l'anarchie et les Stuart.*

l'un et l'autre. The exact force of *l'un et l'autre* is easily brought out in reading by stressing 'both'.

ses attentats: *un attentat* is a criminal attempt on some principle of law and order, a lawless act, a high-handed, or unconstitutional, action.

prudent génie: *prudent* here has probably its original strength of 'fore-seeing' (Latin *pro-videns*), 'far-sighted', 'providing for the future'.

persévérante volonté is 'unswerving (unbending, unflagging) will-power' or 'persistent will'.

For *ne purent surmonter* 'could not surmount' scarcely renders the Past Historic, the force of which (see p. 57, § 44) is better shown by 'proved unable'.

The phrase *comblé de pouvoir et de gloire* is not easily translated. By what steps can we arrive at a translation? We must first grasp the essential meaning of *comblé*, 'full to overflowing', cp. *la salle est comble*; *comblé de pouvoir* is thus said of a man who has had power heaped upon him, who possesses more power than he really requires; *comblé de gloire* is 'laden with glory', just as *comblé de richesses* is 'laden with wealth'. But we cannot say 'laden with power'. Neither can we find for *comblé* an English word which will go both with 'power' and with 'glory'. We must therefore content ourselves with translating *comblé de gloire* as 'laden with glory' and express *comblé de pouvoir* as best we may, for instance by 'all-powerful'.

pour son propre compte: 'as for himself', 'in his own person'.

'He failed in both projects; his lawless actions had raised up for him obstacles which neither his far-seeing mind nor his persistent will proved able to surmount. All-powerful and laden with glory, so far as he himself was concerned, he died disappointed in his dearest hopes, leaving after him as his successors only the two foes he had strenuously fought—anarchy and the Stuarts.'

Suggested Rendering

And yet Cromwell died a sad man—sad not only to die, but also, and chiefly, to die without having attained his true and final aim. For all his egoism, he was too high-minded to be entirely satisfied with the loftiest rank, so long as it was merely personal and transitory, even as he himself was in this world. Weary of the manifold ruin he had wrought, he had set his heart on restoring to his country a regular and settled government, the only government that suited it, a King and Parliament. And at the same time, with ambitions reaching beyond the grave, with that thirsting after permanence which is the stamp of true greatness, he aspired to leaving his name and lineage in possession of the supreme power, in the days to come. He failed in both projects; his lawless actions had raised up for him obstacles which neither his far-seeing mind nor his persistent will proved able to surmount. All-powerful and laden with glory, so far as he himself was concerned, he died disappointed in his dearest hopes, leaving after him as his successors only the two foes he had strenuously fought—anarchy and the Stuarts.

41. *AU BORD DE L'EUROTAS*

VOCABULARY

un oreiller, pillow.
le laurier, laurel (tree), bay.
la voie lactée, milky way.
l'aube (n.f.), dawn.
le mugissement, bellowing, roar.
le bûcher, log fire.
la borne, boundary, bound.
le soc, share.
la sueur, sweat, perspiration.

Après le souper, Joseph apporta ma selle, qui me servait ordinairement d'oreiller; je m'enveloppai[1] dans mon manteau, et je me couchai au bord de l'Eurotas, sous un laurier. La nuit était si pure et si sereine que la voie lactée formait comme[2] une aube réfléchie par l'eau du fleuve, et à la clarté de laquelle on aurait pu lire. Je me rappelle encore le plaisir que j'éprouvais autrefois à me reposer ainsi dans les bois de l'Amérique, et surtout à me réveiller au milieu de la nuit. J'écoutais[3] le bruit du vent dans la solitude, le mugissement d'une cataracte éloignée, tandis que mon bûcher, à demi éteint, rougissait en dessous le feuillage des arbres[4]. J'aimais jusqu'à[5] la voix de l'Iroquois lorsqu'il élevait un cri du sein des forêts et qu'à la clarté des étoiles, dans le silence de la nature, il semblait proclamer sa liberté sans bornes. Tout cela plaît à[6] vingt ans, parce que la vie se suffit pour ainsi dire à elle-même; mais, dans un âge plus mûr, l'esprit revient à des goûts plus solides: il veut surtout se nourrir des souvenirs et des exemples de l'histoire. Je dormirais encore volontiers au bord de l'Eurotas et du Jourdain[7], mais je n'irais plus chercher une terre nouvelle qui n'a point été déchirée par le soc de la charrue; il me faut à présent de vieux pays, des champs dont les sillons m'instruisent et où je retrouve, homme que je suis, le sang, les larmes et les sueurs[8] de l'homme.

CHATEAUBRIAND.

NOTES

Eurotas: the river that flows through the plain of Sparta (Greece). 1 Is the homonym the best translation? 2 See p. 65, § 51. 3 To what time does *écoutais* refer? Make this clear in your translation. 4 Be very careful in translating the last phrase; try to see the picture. Here *rougir* does *not* mean 'to blush'. 5 See p. 70, § 56. 6 The construction requires care. 7 The Eurotas is classical, the Jordan biblical. 8 *le sang* refers to battles; *les larmes* to sorrows; *les sueurs* to toils.

42. *LA FUITE DU TEMPS*

VOCABULARY

obstrué, obstructed, veiled, hidden. *s'enfuir*, to flee.
ridé, wrinkled, furrowed.

Le soleil s'est couché ce soir dans les nuées,
Demain viendra l'orage, et le soir, et la nuit;
Puis l'aube, et ses clartés de vapeurs obstruées[1],
Puis les nuits, puis les jours, pas du temps qui s'enfuit!

Tous ces jours passeront; ils passeront en foule
Sur la face des mers, sur la face des monts,
Sur les fleuves d'argent, sur les forêts où roule
Comme[2] un hymne confus des morts que nous aimons.

Et la face des eaux, et le front des montagnes,
Ridés et non vieillis, et les bois toujours verts
S'iront rajeunissant[3], le fleuve des campagnes
Prendra sans cesse aux[4] monts le flot qu'il donne aux
mers.

Mais moi, sous chaque jour courbant plus bas ma tête,
Je passe, et, refroidi sous ce soleil joyeux,
Je m'en irai bientôt, au milieu de la fête,
Sans que rien manque au monde immense et radieux!

VICTOR HUGO.

NOTES

1 What word does *obstruées* qualify? 2 See p. 65, § 51. 3 Progressive, 'will go on getting younger'. 4 Does *aux* mean 'to the'? Make sense.

43. *LES PETITS ENFANTS*

VOCABULARY

laid, ugly.
agréable, pleasant.
l'impuissance (n.f.), powerlessness.
méchant, *here* wicked, cruel.
attachant, absorbing, engrossing.
déformé, put out of shape, distorted, spoiled.
la féerie, fairyland.
poétique, poetical, romantic.
moyen, average.

Un petit enfant, c'est d'abord, quand il est joli ou seulement quand il n'est pas laid, la créature du monde la plus agréable à voir[1], la plus gracieuse par ses mouvements, la plus noble par son ignorance du mal, son impuissance à être méchant ou vil. Un petit enfant, c'est aussi la créature la plus aimée d'autres êtres, dont il est la raison de vivre, pour qui il est la suprême affection, la plus chère espérance, souvent l'unique intérêt. Et surtout un petit enfant, c'est pour un philosophe le sujet d'observation le plus attachant. C'est un homme tout neuf, non déformé, parfaitement original; c'est l'être qui reçoit des choses et du monde entier les impressions les plus directes et les plus vives, pour qui tout est étonnement et féerie; qui, cherchant à comprendre le monde, imagine des explications incomplètes qui en[2] respectent le mystère et sont par là éminemment poétiques. Plus tard, l'homme moyen accepte des explications qu'il croit définitives[3]; il perd le don de s'étonner, de s'émerveiller, de sentir le mystère des choses. Ceux qui conservent ce don sont le[4] très petit nombre, et ce sont eux[5] les poètes et les vrais philosophes.

JULES LEMAÎTRE.

NOTES

1 Arrange carefully. 2 To what word does *en* refer? 3 For *définitif*, see p. 10, § 7. 4 Not 'a'. 5 Translate idiomatically.

44. *CHAGRIN D'AUTOMNE*

VOCABULARY

le labour, ploughing. *entonner*, chant, intone. *féconder*, to fertilize, render fruitful. *le cerveau*, brain.

Les lignes du labour[1] dans les champs, en automne,
Fatiguent l'œil, qu'à peine un toit fumant[2] distrait,
Et la voûte du ciel tout entière apparaît,
Bornant d'un cercle nu la plaine monotone.

En des âges perdus dont la vieillesse étonne,
Là même a dû grandir une vierge forêt,
Où le chant des oiseaux sonore et pur vibrait,
Avec l'hymne qu'au vent le clair feuillage entonne[3].

Les poètes chagrins redemandent aux bras
Qui font ce plat désert sous des rayons sans voile
La verte nuit des bois que le soleil étoile[4];

Ils pleurent, oubliant, dans leurs soupirs ingrats,
Que des[5] mornes sillons sort le pain qui féconde
Leurs cerveaux, dont le rêve est plus beau que le monde.

SULLY PRUDHOMME.

NOTES

1 See p. 25, § 16. 2 Do we say 'a smoking roof'? 3 Prose order? 4 Study the construction of these three lines before translating, and try to *see* what the poet means by *étoile* which is here a verb. 5 Construction?

45. *LE HOBEREAU*

VOCABULARY

e hobereau, country squire.
un fouilleur, digger, searcher.
à moitié, half.
un pardon, a Breton religious festival.
un chemin creux, (sunk) lane.
la barrière, (barred) gate.
lever, (of grain) to spring up, grow, shoot.
une épine, thorn.
écarté, pushed aside.
une pincée, tuft.
fauve, tawny, brown.
la gîtée, lair, form.
un autour, goshawk, hawk.
le vacarme, uproar, hubbub.

M. de Jaoüen n'était pas sans lecture[1]; il savait du passé, surtout de son passé à lui[2], l'histoire de son sang à travers la Bretagne et les temps, plus de choses en somme que n'en[3] racontent, dans un fort volume, les fouilleurs de bibliothèques, gens de simple curiosité que les vieilles chroniques amusent, mais qui ne les ont pas vécues, qui ne les continuent point et ne les comprennent qu'à moitié. On le rencontrait partout, toujours un peu à l'écart[4]; dans les chasses[5], dans les repas de noces paysannes et dans les pardons. On le voyait souvent dans les chemins creux, regardant, à la barrière des champs, si le froment levait ou mûrissait, si le pommier promettait du cidre, et peut-être si, entre les épines écartées d'un buisson, une pincée de poils fauves et l'herbe couchée en ronde n'indiquaient pas la gîtée d'un lièvre. Au soir des jours d'automne, il rapportait[6], dans chaque main, une paire d'oiseaux et il les jetait[6] sur la table: "Voilà le dîner de demain, les petits!" Il[7] s'élevait des cris, comme dans le nid d'un autour. La servante accourut au vacarme; de son bras en faucille[8] elle balayait, sur la table, les oiseaux et les plumes envolées[9], les jetait dans son tablier tendu et regagnait sa cuisine.

RENÉ BAZIN.

NOTES

1 See p. 71, § 56, SANS. 2 *son...à lui*, 'his own'. 3 Exact construction? 4 See p. 42, § 28. 5 'shooting-party', 'hunting-expedition'; 'shoot' as in 'He was wont to be present at the great *shoots*' (W. E. Norris). 6 Tense? English form? 7 Personal or impersonal? 8 *Une faucille* is 'a sickle': try to visualize the scene. 9 *envolées*, 'which had flown off', i.e. 'loose'.

46. *LES JARDINS SOUS LE GEL*

VOCABULARY

le gel, frost.
le giron, lap.
le platane, plane-tree.
le couvert, covert.
le buis, box-wood.
figé, fixed, frozen.
s'acharner à, to attempt furiously to, to work implacably to.

La pompe a gelé; mais l'eau dans le puits
Est tiède au giron de la Mère-Terre.
Le platane est nu; mais autour de lui,
Les feuilles ont l'or des grands dignitaires,
Nids, ruchers[1], fontaine ont tous dû se taire,
Et leur voix sommeille au creux des couverts,
Les arbres vaincus se décapitèrent[2],
Mais j'en sais de grands qui sont toujours verts.

Le sentier bordé de bouquets de buis
Est sec d'un sang noir figé dans l'artère,
Et l'on ne sait plus où il vous conduit,
Tant le dur silence est lourd de mystère.
Le vent, qui n'a pas un bon caractère[3],
S'acharne à flétrir les espoirs divers
Que doit colorer l'avril volontaire,
Mais j'en sais de grands qui sont toujours verts.

GEORGES DELAQUYS.

NOTES

1 If *une ruche* is 'a bee-hive', what is *un rucher*? 2 *se décapitèrent*, a strange use of the Past Historic = *sont décapités*. 3 *Not* 'character'.

47. *LA BARQUE DU PÊCHEUR*

VOCABULARY

l'anse (n.f.), creek.
algues (n.f.pl.), seaweed.
glauque, gray-green.
la marée, tide.
effleurer, to skim.
le gouvernail, helm, rudder.
s'affaisser, to drop down.
le sillage, wake.

Au fond[1] d'une petite anse, sous une falaise creusée à sa base par les flots, entre les rochers où pendaient de longues algues d'un vert glauque, deux hommes, l'un jeune, l'autre âgé, mais robuste encore, appuyés contre une barque de pêcheur, attendaient la marée qui montait lentement, à peine effleurée par une brise mourante. Quelque temps après, on voyait la barque s'éloigner du rivage et s'avancer vers la haute mer, la proue relevée, laissant derrière elle un ruban d'écume blanche. Le vieillard, près du gouvernail, regardait les voiles qui tantôt s'enflaient, tantôt s'affaissaient, comme des ailes fatiguées. Puis, retombant[2] dans ses pensées, on lisait sur son front bruni toute une vie de labeur et de combat soutenu sans fléchir jamais. Le reflux[3] creusait dans la mer calme des vallons où se jouait la pétrelle, gracieusement balancée sur les ondes luisantes et plombées. Sur la pointe noire d'un rocher le lourd cormoran reposait immobile. Le moindre accident[4], un léger souffle, un jet de lumière, variait l'aspect de ces scènes changeantes. Le jeune homme, replié[2] en soi, les voyait comme on voit en songe. Son âme flottait au bruit du sillage, semblable au son monotone et faible dont la nourrice endort l'enfant. F. LAMENNAIS.

NOTES

1 See p. 42, § 28. 2 Note the prefix. 3 If *flux* means 'incoming tide', what does *reflux* mean? 4 Is this really an 'accident'? See p. 23, § 16.

48. *LA SŒUR*

VOCABULARY

l'officine (n.f.), dispensary.
un cabinet, a private room.
contrôler, to check.
le registre de visite, clinical chart.
la chance, luck.
de garde, on duty.
se promettre, to look forward to.
le palier, landing.
les béquilles (n.f.), crutches.

Elle était presque une famille pour les malades, tant elle entrait dans leurs affections comme une confidente, dans leurs pensées comme une parente, dans leurs larmes comme une amie. Sans cesse on la voyait marcher d'un lit à un autre, avec quelque chose à la main, avec son cœur dans les yeux, passant de celle-ci à celle-là, allant de l'officine à la salle[1], de la salle à son cabinet, additionnant[2], contrôlant, vérifiant, pliée en deux sur les registres de visite, sans s'arrêter ni prendre le temps de s'asseoir. Sa robe passait et repassait, toujours allant. Aussi[3] était-elle adorée et vénérée. Aux malades qui arrivaient, les malades déjà vieilles dans la salle parlaient de la chance qu'elles avaient, de la bonne sœur qu'elles allaient avoir. Même dans les autres salles, on faisait attention aux nuits où elle devait être de garde; le soir, d'un lit à l'autre, on se promettait sa ronde; et quand, dans le jour, elle descendait l'escalier, les convalescents qui, sur le palier de la salle des hommes, fumaient leur pipe en se promenant avec des béquilles, la saluaient d'un grand coup de bonnet de coton. E. ET J. DE GONCOURT.

NOTES

1 What is the word used in an English hospital? 2 'adding' or 'adding up'? 3 See p. 128.

49. *GAMBETTA*

VOCABULARY

une acclamation, shout.
ramassé, thick-set, squat.
encadré de, framed in, set in.
fourni, close, full.
l'élu (n.m.), the elected representative, the chosen (one).
accru, p.p. of *accroître*, increased.
l'envahissement (n.m.), invasion.
la barre, tiller, helm.

Une acclamation retentit: Vive Gambetta! Sur un balcon de pierre, un homme venait de paraître. De taille plutôt ramassée, les épaules larges, une figure pleine encadrée d'une barbe noire et fournie, Léon Gambetta promena[1] sur la foule un regard dominateur. Tous eurent cette sensation nette: quelqu'un! Tous contemplaient le jeune député qu'une récente fortune politique environnait pour la plupart[2] d'un éclatant prestige, pour d'autres de suspicion. L'avocat devenu homme d'État, l'élu de Paris et de Marseille, arrivait, précédé d'une belle réputation d'éloquence, d'une autorité chaque jour accrue par deux ans de sage et courageuse opposition, autorité à laquelle ajoutait encore sa part dans les derniers événements. Quoique ayant blâmé la guerre avant d'en voter la déclaration, il s'était depuis ardemment efforcé à la servir, en proie à cette idée fixe: faire de chaque citoyen un soldat. Quoique ayant blâmé l'envahissement du Corps législatif au 4 septembre, il avait su prendre à temps la barre en main, diriger, sinon dominer, les événements.

PAUL ET VICTOR MARGUERITTE.

NOTES

1 *promener le regard sur*, 'to look round on'; 'glance over', 'run one's eyes over'. 2 *pour la plupart* is balanced by *pour d'autres*.

50. *LES BLESSURES*

VOCABULARY

le baume, balm.
assainir, to make healthy, purify.
maux, plur. of *mal*.
guérir, to cure, heal.
la morsure, bite, gnawing.
gît, 3rd sing. pres. ind. of *gésir*, to lie.
meurtrir, to bruise, mangle.
selon, according to.
le renouveau, revival (*poet.* spring).

Le soldat frappé tombe en poussant de grands[1] cris;
On l'emporte; le baume assainit la blessure,
Elle se ferme un jour; il marche, il se rassure,
Et, par un beau soleil, il croit ses maux guéris.

Mais au premier retour d'un ciel humide et gris,
De l'ancienne douleur il ressent la morsure[2];
Alors la guérison ne lui paraît pas sûre,
Le souvenir du fer gît dans ses flancs meurtris.

Ainsi, selon le temps[3] qu'il fait dans ma pensée,
A la place où mon âme autrefois fut blessée
Il est[4] un renouveau d'angoisse que je crains;

Une larme, un chant triste, un seul mot dans un livre,
Nuage[5] au ciel limpide où je me plais[6] à vivre,
Me fait sentir au cœur la dent des vieux chagrins.

SULLY PRUDHOMME.

NOTES

1 Is this 'great'? 2 Prose order? 3 Metaphor? 4 See p. 53, § 39. 5 See p. 37, § 24. 6 See 62, § 49.

51. *CIMETIÈRE DE VILLAGE*

VOCABULARY

cimetière, see p. 92.
tenter, to tempt, attempt, try.
toutefois, indeed.
le buisson, bush.
le pâtre, shepherd.
la glèbe, sod, clod.
la portée, reach; *à leur* —, to their hand, within their reach.
témoigner de, to bear witness to.
inédit (*lit.* unpublished), unknown to the world.

Je n'ai jamais passé à côté d'un[1] cimetière de village sans être tenté de questionner la mort et de lui[2] demander le secret des diverses générations qui sont venues finir là. Qu'ont fait ces hommes quand ils étaient debout[3]? Qu'ont-ils pensé, si toutefois ils ont pensé? Aucune voix ne répond à cette question: le vent souffle à travers les buissons du sentier; la mort garde le silence. Beaucoup, sans doute, ont ignoré[4] leur âme; pâtres ou laboureurs, ils ont retourné la glèbe ou conduit leurs troupeaux, troupeaux eux-mêmes d'un ordre plus élevé. Mais d'autres aussi, mieux servis par la destinée, ont porté leur vie plus haut; ils ont eu toutes les bonnes pensées ou accompli les fortes œuvres que la Providence des humbles avait mises à leur portée. Maintenant ils sont couchés là, et aucune trace après eux, pas même une pierre, ne témoigne de leur passage. Qu'un héros inédit, aussi grand par l'âme que l'on peut l'être ici-bas, fasse[5] le bien modestement, sans quitter sa vallée, est-ce que l'histoire le connaîtra? Est-ce qu'elle daignera retourner la tête pour le regarder? Non, celui-là vit ignoré[4] et meurt comme il a vécu. Son heure venue[6], il tombe à l'écart[7]. La terre le dévore tout entier sans que sa vie, prolongée après lui en écho, retentisse[8] dans le souvenir de personne. Il a passé.

EUGÈNE PELLETAN.

NOTES

1 Distinguish *à côté de* from *du côté de*. 2 Construction? 3 *Not* 'standing' or 'upright'. 4 See p. 25, § 16, IGNORER. 5 'Let him do', etc., i.e. 'If he does', 'Suppose he does'. 6 See p. 37, § 24. 7 He is out of the main stream of human life, apart from the great world. 8 *retentir* often means 'to echo', but here we must find another word, e.g. 'to linger'.

52. *LES TÉMÉRAIRES*

VOCABULARY

téméraire, rash, daring, reckless.
enflure, swelling.
la voilure, (collective) sails.
gracieux, graceful.
le sillage, wake.
sombrer, to sink, founder.
ravi, transported.
agiter, to think excitedly of, plan feverishly.

Du pôle il va tenter les merveilleux hivers,
Il part, le grand navire[1]! Une puissante enflure
Au souffle d'un bon vent lève et tend la voilure,
Sur trois beaux mâts portant neuf vergues en travers.
Il est parti. Là-bas, au soleil, dans les airs
Traînant son pavillon comme une chevelure[2],
Il a pris sa superbe et gracieuse allure,
Et du côté du nord[3] gagne les hautes mers.
D'un œil triste je suis[4] au loin son blanc sillage;
Il va sombrer peut-être au but de son voyage,
Par des géants de glace étreint de toutes parts[1]!
Et près de moi, debout, l'enfant du capitaine,
Dans la brise ravi vers la brume lointaine,
Agite dans son cœur d'aventureux départs.

SULLY PRUDHOMME.

NOTES

1 Prose order? See p. 47, § 32. 2 Cp. *Le Cygne*, by the same poet:

...laissant les herbages épais
Traîner derrière lui comme une chevelure.

'with thick-clustering weeds trailing behind him like floating tresses'. 3 Cp. *Le Cygne*: *du côté de l'azur*, 'towards the blue depths'. 4 See p. 9, § 7.

53. *LES CYCLADES*

VOCABULARY

séduisant, seductive.
qualifier de, to describe as.
inonder, to flood.
enchâsser, to enchase, set (as a precious stone).
un inconvénient, disadvantage, shortcoming.
la somptuosité, sumptuousness.
interdit, forbidden, denied.
un parvenu, upstart.

Les Cyclades sont un des endroits du monde auquel l'épithète de séduisant s'applique[1] avec le plus de vérité.

Pourtant beaucoup d'entre elles peuvent être qualifiées en toute justice de rochers stériles; mais au sein de ces mers de la Grèce, où la main des dieux les a semés, ces rochers brillent comme autant de pierres précieuses. La lumière qui les inonde au milieu d'une atmosphère sans tache, et les flots d'azur qui les enchâssent, en[2] font, suivant les heures du jour, autant d'améthystes, de saphirs, de rubis, de topazes. La réalité est stérile, pauvre, assez nue, certainement mélancolique; mais ces inconvénients s'effacent sous une majesté et une grâce incomparables. Les Cyclades donnent l'idée de très grandes dames nées et élevées au milieu des richesses et de l'élégance. Aucune des somptuosités du luxe le plus raffiné ne leur a été inconnue. Mais des malheurs sont venus les frapper, de grands, de nobles, malheurs; elles se sont retirées du monde avec les débris de leur fortune; elles ne font plus de visites[3], elles ne reçoivent personne; néanmoins ce sont toujours de grandes dames, et du passé[4] il leur demeure, comme le suprême raffinement interdit aux parvenues, une sérénité charmante et un sourire adorable. COMTE DE GOBINEAU.

NOTES

1 Might be slightly expanded. See p. 37, § 24. 2 *font de* —; *quoi?* 3 'visits'? Or 'calls'? 4 Construction?

54. *LE BOUC*

VOCABULARY

le bouc, he-goat.
entraîner, to drag (see p. 18, § 13).
reculer, to recoil, to back.
fougueux, fiery, spirited.
renverser, to throw back.
le torse, torso, chest, trunk.
étreindre, to clasp *or* hold tightly, squeeze.
se garer, to protect oneself, avoid.
oblique, slanting.
se réjouir, to rejoice.
essuyer, to wipe, dry.
coller, to stick, cling.
l'orgueil (n.m.), pride.

Le petit Palémon, grand de huit ans à peine,
Maintient en vain[1] le bouc qui résiste et l'entraîne,
Et le force à courir à travers le jardin,
Et brusquement recule et s'élance soudain.

Ils luttent corps à corps; le bouc fougueux s'efforce;
Mais l'enfant, qui s'arc-boute[2] et renverse le torse,
Étreint le cou rebelle entre ses petits bras,
Se gare de la corne oblique et, pas à pas,
Rouge, serrant les dents, volontaire, indomptable,
Ramène triomphant le bouc noir à l'étable.
Et Lysidé, sa mère aux belles tresses d'or,
Assise au seuil avec un bel enfant qui dort,
Se réjouit à voir[3] sa force et son adresse,
L'appelle et, souriante, essuie avec tendresse
Son front tout en sueur où collent ses cheveux;
Et l'orgueil maternel illumine ses yeux. ALBERT SAMAIN.

NOTES

1 Does this mean 'maintain in vain'? 2 An *arc-boutant* is a flying buttress: *s'arc-bouter* is 'to brace oneself' in a curved position like such a buttress. 3 *se réjouir de* voir, 'to rejoice *to* see'. What does *se réjouir à* mean?

55. *À BICYCLETTE*

VOCABULARY

s'aviser, to take it into one's head.
fou, *folle*, has a great variety of meanings: *here* 'madly-careering' or 'giddy' or perhaps 'free-running' would suit; cp. *roue folle* = *roue libre* = 'free wheel'.
la buée, steam, mist.
bleuissant, tinting with blue.
fêter, to celebrate, welcome.
le baiser, kiss.
dévaler, to run swiftly down, to coast.
la pente, slope.
le sol, ground.
raser, to graze, skim.
affolé de, mad with.
défiler, to rush past.
le vertige, dizziness, giddiness.
la senteur, scent.
mouillé, wet, damp.
picorer, to peck.
le fourré, thicket, brushwood.
le chevreuil, roe deer.
retardataire, laggard, straggler.
la course, expedition.

Quand un Français s'avisera-t-il[1] de voyager en France et de raconter ce qui s'y voit pour l'émerveillement de ses concitoyens? Ainsi je pensais hier matin, aux premiers rayons du soleil, emporté par une folle bicyclette sur la route de Rambouillet à Clairefontaine. La rosée remontait[2] au ciel en une claire buée bleuissante, traversée de rayons d'or. Tout le ciel brillant fêtait la venue du soleil, et la terre, caressée d'une brise matinale, se préparait aux baisers du midi. Cependant la machine courait, dévalant les longues pentes, et le coureur[3] inconscient de tout effort, insensible au contact du sol, comme un oiseau rasant la terre, affolé de vitesse, s'enivrait[4] de l'espace, et du ciel, et du vent. Le paysage défilait dans un vertige, et bientôt les senteurs mouillées de l'automne apportaient la bienvenue de la forêt. Sur la route, à cent pas, des lapins sautaient[5] d'un mouvement mécanique, des faisans picoraient avant de rentrer au fourré, un chevreuil en deux sauts franchissait la route; tous les retardataires des courses de la nuit regagnaient le coin de feuillée qui leur donne la paix du jour. G. CLEMENCEAU.

NOTES

1 Be careful with the arrangement. 2 Why *re*-montait? 3 Does *coureur* here mean 'runner'? 4 *ivre*, 'intoxicated', 'drunk', often figuratively, e.g. *ivre de joie*: *s'enivrer de*, 'to be intoxicated with'. 5 Is 'leapt' satisfactory? How do rabbits move about?

56. *LORD BYRON*

VOCABULARY

ébranler, to set in motion, stir, excite. *fantastique*, fantastic; *here* romantic. *le crépuscule*, twilight.

J'entendis parler pour la première fois de lui par un de mes anciens amis qui revenait d'Angleterre en 1819[1]. Le seul récit de quelques-uns de ses poèmes m'ébranla l'imagination. Je savais mal l'anglais alors, et on[2] n'avait rien traduit de Byron encore. L'été suivant, me trouvant à Genève[3], un de mes amis qui y résidait me montra un soir, sur la grève du lac Léman, un jeune homme qui descendait de bateau et qui montait à cheval pour rentrer dans une de ces délicieuses villas réfléchies dans les eaux du lac. Mon ami me dit que ce jeune homme était un fameux poète anglais, appelé lord Byron. Je ne fis qu'[4]entrevoir son visage pâle et fantastique à travers la brume du crépuscule. J'étais alors bien inconnu, bien pauvre, bien découragé de la vie. Ce poète misanthrope, jeune, riche, élégant de figure, illustre de nom, déjà célèbre de génie, voyageant à son gré ou se fixant à son caprice dans les plus ravissantes contrées du globe, ayant des barques à lui[5] sur les vagues, des chevaux sur les grèves, passant l'été sous les ombrages des Alpes, les hivers sous les orangers de Pise, me paraissait le plus favorisé des mortels. Il fallait que ses larmes vinssent de quelque source de l'âme bien profonde et bien mystérieuse pour donner tant d'amertume à ses accents, tant de mélancolie à ses vers. Cette mélancolie même était un attrait de plus pour mon cœur. LAMARTINE.

NOTES

1 Rearrange the order of the sentence, which is awkward. 2 Use the Passive. 3 This participial construction is not quite correct; better translate by a clause. 4 See p. 66, § 52. 5 'of his own'.

57. *LA FUTAIE*

VOCABULARY

la futaie, see p. 35, § 23.
le fût, stem, trunk.
le hêtre, beech.
svelte, slim.
la ramure, branches.
éclairci, cleared.
débarrassé, rid.
les broussailles (n.f.), brushwood, undergrowth.
verdissant, pres. p. of *verdir*, to turn green.
profiler, show in outline, silhouette.
le pilier, pillar, column.
la nef, nave (of church).
le cierge, (wax) candle, taper.
âcre, pungent.
le charbonnier, charcoal-burner.

Nous avons pris le chemin des[1] bois de Fosses, et, au bout d'un quart d'heure, nous nous sommes trouvés sous les grands fûts de la *réserve*[2]. Quelle belle chose qu'une futaie à l'heure du soir où[3] le soleil glisse ses rayons obliques sous le couvert! Les hêtres et les chênes élancent droit vers le ciel leurs troncs sveltes et nus, surmontés d'une ramure opaque. Le sol éclairci et débarrassé de broussailles laisse le regard plonger dans les intimes profondeurs de la forêt; une lumière verdissante et mystérieuse baigne la futaie où les pas et les voix deviennent plus sonores. De tous côtés, les hêtres profilent leurs blanches colonnades. C'est comme un temple aux mille piliers puissants, aux nefs spacieuses et sombres, où, tout au loin, des pluies de rayons lumineux brillent dans l'ombre comme des lueurs de cierges. Tandis que nous cheminions silencieux et recueillis, une âcre odeur de fumée se répandait sous les branches. — Les charbonniers ne sont pas loin, dit Tristan.

ANDRÉ THEURIET.

NOTES

1 Cp. *la route de Paris*, 'the highway to Paris', 'the Paris road'. 2 *la réserve*, keep the technical French word '*réserve*' or translate by 'preserve'. See p. 35, § 23. 3 Is this 'where'?

58. *LA CHUTE DE NAPOLÉON*

VOCABULARY

planer, to soar.
foudroyant, as of lightning, flashing like a thunderbolt.
fondre, to swoop down.
ployé, bent double, huddled up.
infécond, barren.

Oui, l'aigle, un soir, planait aux voûtes éternelles,
Lorsqu'un grand coup de vent lui cassa les deux ailes;
Sa chute fit dans l'air un foudroyant sillon;
Tous alors sur son nid fondirent pleins de joie;
Chacun selon ses dents se partagea la proie;
L'Angleterre prit l'aigle[1], et l'Autriche l'aiglon[1].

Vous savez ce qu'on fit du géant historique.
Pendant six ans l'on vit, loin derrière l'Afrique[2],
Sous le verrou des rois prudents,
— Oh! n'exilons personne, oh! l'exil est impie! —
Cette grande figure en sa cage accroupie,
Ployée, et les genoux aux dents.

Encor si[3] ce banni n'eût rien aimé sur terre!
Mais les cœurs de lion sont les vrais cœurs de père;
Il aimait son fils, ce vainqueur!
Deux choses lui restaient dans sa cage inféconde[4],
Le portrait d'un enfant et la carte du monde,
Tout son génie et tout son cœur!

VICTOR HUGO.

NOTES

1 *l'aigle* represents Napoleon; *l'aiglon*, his son, the King of Rome. 2 In Saint Helena. 3 'If only'. The sense is almost 'It would not have mattered so much if', etc. 4 Exiled in that lonely island Napoleon's abilities were useless to the world.

59. *IL FAUT SUIVRE LA NATURE*

VOCABULARY

un mets, a meat, dish. *se garantir de*, to protect oneself from.

Je resterais toujours aussi près de la nature qu'il serait possible, pour flatter[1] les sens que j'ai reçus d'elle, bien sûr que plus elle mettrait du sien[2] dans mes jouissances, plus j'y trouverais de réalité. Si je voulais goûter un mets du bout du monde, j'irais plutôt l'y chercher, que de l'en[3] faire venir; car les mets les plus exquis manquent toujours d'un assaisonnement qu'on n'apporte pas avec eux, et qu'aucun cuisinier ne leur donne[4], l'air du climat qui les a produits. Par la même raison je n'imiterais pas ceux qui, ne se trouvant bien qu'où ils ne sont point, mettent toujours les saisons en contradiction avec elles-mêmes; qui vont en Italie en hiver pour y chercher l'été, sans songer qu'en croyant fuir la rigueur des saisons ils la trouvent dans les lieux où l'on n'a point appris à s'en garantir. J.-J. ROUSSEAU.

NOTES

1 *flatter*, here 'to humour', 'to indulge' rather than 'to flatter'. 2 Cp. *Il faut y mettre du sien*, 'One must put something of one's own into it'. 3 What does *en* refer to? 4 'can give'. See p. 37, § 24.

60. *LE PROVINCIAL*

VOCABULARY

la mode, fashion. *éblouir*, to dazzle. *l'effet* (n.m.), reality.

Dorante. A ne rien déguiser, Cliton, je te confesse
Qu'à Poitiers j'ai vécu comme vit la jeunesse;
J'étais en ces lieux-là de beaucoup de métiers;
Mais Paris, après tout, est bien loin de Poitiers.
Le climat[1] différent veut une autre méthode;
Ce qu'on admire ailleurs est ici hors de mode:
La diverse façon de parler et d'agir
Donne aux nouveaux venus souvent de quoi rougir.
Chez les provinciaux on prend ce qu'on rencontre;
Et là, faute de mieux, un sot passe à la montre[2].
Mais il faut à Paris bien d'autres[3] qualités:
On ne s'éblouit point de ces fausses clartés[4];
Et tant d'honnêtes gens[5], que l'on y voit ensemble,
Font qu'on est mal reçu, si l'on ne leur ressemble.
Cliton. Connaissez mieux Paris, puisque vous en parlez.
Paris est un grand lieu plein de marchands mêlés[6];
L'effet n'y répond pas toujours à l'apparence:
On s'y laisse duper autant qu'en lieu de France.

CORNEILLE.

NOTES

1 'atmosphere' rather than 'climate'. 2 *la montre* is 'the review' of the citizen-soldiers of former times: we say 'to pass in the crowd', in much the same way. 3 See p. 50, § 35, AUTRE. 4 See p. 50, § 36. 5 *les honnêtes gens*, 'well-bred people', 'gentlefolks'. 6 *marchands mêlés*, 'doubtful characters'.

SECTION IV

MODEL LESSON IV

CAMILLE. O mes frères !
LE VIEIL HORACE. Tout beau, ne les pleurez pas tous;
Deux jouissent d'un sort dont leur père est jaloux.
Que des plus nobles fleurs leur tombe soit couverte,
La gloire de leur mort m'a payé de leur perte:
Ce bonheur a suivi leur courage invaincu,
Qu'ils ont vu Rome libre autant qu'ils ont vécu
Et ne l'auront point vue obéir qu'à son prince,
Ni d'un État voisin devenir la province.
Pleurez l'autre, pleurez l'irréparable affront
Que sa fuite honteuse imprime à notre front;
Pleurez le déshonneur de toute notre race,
Et l'opprobre éternel qu'il laisse au nom d'Horace.
JULIE. Que vouliez-vous qu'il fît contre trois?
LE VIEIL HORACE. Qu'il mourût,
Ou qu'un beau désespoir alors le secourût.
N'eût-il que d'un moment reculé sa défaite,
Rome eût été du moins un peu plus tard sujette;
Il eût avec honneur laissé mes cheveux gris,
Et c'était de sa vie un assez digne prix.

CORNEILLE.

1. CAMILLE. *O mes frères!*
LE VIEIL HORACE. *Tout beau, ne les pleurez pas tous;*
Deux jouissent d'un sort dont leur père est jaloux.
Que des plus nobles fleurs leur tombe soit couverte,
La gloire de leur mort m'a payé de leur perte.

In translating such a passage our hands are tied. Within the narrow limits of rigid accuracy we can do little to reproduce the power and the beauty of the original. Corneille and Racine with their Classical verse do not give the translator a chance when his medium is prose. In these conditions to translate *con amore* is difficult, often impossible. It is true that we are entitled to use archaic and Biblical English and to drop occasionally into blank verse. But unless we abandon our principles and paraphrase instead of translating (and thereby run the risk of forfeiting marks), we must consider the exercise mainly as testing knowledge of Classical diction and seventeenth-century constructions, and tackle the passage conscientiously, if without much enthusiasm. The translation will be at best somewhat wooden. But it can at least be accurate, if we observe such points as the following:

Camille...Le vieil Horace...Julie. Although the characters in French Classical drama have Classical names, they are themselves generally more French than Greek or Roman. We should thus perhaps retain a name like *Émilie* in preference to Latin 'Æmilia' or English 'Emily'. But the matter demands considerable tact. Thus either *Camille* or 'Camilla', *Julie* or 'Julia' will do, but 'old Horace' will not! On the analogy of 'Pliny the Elder' we might say 'Horace (or Horatius) the Elder'.

Tout beau: the phrase seems to moderns somewhat trivial, as if meaning 'Gently', but it was used like the Shakespearean 'Soft'.

ne les pleurez pas tous: 'do not weep for them all' would be unfortunate. The Horatian brothers, being only three in number, are hardly to be referred to as 'them all'. The case is met by 'Weep not for all'.

Deux jouissent d'un sort: 'Two are happy in a fate' or, as in older English, 'Two enjoy a fate', cp. a 1577 quotation in the *Oxford English Dictionary*:

What shall I speak of Pertinax and what of Julian?
Enjoyed not both they one kinde of *death*?

des plus nobles fleurs: 'with the noblest flowers', i.e. those reserved for the most honoured dead.

tombe: not so much 'grave' as the raised Roman 'tomb'; hence *couverte*, 'covered' or 'heaped' and not 'strewn'.

leur perte: 'their loss' might just possibly convey a wrong meaning, viz. 'the loss which *they* have suffered', whereas it means 'the loss of them'. If so, it would be permissible to alter it to '*my* loss'.

'CAMILLA. O my brothers!
HORATIUS THE ELDER. Soft! Weep not for all. Two enjoy a fate their sire doth envy them. With flowers most noble let their tomb be heaped. The glory of their death hath recompensed me for their loss.'

2. *Ce bonheur a suivi leur courage invaincu,*
Qu'ils ont vu Rome libre autant qu'ils ont vécu
Et ne l'auront point vue obéir qu'à son prince,
Ni d'un État voisin devenir la province.

a suivi: *suivre* here, as frequently, means 'to attend'; cp. *les suivants du roi*, 'The King's attendants'.

ne...point...que: this turn is equivalent to 'not... except', and *point*, being stronger than *pas*, can be rendered here by 'never'.

son prince: not 'her prince', but (see p. 55, § 42) 'her *own* prince'; *prince* may, as in English, be *any* 'ruler', such as the king of early Roman times.

la province: 'the appanage' or 'the province', as when some people said in 1914, 'France must not become a German *province*'.

'This blessing hath attended their unvanquished courage, that so long as life was in them they beheld Rome free. Never shall they have seen her obey any but her own king, nor of a neighbour State become the province.'

3. *Pleurez l'autre, pleurez l'irréparable affront*
Que sa fuite honteuse imprime à notre front;

Pleurez le déshonneur de toute notre race,
Et l'opprobre éternel qu'il laisse au nom d'Horace.

Pleurez l'autre. It is difficult to render this exactly; *l'autre* is of course the remaining brother, the only survivor, but one reason why he is referred to merely as *l'autre* is that the old man is unwilling to mention the name of a son who, he thinks, has disgraced him. For such cases *l'autre* is still in present-day French a useful phrase. But we do not happen to use 'the other' in this way. To say 'the other one' or 'the remaining one' or 'the third' would be ridiculous. Perhaps 'Weep for him that yet liveth' will suit.

irréparable: English 'irreparable' is a poor substitute because of its short syllables; 'beyond repair' is better; cp. Fletcher: 'We have suffered beyond *all repair of honour*' (*Cent. Dict.*).

opprobre éternel: 'perpetual shame' is the Biblical phrase, but it would make an unpleasant rime with 'name' unless the order were inverted.

il laisse: *il* does not stand for *le déshonneur*, but for *l'autre*; *laisser*, 'to leave as a legacy', 'to bequeath to'.

'Weep for him who yet liveth, weep for the disgrace beyond repair that his dastard flight doth brand upon our brow; weep for the dishonour of all our house, for the shame perpetual he leaveth to the Horatian name.'

4. JULIE. *Que vouliez-vous qu'il fît contre trois?*
LE VIEIL HORACE. *Qu'il mourût,*
Ou qu'un beau désespoir alors le secourût.
N'eût-il que d'un moment reculé sa défaite,
Rome eût été du moins un peu plus tard sujette;
Il eût avec honneur laissé mes cheveux gris,
Et c'était de sa vie un assez digne prix.

Que vouliez-vous, etc. It will be noticed that Julia uses the second person plural, as was the respectful seventeenth-century custom, whereas in Shakespeare 'thou' was permissible. The construction is easily understood by considering the form it would have in the Present Tense, as in the simple phrase: *Que voulez-vous que j'y fasse?* 'What do you wish me to do in the matter?' 'What would you have me do?' or even 'What can I do?' This, used in the Past with the Imperfect, gives 'What would'st thou have had him do?' i.e. 'What could he do?' The natural English construction would be 'What could he do against three?'—to which Horatius in his anger would retort 'Die!' But this would not allow for the continuance of the French construction, which makes *secourût* also depend on *vouliez-vous*; it would have to be followed by e.g. 'or draw courage from despair'. On the other hand, keeping the construction means losing the conciseness and the force of the original.

un beau désespoir: not 'some noble despair' nor (with too marked an allusion to Tennyson) 'some divine despair', but rather 'splendid desperation'; *le désespoir* does duty for both 'despair' and 'desperation' and the latter seems the sense here intended. Perhaps the phrase 'the valour of despair' will do.

reculé sa défaite: 'staved off his defeat' would be exact, but somewhat trivial; 'retarded' is better here.

sujette: 'a slave', 'enslaved' or (archaic) 'enthralled'.

c'était. The construction is suddenly altered; not 'it would have been' as we might have expected from the preceding *eût*, but 'it was', expressing a general fact independent of the particular situation, i.e. such a result *was* an adequate price for his life, whether actually he did or did not decide to sell it.

'Julia. What would'st thou have had him do against three?

HORATIUS THE ELDER. I would that he had died! Or that the valour of despair had come to help him then. Had he, by but one moment, retarded his defeat, Rome had been at least somewhat the later enthralled. In honour had he left my grey hairs, and for his life 'twas surely price enough.'

SUGGESTED RENDERING

CAMILLA. O my brothers!

HORATIUS THE ELDER. Soft! Weep not for all. Two enjoy a fate their sire doth envy them. With flowers most noble let their tomb be heaped. The glory of their death hath recompensed me for their loss. This blessing hath attended their unvanquished courage, that so long as life was in them they beheld Rome free. Never shall they have seen her obey any but her own king, nor of a neighbour State become the province. Weep for him who yet liveth, weep for the disgrace beyond repair that his dastard flight doth brand upon our brow; weep for the dishonour of all our house, for the shame perpetual he leaveth to the Horatian name.

JULIA. What would'st thou have had him do against three?

HORATIUS THE ELDER. I would that he had died. Or that the valour of despair had come to help him then. Had he, by but one moment, retarded his defeat, Rome had been at least somewhat the later enthralled. In honour had he left my grey hairs, and for his life 'twas surely price enough.

61. *COUCHER DE SOLEIL*

VOCABULARY

l'écran (n.m.), screen (for magic-lantern, etc.). *l'âtre* (n.m.), hearth.

Vers le grand soleil d'or qui, par l'ombre insulté,
Ramène sur son front sa pourpre qu'il déploie,
Là-bas, vers l'incendie énorme qui flamboie
Sous l'écran violet de l'âtre illimité[1],

Il vole, il vole, épris d'un désir indompté,
L'oiseau gris qui du gouffre[2] et des flots fait sa joie;
Dans cette pourpre ardente il s'enfonce, il se noie,
Et qui le voit du bord le voit dans la clarté.

Jamais il n'atteindra l'astre[3] divin: qu'importe?
— Ainsi vers l'Idéal un saint amour m'emporte,
Heureux si je pouvais, dans mes rapides[4] jours,

Loin des réalités et des laideurs humaines,
Sans l'atteindre jamais m'en approchant[5] toujours,
Apparaître baigné de ses lueurs lointaines!

JULES LEMAÎTRE.

NOTES

1 The whole western sky is the *âtre*; the sunset the *incendie*. 2 See p. 24, § 16, GOUFFRE. 3 See p. 41, § 27, *astre*. 4 See p. 38, § 25. 5 On the force of the Present Participle, see p. 58, § 45.

62. *GUY DE MAUPASSANT*

VOCABULARY

franc, free, free-spoken, natural.
conteur, story-teller.
avoir un goût de terroir, to be redolent of the soil, have a local flavour.
madré, cunning, 'canny.'
matois, sly.
gabeur, fond of drawing the long bow.
outre-tombe, beyond the grave.
le coquin, scamp, rascal.

M. de Maupassant est certainement un des plus francs conteurs de ce pays[1], où l'on fit[2] tant de contes, et de si bons. Sa langue forte, simple, naturelle, a un goût de terroir qui nous la fait aimer chèrement. Il possède les trois grandes qualités de l'écrivain français, d'abord la clarté, puis encore la clarté et enfin la clarté. Il a l'esprit de mesure et d'ordre qui est celui de notre race. Il écrit comme vit un bon propriétaire normand, avec économie et joie. Madré, matois, bon enfant, assez gabeur, n'ayant honte que de sa large[3] bonté native, attentif à cacher ce qu'il y a d'exquis dans son âme, plein[4] de ferme et haute raison, point rêveur[4]; peu curieux des choses d'outre-tombe, ne croyant qu'à ce qu'il voit, ne comptant que sur ce qu'il touche, il est de chez nous, celui-là; c'est un pays[5]!...Il est plus varié dans ses types, plus riche dans ses sujets qu'aucun autre conteur de ce temps. On ne trouve guère d'imbéciles ni de coquins qui ne soient bons pour lui[6] et qu'il ne mette en passant dans son sac.

ANATOLE FRANCE.

NOTES

1 *ce pays* = Normandy. 2 Why the Past Historic? 3 'expansive'? or 'generous'? 4 Note the gender—and the construction. 5 'fellow-countryman', 'brother-Frenchman'. 6 'good for his purposes', 'fair game for him'.

63. (*Ptolemy is warned by his minister against receiving Pompey in Egypt*)

VOCABULARY

la saison, season, time.
balancer, to weigh.
en butte, aimed at.
la curée, quarry, the parts of the deer given to the hounds.

Sire, quand par le fer[1] les choses sont vidées[2],
La justice et le droit sont de vaines idées;
Et qui[3] veut être juste en de telles saisons
Balance le pouvoir, et non pas les raisons.
Voyez donc votre force; et regardez Pompée,
Sa fortune abattue, et sa valeur trompée.
César n'est pas le seul qu'il fuie en cet état:
Il fuit et le reproche et les yeux du sénat,
Dont plus de la moitié piteusement étale
Une indigne curée aux vautours de Pharsale[4];
Il fuit Rome perdue; il fuit tous les Romains,
A qui par sa défaite il met les fers[1] aux mains.
Auteur des maux de tous, il est à tous en butte,
Et fuit le monde entier écrasé sous sa chute.
Le défendrez-vous seul[5] contre tant d'ennemis?
L'espoir de son salut en lui seul était mis.

CORNEILLE.

NOTES

1 What is the plain English for *fer* here? 2 Cp. *vider une querelle*, 'to settle a quarrel'. 3 Note omission of antecedent. Supply in translating. 4 At the battle of Pharsalus, 48 B.C.,

Caesar routed Pompey. 5 To whom does *seul* refer? Decide from the context.

64. *L'ARRIVÉE AU JAPON*

VOCABULARY

vent debout, a head wind.
surplomber, to overhang.
un fouillis, confused mass.
un couloir, corridor, passage.
une paroi, partition, inner wall.
un décor, stage scenery.
le large, the open sea.
frôler, to brush, graze.
froisser, to ruffle.
un store, window-blind.
une nef, a ship.

Tout le long de l'horizon, on vit bientôt comme[1] une lourdeur en l'air, comme un voile pesant sur les eaux, et peu à peu, dans cette sorte de grande nuée confuse, se découpèrent des montagnes. Nous avions[2] vent debout, comme si ce pays eût soufflé[3] de toutes ses forces contre nous pour nous éloigner de lui. La mer, les cordages, le navire étaient agités et bruissants[4].

Vers trois heures du soir, toutes ces choses lointaines s'étaient rapprochées[2], jusqu'à nous surplomber de leurs masses rocheuses ou de leurs fouillis de verdure, et nous entrions[2] maintenant dans une espèce de couloir ombreux, entre deux rangées de montagnes, qui se succédaient avec une bizarrerie symétrique—comme les parois d'un décor tout en profondeur.

La grande brise du large, brusquement tombée, avait fait place au calme; et, dans cette vallée, il[5] se faisait une étonnante musique de cigales. Nous frôlions au passage de grandes jonques, qui glissaient tout doucement sur l'eau à peine froissée; leurs voiles blanches, tendues sur des vergues horizontales, retombaient[6] mollement, drapées à mille plis comme des stores, leurs poupes compliquées se relevaient en château, comme celles des nefs du moyen âge. Au milieu de ce vert intense, elles avaient une blancheur neigeuse.

PIERRE LOTI.

NOTES

1 See p. 65, § 51. 2 Note the tense. 3 'had blown'? or 'had been blowing'? 4 *bruissant*, 'noisy', 'boisterous', from the verb *bruire*, connected with *bruit*. 5 Personal or Impersonal? 6 See p. 19, § 13.

65. (*Le Comte de Gormas, father of Chimène, is angry because Don Diègue, father of Rodrigue, has been appointed 'gouverneur' of the heir to the Spanish throne*)

VOCABULARY

répondre à, here to do justice to, come up to. *le nerf*, sinew.

LE COMTE. Les exemples vivants sont d'un autre[1] pouvoir;
Un prince dans un livre apprend mal son devoir.
Et qu'a fait après tout ce grand nombre d'années,
Que[2] ne puisse égaler une de mes journées?
Si vous fûtes vaillant, je le suis aujourd'hui,
Et ce bras du royaume est le plus ferme appui[3].
Grenade et l'Aragon tremblent quand ce fer brille;
Mon nom sert de rempart à toute la Castille:
Sans moi, vous passeriez bientôt sous d'autres lois,
Et vous auriez bientôt vos ennemis pour rois.
Chaque jour, chaque instant, pour rehausser ma gloire,
Met lauriers sur lauriers, victoire sur victoire.
Le prince à mes côtés ferait dans les combats
L'essai de son courage à l'ombre de mon bras;
Il apprendrait à vaincre en me regardant faire,
Et pour répondre en hâte à son grand caractère,
Il verrait...
DON DIÈGUE. Je le sais, vous servez bien le roi:
Je vous ai vu combattre et commander sous moi.
Quand l'âge dans mes nerfs a fait couler sa glace,
Votre rare valeur a bien rempli ma place;
Enfin, pour épargner les discours superflus,
Vous êtes aujourd'hui ce qu'autrefois je fus.

CORNEILLE.

NOTES

1 For this sense of *autre* see p. 50, § 35, AUTRE. 2 Case?
3 Prose order?

66. *ALPHONSE DAUDET*

VOCABULARY

l'aisance (f.), ease of manner.
laborieux, laboured.
voulu, intentional, studied.
plat, uninteresting, dull.
brutal, crude.

M. Daudet traîne tous les cœurs après lui; car il a le charme, aussi indéfinissable dans une œuvre d'art que dans un visage féminin, et qui pourtant n'est pas un vain mot puisque de très grands écrivains ne l'[1] ont pas. Le charme, c'est peut-être une certaine aisance heureuse, une fleur de naturel même dans le rare et le recherché; c'est, en tout cas, quelque chose d'incompatible avec des qualités trop laborieuses et trop voulues; ainsi le charme ne se rencontre guère chez les chefs d'école. On peut remarquer[2] aussi que le charme ne va pas sans un cœur aisément ému et qui ne craint pas de le[1] paraître. Il ne faut donc pas le[1] demander à ceux qui font profession de ne peindre que des réalités plates ou brutales, ou qui affectent de n'être curieux que du monde extérieur. Ce charme, quel qu'il soit, est une des puissances de M. Alphonse Daudet.

JULES LEMAÎTRE.

NOTES

1 What does *le* stand for here? 2 Is this equal to 'remark'?

67. (*The Cid describes the stratagem by which he has defeated the Moors who intended to invade Spain*)

VOCABULARY

le flux, incoming tide. *abuser*, to deceive.

DON RODRIGUE. Cette obscure clarté[1] qui tombe des étoiles
Enfin avec le flux nous fait voir trente voiles;
L'onde s'enfle dessous, et d'un commun effort
Les Maures et la mer montent jusques au port.
On les laisse passer; tout leur paraît tranquille;
Point de soldats au port, point aux murs de la ville.

Notre profond silence abusant leurs esprits,
Ils n'osent plus douter de nous avoir surpris;
Ils abordent sans peur, ils ancrent, ils descendent[2]
Et courent se livrer aux mains qui les attendent.
Nous nous levons alors, et tous en même temps
Poussons jusques au ciel mille cris éclatants.
Les nôtres, à ces cris, de nos vaisseaux répondent;
Ils paraissent[3] armés, les Maures se confondent,
L'épouvante les prend à demi descendus;
Avant que de combattre ils s'estiment perdus.
Ils couraient au pillage, et rencontrent la guerre;
Nous les pressons sur l'eau, nous les pressons sur terre,
Et nous faisons courir des ruisseaux de leur sang,
Avant qu'aucun résiste ou reprenne son rang.

CORNEILLE.

NOTES

1 Note the oxymoron or apparent self-contradiction.
2 Note the order of the three actions described in this line.
3 Beware of ambiguity.

68. *SAINT-MALO*

VOCABULARY

le varech, sea-weed.
les remparts (m. pl.), city-walls.
une lucarne, dormer-window.
une girouette, vane, weather-cock.
un pan, stretch.
une meurtrière, loop-hole.
le bassin, basin, dock.
vaseux (*la vase*, ooze), miry, slimy.
le chantier, shipbuilding yard.
la marmite, cauldron.
le goudron, pitch.
les copeaux (m. pl.), shavings.

Les vagues battent contre les murs et, quand il est marée basse, déferlent[1] à leur pied sur le sable. De petits rochers couverts de varechs surgissent de la grève à ras du sol, comme des taches noires sur cette surface blonde. Les plus grands, dressés à pic et tout unis, supportent de leurs sommets inégaux la base des fortifications, en prolongeant ainsi la couleur grise et en augmentant la hauteur.

Au-dessus de cette ligne uniforme de remparts, on

voit les toits des maisons serrés[2] l'un près de l'autre, avec leurs petites lucarnes ouvertes, leurs girouettes découpées qui tournent, et leurs cheminées de poterie rouge dont les fumées bleuâtres se perdent dans l'air.

Tout à l'entour sur la mer s'élèvent d'arides îlots sur lesquels on distingue de loin quelques pans de mur percés de meurtrières. En face de la ville, rattaché à la terre ferme par une longue jetée qui sépare le port de la pleine mer, de l'autre côté du bassin s'étend le quartier de Saint-Servan, couché tout à son aise dans une grande prairie vaseuse. A l'entrée se dressent les quatre tours du château, noires du haut en bas. Cela seul nous récompense d'avoir fait ce long circuit sur la grève, en plein soleil de juillet, au milieu de chantiers, parmi les marmites de goudron qui bouillaient et les feux de copeaux dont on flambait[3] la carcasse des navires.

FLAUBERT.

NOTES

1 *déferler* is said of the wave curling just before it breaks.
2 Make it clear which word the English participle goes with.
3 *flamber la carcasse d'un navire*, 'to cleanse with fire the bottom of a ship', technically 'to bream': *carcasse* usually = *charpente*, 'framework', but here 'hull'.

69. *LE ROI DE ROME*

VOCABULARY

le hochet, plaything, bauble.
épaissir, see p. 17, § 12.
le chevet, pillow.
fonder, to found, lay foundations.
la cognée, (woodcutter's) axe, hatchet.
doter, to dower.
le relais, relay, stage.

O revers ! ô leçon ! — Quand l'enfant de cet homme
Eut reçu pour hochet la couronne de Rome;
Lorsqu'on l'eut revêtu d'un nom qui retentit;
Lorsqu'on eut bien montré son front royal qui tremble
Au peuple émerveillé qu'on puisse[1] tout ensemble
    Être si grand et si petit;

Quand son père eut pour lui gagné bien des batailles;
Lorsqu'il eut épaissi de vivantes murailles[2]
Autour du nouveau-né riant sur son chevet;
Quand ce grand ouvrier, qui savait comme on fonde,
Eut, à coups de cognée, à peu près fait le monde
Selon le songe qu'il rêvait;

Quand tout fut préparé par les mains paternelles
Pour doter l'humble enfant de splendeurs éternelles;
Lorsqu'on eut de sa vie assuré les relais[3];
Quand pour loger un jour ce maître héréditaire,
On eut enraciné bien avant dans la terre
Les pieds de marbre des palais;

Lorsqu'on eut pour sa[4] soif posé devant la France
Un vase tout rempli du vin de l'espérance,—
Avant qu'il eût goûté de ce poison doré,
Avant que de sa lèvre il eût touché la coupe,
Un cosaque[5] survint qui prit l'enfant en croupe
Et l'emporta tout effaré!

VICTOR HUGO.

NOTES

1 Examine carefully the construction. 2 Keep the metaphor but do not translate word by word. 3 Prose order? 4 What does *sa* refer to? 5 Not to be understood literally: cp. p. 170, Passage 58, l. 6.

70. *LA PROPRIÉTÉ*

VOCABULARY

s'aviser, to take into one's head, to think fit.
un pieu, stake.
l'industrie (f.), skill.

Le premier qui ayant enclos un terrain s'avisa de dire *ceci est à moi*, et trouva des gens assez simples pour le croire, fut le vrai fondateur de la société civile. Que de crimes, de guerres, de meurtres, que de misères et d'horreurs n'eût[1] point épargnés au genre humain celui[2] qui, arrachant les pieux ou comblant le fossé, eût[1] crié à ses semblables: "Gardez-vous d'écouter[3] cet imposteur; vous êtes perdus si vous oubliez que les fruits sont à tous et que la terre n'est à personne!" Mais il y a grande apparence qu'alors les choses en étaient déjà venues au point de ne pouvoir plus durer comme elles étaient: car cette idée de propriété, dépendant de beaucoup d'idées antérieures qui n'ont pu naître que successivement, ne se forma pas tout d'un coup dans l'esprit humain: il fallut faire bien des progrès, acquérir bien de l'industrie et des lumières[4], les transmettre et les augmenter d'âge en âge, avant que d'arriver à ce dernier terme de l'état de nature. J.-J. ROUSSEAU.

NOTES

1 See p. 56, § 43. 2 'he' or 'one'? See p. 51, § 37. 3 See p. 65, § 52. 4 See p. 50, § 36.

71. *RÊVERIE*

VOCABULARY

l'astre (n.m.), *here* star, day-star.
dorer, to gild.
rouiller, to rust.
mauresque, Moorish.
inouï, unheard of, marvellous.
la fusée, rocket.
la gerbe, sheaf.
épanoui, expanded, full-blown, outspread.
rembruni, dusky (see p. 20, § 13).
denteler, to jag, notch, indent.

Oh! laissez-moi! c'est l'heure où l'horizon qui fume[1]
Cache un front inégal[2] sous un cercle de brume,
L'heure où l'astre géant rougit et disparaît.
Le grand bois jaunissant[3] dore seul la colline.
On dirait qu'en ces jours où l'automne décline,
Le soleil et la pluie ont rouillé la forêt.

Oh! qui fera surgir soudain, qui fera naître,
Là-bas, — tandis que seul je rêve à la fenêtre
Et que l'ombre s'amasse au fond du corridor, —
Quelque ville mauresque, éclatante, inouïe,
Qui, comme la fusée en gerbe épanouie,
Déchire ce brouillard avec ses flèches d'or?

Qu'elle[4] vienne inspirer, ranimer, ô génies,
Mes chansons, comme un ciel d'automne rembrunies[5],

Et jeter dans mes yeux son magique reflet,
Et longtemps, s'éteignant en rumeurs étouffées,
Avec les mille tours de ses palais de fées,
Brumeuse, denteler[2] l'horizon violet! VICTOR HUGO.

NOTES

1 Would 'which is smoking' mean anything here? 2 These two words *inégal* and *denteler* express the same idea. 3 See p. 17, § 12. 4 What noun does *elle* refer to? 5 What noun does *rembrunies* go with?

72. *LEVER DE SOLEIL*

VOCABULARY

une friche, waste *or* fallow land.
semer, to sow, plant, scatter.
le genévrier, the juniper(-bush).
arroser, to water.
d'en face, opposite.
la côte, the hillside.
se déchirer, to be rent, break up.
un flocon, flake, wisp.
miroiter, to glisten, glitter.
le tapage, noise, racket, din.

Le pays que nous avions devant les yeux m'était totalement inconnu. A nos pieds, une friche semée de genévriers descendait jusque dans une gorge profonde, dont le creux était sans doute arrosé par un ruisseau, car il[1] s'en dégageait un ruban de brouillard qui serpentait comme une fumée au pied du coteau et nous voilait le fond du vallon. La colline d'en face était couverte de vignes, et au-dessus de nos têtes, dans le ciel d'un bleu fin, il y avait déjà une musique d'alouettes. Au fond de la vallée brumeuse, une horloge d'église sonna cinq heures. Le soleil se montra[2] tout rouge au-dessus des vignes mouillées de rosée; puis ses rayons glissèrent le long de la côte dans le brouillard, qui s'argenta tout à coup, se déchira, s'enleva en minces flocons blancs et finalement se dissipa pour nous laisser voir un ruisseau qui miroitait, des prés tout jaunes et violets dans leur pleine maturité, enfin au loin, à l'entrée de la gorge, un village dont les vitres roses étincelaient. En même temps des coqs chantèrent[3], la corne d'un pâtre résonna dans les rues du village et des mugissements de vaches lui répondirent du fond des étables. Ce gai soleil, ces prés en fleur, la musique des alouettes, tout ce tapage du réveil me redonnèrent un peu de courage. ANDRÉ THEURIET.

NOTES

1 Construction? 2 Do we say 'the sun showed itself'? How do we express the picture? 3 This use of the Past Historic with *en même temps* is not quite correct: the Imperfect would be more natural.

73. (*Narcissus, Nero's evil genius, urges him to disregard the opinion of the Roman people*)

VOCABULARY

la pente, inclination. *façonné*, fashioned, accustomed.

Néron. Mais, Narcisse, dis-moi, que veux-tu que je fasse?
Je n'ai que trop de pente à punir son audace;
Et, si je m'en croyais, ce triomphe indiscret
Serait bientôt suivi d'un éternel regret.
Mais de tout l'univers quel sera le langage?
Sur les pas des tyrans veux-tu que je m'engage[1],
Et que Rome, effaçant tant de titres d'honneur,
Me laisse pour tout nom celui d'empoisonneur?
Ils mettront ma vengeance au rang des parricides.

Narcisse. Et prenez-vous, seigneur, leurs caprices pour guides?
Avez-vous prétendu[2] qu'ils se tairaient toujours?
Est-ce à vous de prêter l'oreille à leurs discours?
De vos propres désirs perdez-vous la mémoire?
Et serez-vous le seul que vous n'oserez croire?
Mais, seigneur, les Romains ne vous sont point connus.
Non, non, dans leurs discours ils sont plus retenus.
Tant de précaution affaiblit votre règne:
Ils croiront, en effet, mériter qu'on les craigne.
Au joug depuis longtemps ils se sont façonnés;
Ils adorent la main qui les tient enchaînés. RACINE.

NOTES

1 *s'engager* is properly 'to enter upon' (a path). 2 See p. 26, § 16, PRÉTENDRE.

74. (*Le Roi d'Espagne parle à un de ses courtisans*)

VOCABULARY

grand, *here* grandee.
se prendre de bec avec, to quarrel, squabble with.
ramper, to crawl.
la couleuvre, snake.
dévider, to unwind, develop.
la fange, slime, mud.
sinistre, evil.

Je t'ai fait comte, grand de Castille, et marquis.
Agir par ruse, ou bien par force, t'est facile;
Tu te prendrais de bec avec tout un concile
Ou tu le chasserais, le démon en[1] fût-il.
Tu sais être hardi tout en restant subtil.
Quoique fait pour ramper, tu braves la tempête.
Tu saurais, s'il le faut, pour quelque coup de tête[2]
Te risquer, et, toi vieux[3], mettre l'épée au poing.
Tu conseilles le mal, mais tu ne le fais point.
Tu me conviens. J'observe en riant tes manœuvres.
J'ai du plaisir à voir serpenter les couleuvres.
Tes projets que, pensif, tu dévides sans bruit,
Sorte de fil[4] flottant qui se perd dans la nuit,
Tes talents, ton esprit, ta fortune, ta fange,
Tout cela fait de toi quelque chose d'étrange,
De sinistre et d'ingrat dont j'aime à me servir.

VICTOR HUGO.

NOTES

1 What does *en* stand for? Examine construction. 2 'some rash notion', 'ill-considered act'. 3 Expand. 4 Note, and translate, the metaphor in *dévides*, *fil*, *se perd*.

75. *LA NORMANDIE FRANÇAISE*

VOCABULARY

quand même, in spite of all, all the same.
conclu, arranged, agreed upon.
le pire, worst; *here* blackest.
un soubresaut, convulsive start.

Attachée à la terre française, la Normandie voulut[1] rester France à tout prix, quand même. Et, sur ce point, jamais la vaillante province n'a un seul instant hésité. Elle s'est donnée, et c'était un splendide cadeau qu'elle faisait. Car les rois de France ne pouvaient guère se passer d'elle pour constituer le royaume. Assise sur la basse Seine, tenant l'entrée et la sortie de Paris, sa défection ou seulement sa neutralité eussent[2] rejeté le centre vers le midi et changé probablement le cours de notre destinée. La conquérir, si elle ne l'eût pas voulu, et appuyée qu'elle eût[2] été toujours par les ennemis des rois, c'eût été une rude entreprise. Mais, avec elle et par elle, au contraire, tout devenait facile. Et c'est ainsi, en effet, que les choses se passèrent. A partir de[3] Jean Sans-Terre, la Normandie se tourna, une bonne fois[4], vers la France, et, étant gagnée, le cœur ouvert[5], la main fut prise et le mariage conclu. Depuis lors, il n'y eut plus de regret ni même d'arrière-pensée. Dans les pires moments, quand l'invasion pesait sur la province et que tout le monde souffrait tant, les bouches se taisaient, mais l'âme restait fidèle, et l'on sentait bien, à[6] un frémissement et à un soubresaut continuel, que la pensée était ailleurs, et que, s'il fallait attendre cent ans, eh bien! on attendrait cent ans. HANOTAUX.

NOTES

1 See p. 57, § 44. 2 Note mood and tense. 3 Cp. *à partir d'aujourd'hui*, 'from to-day onwards'. 4 = *une fois pour toutes*. 5 Expand. 6 See p. 68, § 55.

76. *LE MOYEN ÂGE*

VOCABULARY

le faîte, roof-top.
rabougri, stunted.
le pignon, gable.
aigu, sharp, pointed.
les réseaux, net-work, tracery.
exigu, tiny.
le preux, warrior (mediaeval).
une ogive, (Norman) arch.
moresque, Moorish.
verdir, to turn green.
le donjon, donjon, tower, keep.
la cigogne, stork.
effleurer, to graze, brush, skim over.
paré, adorned, decked, arrayed.

Quand je vais poursuivant mes courses poétiques,
Je m'arrête surtout aux vieux châteaux gothiques.
J'aime leurs toits d'ardoise aux reflets bleus et gris,

Aux faîtes couronnés d'arbustes rabougris;
Leurs pignons anguleux, leurs tourelles aiguës;
Dans les réseaux de plomb leurs vitres exiguës[1],
Légendes du vieux temps où les preux et les saints
Se groupent dans l'ogive en fantasques dessins;
Avec les minarets moresques, la chapelle,
Dont la cloche qui tinte à la prière appelle[2].
J'aime leurs murs verdis, par l'eau du ciel lavés,
Leurs cours où l'herbe croît à travers les pavés;
Au sommet des donjons leurs girouettes frêles
Que la blanche cigogne effleure de ses ailes;
Leurs ponts-levis tremblants, leurs portails blasonnés
De monstres, de griffons bizarrement ornés[1];
Leurs larges escaliers aux marches colossales,
Leurs corridors sans fin[3] et leurs immenses salles,
Où[2], comme une voix faible, erre et gémit le vent,
Où, recueilli dans moi, je m'égare en rêvant,
Paré de souvenirs d'amour et de féerie,
Le brillant moyen-âge et la chevalerie.

THÉOPHILE GAUTIER.

NOTES

1 Prose order? The *réseaux de plomb* are the 'lead-work' of the windows. 2 Construction? 3 See p. 71, § 56, SANS.

77. *LE "CHAOS"*

VOCABULARY

le genévrier, juniper (-bush).
le Gave, the torrent (running in a deep narrow bed); see p. 34, § 23.
fracassé, shattered.
broyé, crushed.
une cassure vive, sharp break.
âpre, rugged, harsh.
se froisser, to crush one another.
la traînée, track, trail.
roussi, scorched, reddened.

Après Gèdres est une vallée sauvage qu'on nomme le Chaos et qui est bien nommée. Là, au bout d'un quart d'heure, les arbres disparaissent, puis les genévriers et les buis, enfin les mousses; on ne voit plus le Gave, tous les bruits cessent. C'est la solitude morte et peuplée de débris. Trois avalanches de roches et de cailloux écrasés sont descendues de la cime jusqu'au fond.

L'effroyable marée, haute et longue d'un quart de lieue[1], étale comme des flots ses myriades de pierres stériles et la nappe inclinée semble encore glisser pour inonder la gorge. Ces pierres sont fracassées et broyées; leurs cassures vives et leurs pointes âpres blessent l'œil; elles se froissent et s'écrasent encore. Pas un buisson, pas un brin d'herbe; l'aride traînée grisâtre brûle sous un soleil de plomb[2]; ses débris sont roussis d'une teinte morne, comme dans une fournaise. Une montagne ruinée est plus désolée que toutes les ruines humaines.

TAINE.

NOTES

1 Express in natural English: for *une lieue* see p. 34, § 22.

2 Seems to mean 'leaden' either of colour (cp. *un soleil d'eau*, 'a watery sun'), or as shedding a heavy, close heat: *le soleil donne à plomb*, 'the sun is shining straight down on us'.

78. (*Prusias II, King of Bithynia* (*2nd cent.* B.C.), *had two sons, Nicomedes and Attalus. The Romans wished the younger son, Attalus, to succeed his father.*)

VOCABULARY

l'effet, see p. 77, § 59.
la vertu, virtue; courage.
insigne, signal, eminent.
l'éclat (n.m.), magnificence.

Nicomède. Eh bien! s'il est besoin de répondre autre chose,
Attale doit régner, Rome l'a résolu;
Et puisqu'elle a partout un pouvoir absolu,
C'est aux rois d'obéir alors qu'elle commande.
Attale a le cœur grand, l'esprit grand, l'âme grande,
Et toutes les grandeurs dont se fait un grand roi;
Mais c'est trop que d'en[1] croire un Romain sur sa foi.
Par quelque grand effet voyons s'il en[2] est digne,
S'il a cette vertu, cette valeur insigne:
Donnez-lui votre armée, et voyons ces grands coups;
Qu'il en[2] fasse pour lui[2] ce que j'ai fait pour vous;
Qu'il règne avec éclat sur sa propre conquête,
Et que de sa victoire il couronne sa tête.

Je lui prête mon bras, et veux dès maintenant,
S'il daigne s'en servir, être son lieutenant. CORNEILLE.

NOTES

1 Cp. *si vous m'en croyez*, 'if you will believe me'. 2 To what noun do these pronouns refer?

79. *L'ORAISON DU SOIR*

VOCABULARY

il sied, 'tis fitting.
s'entendre, to understand one another, reach agreement.
le vautour, vulture.
la calandre, (species of) lark.
éplucher, to shell.
un outil, tool.
un sécateur, pruning-scissors.
un échenilloir (*une chenille*, caterpiller), caterpillar-destroyer.
la nielle, black rust.
un groseillier, currant-bush.

Une Voix dans les branches.

Dieu des oiseaux!

Un Autre.

Ou plutôt — car il sied avant tout de s'entendre
Et le vautour n'a pas le Dieu de la calandre!—
Dieu des petits oiseaux!...

Mille Voix, dans les feuilles.

Dieu des petits oiseaux!...

La première Voix.

Qui pour nous alléger mis de l'air dans nos os[1]
Et pour nous embellir mis du ciel[2] sur nos plumes,
Merci de ce beau jour, de la source où nous bûmes,
Des grains qu'ont épluchés nos becs minutieux,
De nous avoir donné d'excellents petits yeux
Qui voient les ennemis invisibles des hommes,
De nous avoir munis, jardiniers que nous sommes,
De bons petits outils de corne, blonds ou noirs,
Qui sont des sécateurs et des échenilloirs...

La deuxième Voix.

Demain, nous combattrons les chardons et les nielles:
Pardonnez-nous, ce soir, nos fautes vénielles
Et d'avoir dégarni deux ou trois groseilliers.

ROSTAND.

NOTES

1 Cp. Passage 6, line 8. 2 Meaning?

80. *L'ORAISON DU SOIR* (*suite*)

VOCABULARY

le charançon, weevil.
le réseau, net, snare.
le pinson, chaffinch.
l'orge (n.f.), barley.
le mil or *millet*, millet.
un susurrement, whisper, murmur.

La première Voix.

Pour que nous dormions bien, il faut que vous ayez
Soufflé sur nos yeux ronds que ferment trois paupières.
Seigneur, si l'homme injuste, en nous jetant des pierres,
Nous paye de l'avoir entouré de chansons
Et d'avoir disputé[1] son pain aux charançons,
Si dans quelque filet notre famille[2] est prise,
Faites-nous souvenir de Saint François d'Assise
Et qu'il faut pardonner à l'homme ses réseaux
Parce qu'un homme a dit: "Mes frères les oiseaux!"

La deuxième Voix, sur un ton de litanie.

Et vous, François, grand Saint, bénisseur de nos ailes...

Des Milliers de Voix, dans les feuilles.

Priez pour nous!

La Voix.

Prédicateur des Hirondelles,
Confesseur des Pinsons...

Toutes les Voix.

Priez pour nous!

La Voix.

Rêveur
Qui crûtes à notre âme avec tant de ferveur
Que notre âme, depuis, se forme et se précise...

Toutes les Voix.

Priez pour nous!

La première Voix.

Obtenez-nous, François d'Assise,
Le grain d'orge...

La deuxième Voix.

Le grain de blé...

Une autre Voix.

Le grain de mil!

La première Voix.

Ainsi soit-il!

Toutes, dans un susurrement qui court jusqu'au bout de la forêt.

Ainsi soit-il! ROSTAND.

NOTES

1 See p. 41, § 27. 2 'some of our folks.'

SECTION V

81. *UN GROS CHAGRIN*

VOCABULARY

cuirassier, cuirassier, horse-soldier with breastplate = lifeguardsman.
le turco, turco, Algerian infantryman = sepoy.
envahir, to invade, steal over *or* into.
tout plein, *familiar*, a whole lot, heaps.

Trott n'est pas jaloux de sa petite sœur: il l'aime bien à sa manière et il a un trop bon cœur, maître Trott. Il voudrait qu'elle fût toujours contente et n'a pas l'ombre d'un mauvais sentiment contre elle. Non, Trott n'est pas jaloux. Il est triste; il est même très triste. Puisque maintenant on ne fait plus attention à lui, c'est que peut-être son papa et sa maman ne l'aiment plus. Maintenant qu'ils ont un enfant neuf, ils ne se soucient plus du vieux. Trott lui-même, dès qu'on lui a donné sa boîte de cuirassiers en plomb, a tout à fait délaissé ses turcos, qui n'étaient plus très jolis. Pour les grandes personnes, c'est la même chose, évidemment. Oui, maintenant on l'oublie tout à fait.

Une grande peine a envahi le cœur de Trott. On ne l'aime plus du tout. Peut-être un tout petit peu encore, mais pas comme avant. Et quand on a été aimé tout plein, ça n'est pas assez. Trott a le cœur très lourd, un peu comme quand il a mangé trop de tarte aux pommes.

André Lichtenberger.

82. *LE RETOUR*

VOCABULARY

se serrer, to close up, sit closer.
le garnement, urchin, little rascal, scamp.
bénir, to bless.
le pouce, thumb; inch.

Perdican. — Bonjour, mes amis, me reconnaissez-vous?

Chœur de Paysans. — Seigneur, vous ressemblez à un enfant que nous avons beaucoup aimé.

Perdican. — N'est-ce pas vous qui m'avez porté sur votre dos pour passer les ruisseaux de vos prairies, vous qui m'avez fait danser sur vos genoux, qui m'avez pris en croupe sur vos chevaux robustes, qui vous êtes serrés quelquefois autour de vos tables pour me faire une place au souper de la ferme?

Chœur de Paysans. — Nous nous en souvenons, seigneur. Vous étiez le plus mauvais garnement et le meilleur garçon de la terre.

Perdican. — Et pourquoi donc alors ne m'embrassez-vous pas, au lieu de me saluer comme un étranger?

Chœur de Paysans. — Que Dieu te bénisse! Chacun de nous voudrait te prendre dans ses bras; mais nous sommes vieux, Monseigneur, et vous êtes un homme.

Perdican. — Oui, il y a dix ans que je ne vous ai vus, et en un jour tout change sous le soleil. Je me suis élevé de quelques pieds vers le ciel et vous vous êtes courbés de quelques pouces vers le tombeau. Vos têtes ont blanchi, vos pas sont devenus plus lents; vous ne pouvez plus soulever de terre votre enfant d'autrefois. C'est donc à moi d'être votre père, à vous qui avez été les miens.

Alfred de Musset.

83. *SAINT FRANÇOIS À NOËL*

VOCABULARY

convier, to invite. *la chaumine*, thatched cottage, cot.

Un Dieu plein de douceur mit la faiblesse en nous
Afin que nous aimions les faibles et les doux,
Et que l'homme aux petits soit toujours charitable.
Aussi Jésus voulut naître dans une étable.
Or, le bon saint François, lorsque venait Noël,
Pour convier le monde à l'amour fraternel,
Devant ceux que l'orgueil aveuglément domine
Prêchait l'humilité dans une humble chaumine.
Il avait près de lui le bœuf, l'âne; et ceux-ci,
Qu'aimait le pur apôtre, et qui l'aimaient aussi,
Fixaient sur leur ami leur regard grave et tendre,
Et, l'écoutant parler, paraissaient le comprendre.

H. S. C. 1922.

84. *LE JEUNE BERGER*

VOCABULARY

grossier, rough, coarse.
la toile, cloth.
le poil, hair.
teint, p.p. of *teindre*, to dye.
le coutil, canvas.
le seigle, rye.
mal dégrossi, roughly finished.
puiser...dans, to fish out...from.

Il n'est pas bien jour encore dans le village. Je me lève. Mes habits sont aussi grossiers que ceux des petits paysans voisins: ni bas, ni souliers, ni chapeau; un pantalon de grosse toile, une veste de drap bleu à longs poils; un bonnet de laine teint en brun—voilà mon costume. Je jette par-dessus un sac de coutil, qui contient, comme celui de mes camarades, un gros morceau de pain noir mêlé de seigle, un fromage de chèvre, gros et dur comme un caillou, et un petit couteau d'un sou, dont le manche de bois mal dégrossi contient en outre une fourchette de fer à deux longues branches. Cette fourchette sert aux paysans, dans mon pays, à puiser le pain, le lard et les choux dans l'écuelle où ils mangent la soupe. Ainsi équipé, je sors et je vais sur la place du village, près du portail de l'église, sous deux gros noyers. C'est là que, tous les matins, se rassemblent autour de leurs moutons, de leurs chèvres et de quelques vaches maigres les huit ou dix petits bergers avant de partir pour les montagnes. LAMARTINE.

85. *PREMIÈRE VUE DE BONAPARTE*

VOCABULARY

frémir, to quiver. *rentré*, receding. *aigu*, sharp, pointed.

Enfin, pour la première fois je le vis. Il était debout près du bord causant avec Casa-Bianca, capitaine du vaisseau (pauvre *Orient!*), et il jouait avec les cheveux d'un enfant de dix ans, le fils du capitaine. Je fus jaloux de cet enfant sur-le-champ, et le cœur me bondit en voyant qu'il touchait le sabre du général. Mon père s'avança vers Bonaparte et lui parla longtemps. Je ne voyais pas encore son visage. Tout d'un coup il se retourna et me regarda: je frémis de tout mon corps à la vue de ce front jaune entouré de longs cheveux pendants, et, comme sortant de la mer, tout mouillés; de ces grands yeux gris, de ces joues maigres et de cette lèvre rentrée sur un menton aigu. Il venait de parler de moi, car il disait: "Tu vas renvoyer cet enfant en France; je veux qu'il soit fort en mathématiques, et s'il t'arrive quelque chose là-bas, je te réponds de lui, moi; je m'en charge, et j'en ferai un bon soldat." En même temps il se baissa et, me prenant sous les bras, m'éleva jusqu'à sa bouche et me baisa le front.

ALFRED DE VIGNY.

86. *L'AMIRAL COLLINGWOOD*

VOCABULARY

balbutier, to stammer.
la reconnaissance, gratitude, thanks.
l'écume (n.f.), foam.
voûté, bent, bowed.
souhaiter, to wish (esp. of good wishes).

"Vous êtes déjà triste, mon enfant, me dit le bon amiral. J'ai quelques petites choses à vous dire; voulez-vous causer un peu avec moi?"

Je balbutiai quelques paroles vagues de reconnaissance et de politesse qui n'avaient pas le sens commun probablement, car il ne les écouta pas, et s'assit sur un banc, me tenant une main. J'étais debout devant lui.

"Vous n'êtes prisonnier que depuis un mois, reprit-il, et je le suis depuis trente-trois ans. Oui, mon ami, je suis prisonnier de la mer; elle me garde de tous côtés: toujours des flots et des flots; je ne vois qu'eux, je n'entends qu'eux. Mes cheveux ont blanchi sous leur écume, et mon dos s'est un peu voûté sous leur humidité. J'ai passé si peu de temps en Angleterre, que je ne la connais que par la carte. La patrie est un être idéal que je n'ai fait qu'entrevoir, mais que je sers en esclave et qui augmente pour moi de rigueur à mesure que je deviens plus nécessaire. C'est le sort commun et c'est même ce que nous devons le plus souhaiter, que d'avoir de telles chaînes; mais elles sont quelquefois bien lourdes."

ALFRED DE VIGNY.

87. (*Admiral Collingwood's advice to a French Midshipman who is a prisoner on board his Flagship*)

Après quelques minutes, l'amiral revint à moi. "J'ai à vous dire," reprit-il d'un ton plus ferme, "que nous ne tarderons pas à nous rapprocher de la France. Je suis une éternelle sentinelle placée devant vos ports.

Je n'ai qu'un mot à ajouter, et j'ai voulu que ce fût seul à seul: souvenez-vous que vous êtes ici sur votre parole, et que je ne vous surveillerai point; mais, mon enfant, plus le temps passera, plus l'épreuve sera forte. Vous êtes bien jeune encore; si la tentation devient trop grande pour que votre courage y résiste, venez me trouver quand vous craindrez de succomber, et ne vous cachez pas de moi; je vous sauverai d'une action déshonorante que, par malheur pour leurs noms, quelques officiers ont commise. Souvenez-vous qu'il est permis de rompre une chaîne de forçat[1], si l'on peut, mais non une parole d'honneur." Et il me quitta sur ces derniers mots en me serrant la main.

Scottish Leaving Certificate Examination, Lower Grade, 1926.

[1] *forçat*, 'convict'.

88. *LE MISSIONNAIRE*

VOCABULARY

gravir, to climb.
le revers, (opposite) side.
la taille, figure; stature.
cheminer, to wend one's way, to fare.
le bréviaire, breviary (prayer-book).

Les nuages furent bientôt assez dispersés pour nous permettre de quitter notre retraite. Nous sortîmes de la forêt, et nous commençâmes à gravir le revers d'une montagne. Le chien marchait devant nous en portant au bout d'un bâton la lanterne éteinte. Je tenais la main d'Atala, et nous suivions le missionnaire. Il se détournait souvent pour nous regarder, contemplant avec pitié nos malheurs et notre jeunesse. Un livre était suspendu à son cou; il s'appuyait sur un bâton blanc. Sa taille était élevée, sa figure pâle et maigre, sa physionomie simple et sincère. Quand il nous parlait debout et immobile, sa longue barbe, ses yeux modestement baissés, le son affectueux de sa voix, tout en lui avait quelque chose de calme et de sublime. Quiconque a vu, comme moi, le père Aubry cheminant seul avec son bâton et son bréviaire dans le désert, a une véritable idée du voyageur chrétien sur la terre. CHATEAUBRIAND.

89. *VEILLÉE FUNÈBRE*

VOCABULARY

la veillée funèbre, watch, wake.
le flambeau, torch; cresset, flame.
la vestale, vestal virgin.
le cercueil, coffin.
répandre, spread abroad, shed.
le religieux, *here* man of God.
le rameau, bough, branch.
l'amertume (n.f.), bitterness.
la colombe, dove.
le bocage, grove.
décédé, deceased, departed.

La lune prêta son pâle flambeau à cette veillée funèbre. Elle se leva au milieu de la nuit, comme une blanche vestale qui vient pleurer sur le cercueil d'une compagne. Bientôt elle répandit dans les bois ce grand secret de mélancolie qu'elle aime à raconter aux vieux chênes et aux rivages antiques des mers. De temps en temps le religieux plongeait un rameau fleuri dans une eau consacrée, puis, secouant la branche humide, il parfumait la nuit des baumes du ciel. Parfois il répétait sur un air antique quelques vers d'un vieux poète nommé *Job*; il disait:

"J'ai passé comme une fleur; j'ai séché comme l'herbe des champs.

"Pourquoi la lumière a-t-elle été donnée à un misérable et la vie à ceux qui sont dans l'amertume du cœur?"

Ainsi chantait l'ancien des hommes. Sa voix grave et peu cadencée allait roulant dans le silence des déserts. Le nom de Dieu et du tombeau sortait de tous les échos, de tous les torrents, de toutes les forêts. Les roucoulements de la colombe, la chute d'un torrent dans la montagne, les tintements de la cloche qui appelait les voyageurs, se mêlaient à ces chants funèbres, et l'on croyait entendre dans les Bocages de la mort le chœur lointain des décédés, qui répondait a la voix du solitaire.

CHATEAUBRIAND.

90. *LE JEUNE BOHÉMIEN*

VOCABULARY

le naturel, nature.
nomade, wandering.
le métier, trade, profession.
glisser, to glide.
la courbe, curve.
le lévrier, greyhound.
dompter, to tame, break (in).
jongler, to juggle.
un éleveur, trainer.

Silvia.

Et n'ai-je pas le droit de chercher à connaître
Celui qui prétendait dormir sous ma fenêtre?

Zanetto.

Si fait. Je ne veux pas garder l'incognito.
Je suis musicien et j'ai nom Zanetto.
Depuis l'enfance, étant d'un naturel nomade,
Je voyage. Ma vie est une promenade.
Je crois n'avoir jamais dormi trois jours entiers
Sous un toit, et je vis de vingt petits métiers
Dont on n'a pas besoin. Mais, pour être sincère,
L'inutile, ici-bas, c'est le plus nécessaire.
Je sais faire glisser un bateau sur le lac,
Et, pour placer la courbe exquise d'un hamac,
Choisir dans le jardin les branches les plus souples.
Je sais conduire aussi les lévriers par couples
Et dompter un cheval rétif. Je sais encor
Jongler dans un sonnet avec les rimes d'or,
Et suis de plus, mérite assurément très rare,
Éleveur de faucons et maître de guitare.

François Coppée.

91. *L'ALOUETTE*

VOCABULARY

pénible, toilsome.
la devise, motto.
la flèche, arrow.
écarter, to push aside, drive off, keep away.

L'oiseau des champs par excellence, l'oiseau du laboureur, c'est l'alouette, sa compagne assidue, qu'il retrouve partout dans son sillon pénible pour l'encourager, le soutenir, lui chanter l'espérance. *Espoir*, c'est la vieille devise de nos Gaulois, et c'est pour cela qu'ils avaient pris comme oiseau national cet humble oiseau si pauvrement vêtu, mais si riche de cœur et de chant.

C'est la fille du jour. Dès qu'il commence, quand l'horizon s'empourpre et que le soleil va paraître, elle part du sillon comme une flèche, porte au ciel l'hymne de joie. Sainte poésie, fraîche comme l'aube, pure et gaie comme un cœur d'enfant! Cette voix sonore et puissante donne le signal aux moissonneurs. "Il faut partir, dit le père; n'entendez-vous pas l'alouette?" Elle les suit, leur dit d'avoir courage; aux chaudes heures, les invite au sommeil, écarte les insectes. Sur la tête penchée de la jeune fille à demi éveillée, elle verse des torrents d'harmonie....

C'est un bienfait donné au monde que ce chant de lumière, et vous le retrouverez presque en tout pays qu'éclaire le soleil. MICHELET.

92. *SOLEIL D'OCTOBRE*

VOCABULARY

la brume, mist.
brusquement, sharply, suddenly, sudden, abrupt.
le tapis, carpet.
la clairière, clearing, (forest) glade.
le brin, twig, blade (grass).
un osier, willow.
dru, thick.
réfléchir, reflect, ruminate.

Le voilà qui monte en éclairant la brume,
Et le premier rayon qui brusquement s'allume
A toute la forêt donne des feuilles d'or.

Et sur les verts tapis de la grande clairière,
Ferme dans ses sabots, marche en pleine lumière
Une petite fille (elle a sept ou huit ans),
Avec un brin d'osier menant sa vache rousse;
Elle connaît déjà l'herbe fine qui pousse
Vive et drue à l'automne au bord frais des étangs.

Oubliant de brouter, parfois la grosse bête,
L'herbe aux dents, réfléchit et détourne la tête,
Et ses grands yeux naïfs rayonnants de bonté
Ont comme des lueurs d'intelligence humaine:
Elle aime à regarder cette enfant qui la mène,
Belle petite brune ignorant sa beauté.

André Lemoyne.

93. *ROCREUSE*

VOCABULARY

le trou, hole, hollow, spot.
recueilli, peaceful.
jaillir, to spring up, well up.
profiter de, to profit by, take advantage of.
la fente, crack, chink.
s'épancher, to open out.
chuchoter, to whisper.
le bouvreuil, bullfinch.
de toutes parts, on every side.

Mais ce qui fait surtout le charme de Rocreuse, c'est la fraîcheur de ce trou de verdure, aux journées les plus chaudes de juillet et d'août. La Morelle descend des bois de Gagny, et il semble qu'elle prenne le froid des feuillages sous lesquels elle coule pendant des lieues; elle apporte des bruits murmurants, l'ombre glacée et recueillie des forêts. Et elle n'est point la seule fraîcheur: toutes sortes d'eaux courantes chantent sous les bois; à chaque pas des sources jaillissent; on sent, lorsqu'on suit les étroits sentiers, comme des lacs souterrains qui percent sous la mousse, et profitent des moindres fentes au pied des arbres, entre les rochers, pour s'épancher en fontaines cristallines. Les voix chuchotantes de ces ruisseaux s'élèvent si nombreuses et si hautes, qu'elles couvrent le chant des bouvreuils. On se croirait dans quelque parc enchanté, avec des cascades tombant de toutes parts.

É. Zola.

94. *AU TRAVAIL!*

VOCABULARY

ravi, enraptured.
la tâche, task.
retourner, to turn over, till.
le bien, property, land.
le relâche, ceasing, respite.
frais (adv.), freshly, newly.
un aiguillon, goad.
la charrue, plough.
un épi, ear (of corn).
une herbe, herb, weed.
se faner, to wither.

Aimez, ô jeunes gens, et respectez la vie:
Elle est bonne à celui qui va droit son chemin,
Et qui ne garde au fond de son âme ravie
Que le rêve d'hier et l'espoir de demain;

Elle est bonne à tous ceux qui courent à leur tâche,
Comme le laboureur qui se lève au matin,
Et retourne son bien sans plainte et sans relâche,
Malgré la terre dure et le ciel incertain.

Votre aube vient de naître à l'orient tranquille,
Vos bœufs frais attelés se passent d'aiguillon,
Votre charrue est neuve et votre champ fertile;
Déjà l'épi futur germe dans le sillon.

Au travail, au travail! Faites votre journée;
Vous êtes au matin, laissez venir le soir;
Vous êtes en avril, laissez finir l'année;
L'herbe d'ennui se fane où fleurit le devoir...

H. CHANTAVOINE.

95. *LES PRIMEVÈRES*

VOCABULARY

une nappe, table-cloth; sheet.
l'ébène (n.f.), ebony.
le parvis, (temple) court.
tranché, sharply cut, clear cut.
piauler, to cheep.
touffu, tufted, thick.
le frimas, (white) frost, rime.
un asile, asylum, shelter, refuge.
le fardeau, burden, load.
le chaperon, hood.
une ondée, a heavy shower, downpour.
le tablier, apron, pinafore.

Il a neigé toute la nuit. Mes volets mal fermés m'ont laissé entrevoir, dès mon lever, cette grande nappe blanche qui s'est étendue en silence sur la campagne.

Les troncs noirs des arbres s'élèvent comme des colonnes d'ébène sur un parvis d'ivoire; cette opposition dure et tranchée et l'attitude morne des bois attristent éminemment. On n'entend rien: pas un être vivant, sauf quelques moineaux qui vont se réfugier en piaulant dans les sapins, qui étendent leurs longs bras chargés de neige. L'intérieur de ces arbres touffus est impénétrable aux frimas; c'est un asile préparé par la Providence, les petits oiseaux le savent bien.

J'ai visité nos primevères: chacune portait son petit fardeau de neige et pliait la tête sous le poids. Ces jolies fleurs, si richement colorées, faisaient un effet charmant sous leurs chaperons blancs. J'en ai vu des touffes entières recouvertes d'un seul bloc de neige; toutes ces fleurs riantes, ainsi voilées et se penchant les unes sur les autres, semblaient un groupe de jeunes filles surprises par une ondée et se mettant à l'abri sous un tablier blanc. MAURICE DE GUÉRIN.

96. *NUIT DE NEIGE*

VOCABULARY

morne, mournful, dreary.
le chaume, stubble.
s'abattre sur, to swoop down upon.
dépouillé, stripped; *here* bare, leafless.
parcourir, to look over, sweep.

La grande plaine est blanche, immobile et sans voix.
Pas un bruit, pas un son; toute vie est éteinte.
Mais on entend parfois, comme une morne plainte,
Quelque chien sans abri qui hurle au coin d'un bois.

Plus de chansons dans l'air, sous nos pieds plus de chaumes.
L'hiver s'est abattu sur toute floraison.
Des arbres dépouillés dressent à l'horizon
Leurs squelettes blanchis ainsi que des fantômes.

La lune est large et pâle et semble se hâter.
On dirait qu'elle a froid dans le grand ciel austère.
De son morne regard elle parcourt la terre,
Et, voyant tout désert, s'empresse à nous quitter.

Cambridge Senior, 1912.

97. *PAYSAGE NOCTURNE*

VOCABULARY

s'écouler, to flow past, to be spent.
le paysage, landscape.
la lueur, gleam, soft light.
resplendir, to be resplendent *or* brilliant.
frissonner, to quiver, ripple.
un étang, pond, pool.
la pelouse, lawn, green-sward.
éteint, (*lit.* extinguished), plunged in darkness.
découper, to cut out; — *sa silhouette*, to be sharply silhouetted.
le flot, wave, tide.

Parvenu à quelque distance, au moment où le sentier qui gravissait la colline allait descendre l'autre revers, il retourna la tête pour contempler une dernière fois les lieux où s'étaient écoulées plus de vingt années de sa vie. Le parc, le château, tout le paysage à l'entour étaient éclairés des lueurs d'une adorable nuit de septembre qui resplendissait. Les rayons d'une lune argentée s'endormaient sur la cime des grands arbres, ou glissaient en frissonnant sur la face de l'étang, qui brillait au milieu de la pelouse comme une tache de lumière. Sur le fond du ciel étoilé, le château éteint découpait sa grande silhouette majestueuse et sombre. Une seule fenêtre était éclairée; il la reconnut: c'était celle de la chambre où sa mère veillait, pleurait peut-être en pensant à lui. Il resta un moment immobile et silencieux, s'abandonnant au flot montant de ses pensées.

Cambridge Senior, 1918.

98. *LE BERGER*

VOCABULARY

tassé, grouped together, bunched.
brouter, to browse, graze.
insoucieux, heedless, unheeding.
flamboyer, to flame, blaze.
un éblouissement, dazzling splendour.

Voici l'heure incertaine où le soleil décline;
On n'entend d'autre bruit qu'un Angelus lointain.
Quelques moutons, tassés au bas de la colline,
Broutent paisiblement l'herbe fraîche et le thym.

Sur la hauteur, drapé dans sa cape de laine,
Le vieux berger repose à côté de son chien,
Et laisse, insoucieux, par les monts et la plaine,
Errer ses yeux lassés qui ne regardent rien.

. . . .

Pourtant il se fait tard, et le couchant flamboie.
Le jour avec la nuit lutte avant d'expirer;
Dans l'éblouissement de ce grand feu de joie,
La lune peu à peu commence à se montrer.

Le vieux, lui, sur sa roche est toujours immobile,
Et le bon paysan qui rentre à la maison,
Non sans trembler un peu, l'aperçoit qui profile
Sa silhouette d'or sur le rouge horizon.

GABRIEL VICAIRE.

99. *L'ART DE CONTER*

VOCABULARY

vulgaire, common, cheap. *à l'égal de*, just as much as.

L'art de conter est, pour ainsi parler, inné chez les peuples de France et d'Italie; et si spontané, si répandu que soit chez eux ce don, ils sont loin de le considérer comme chose vulgaire; ils en apprécient au contraire toute la valeur. Sans peine apparente et comme en se jouant, ils écrivent, en une prose simple, claire et vive, pareille à l'eau courante, des récits que les ignorants ou les inattentifs prendront pour des riens: eux savent que ce sont des œuvres d'art et qu'elles méritent d'être conservées à l'égal des meilleurs poèmes. De très bonne heure, ils ont eu la révélation des mérites de la prose, la vraie prose, celle qui rejette l'ornement poétique et ne veut plaire que par ses propres moyens, celle qui se fait oublier, comme le fait au théâtre un bon acteur. On ne dit jamais du bon acteur: comme il joue bien! mais on dira: comme il faut qu'il ait bien joué pour nous avoir fait oublier sa personne et croire au personnage représenté! J.-J. JUSSERAND.

100. *INTÉRIEUR*

VOCABULARY

un abat-jour, shade.
fredonner, to hum.
recueilli, lost in one's own thoughts.
bigarré, party-coloured, variegated, motley.
un thème, passage.
sympathique, pleasing.
un camée, cameo.
soyeux, silky, soft.

Le salon est paisible. Au fond, la cheminée
Flambe, par un feu clair et vif illuminée.
Au dehors le vent siffle, et la pluie aux carreaux
Ruisselle avec un bruit pareil à des sanglots.
Sous son abat-jour vert la lampe qui scintille
Baigne de sa clarté la table de famille;
Un vase plein de fleurs de l'arrière-saison
Exhale un parfum vague et doux comme le son
D'un vieil air que fredonne une voix affaiblie.
Le père écrit. La mère, active et recueillie,
Couvre un grand canevas de dessins bigarrés,
Et l'on voit sous ses doigts s'élargir par degrés
Le tissu nuancé de laine rouge et noire.
Assise au piano, sur les touches d'ivoire
La jeune fille essaye un thème préféré,
Puis se retourne et rit. Son profil éclairé
Par un pâle rayon est fier et sympathique,
Et si pur qu'on croirait voir un camée antique.
Elle a vingt ans. Le feu de l'art luit dans ses yeux,
Et son front resplendit, et ses cheveux soyeux
Tombent en bandeaux bruns jusque sur ses épaules.

ANDRÉ THEURIET.

101. *LE TEMPS PERDU*

VOCABULARY

la meute, pack (*usually* of hounds).
un essaim, swarm (*usually* of bees).
pulluler (*lit.* sprout up), throng.
chômer, to be idle, to be out of work.

Si peu d'œuvres pour tant de fatigue et d'ennui!
De stériles soucis notre journée est pleine:
Leur meute sans pitié nous chasse à perdre haleine,
Nous pousse, nous dévore, et l'heure utile a fui...

"Demain! j'irai demain voir ce pauvre chez lui;
Demain je reprendrai ce livre ouvert à peine;
Demain je te dirai, mon âme, où je te mène;
Demain je serai juste et fort...Pas aujourd'hui."

Aujourd'hui, que de soins, de pas et de visites!
Oh! l'implacable essaim des devoirs parasites
Qui pullulent autour de nos tasses de thé!

Ainsi chôment le cœur, la pensée et le livre,
Et, pendant qu'on se tue à différer de vivre,
Le vrai devoir dans l'ombre attend la volonté.

SULLY PRUDHOMME.

102. *LA MOISSON*

VOCABULARY

le froment, wheat.
la faucille, sickle.
accroupi, squatting, crouching.
rétrécir, to make narrower, reduce, contract.
le bluet, cornflower.
le pavot, poppy.

Les blés hauts et dorés, que le vent touche à peine,
Comme un jaune océan ondulent sur la plaine;
D'un long ruban de pourpre, agité mollement,
L'aurore en feu rougit ces vagues de froment,
Et, dans l'air, l'alouette, en secouant sa plume,
Chante, et comme un rubis dans le ciel bleu s'allume.

Mais déjà la faucille est au pied des épis.
Les souples moissonneurs, sur le chaume accroupis,
Sont cachés tout entiers, comme un nageur sous l'onde;
Leur front noir reparaît parfois sur la mer blonde.
Plongeant leurs bras actifs dans les flots de blé mûr,
Ils avancent toujours de leur pas lent, mais sûr;

Leur fer tranchant et prompt, à tous les coups qu'il frappe,
Rétrécit devant eux l'or de l'immense nappe.
Derrière eux, le sillon reparaît morne et gris;
Les bluets sont tombés et les pavots fleuris;
Et le soleil de juin, piquant comme la flèche,
Sur leur couche de paille à l'instant les dessèche.

VICTOR DE LAPRADE.

103. *LE DÉPART PROCHAIN*

VOCABULARY

clapoter, to plash.
moutonner, to show white crests, to be covered with white horses.
haler, to haul.
un thrène (*a Greek word*), dirge.
la vergue, yard (*of mast*).
gonfler, to swell, fill.

Le flot clapote, un homme auprès de nous chantonne;
Des voiles passent comme un vol d'oiseaux blessés.
Ô phare! ô port! demain nous vous aurons laissés
Derrière nous, fuyant sous la mer qui moutonne...

Vois déjà près du môle, au soleil froid d'automne,
Notre vaisseau halé par les haleurs lassés;
Ils tirent pas à pas, et leurs chants cadencés
Font un thrène d'adieux lointain et monotone...

Car tout déjà parle d'adieux! Des matelots
Dans les vergues, bercés sur le péril des flots,
Hissent la voile avec un cri mélancolique;

Et triste comme les adieux, de toute part
Flotte dans l'air humide et le soleil oblique
Le vent qui gonflera nos voiles au départ.

F. GREGH.

104. *LE VIEILLARD*

VOCABULARY

brunir, to make brown *or* dusky.
la pierre = la borne, boundary-stone.
le couchant, sunset.
jadis, of old, of yore, once.
aïeul, forefather, grandfather, grandsire.
farouche, wild, forbidding.

Le soleil déclinait; le soir prompt à le suivre
Brunissait l'horizon; sur la pierre d'un champ,
Un vieillard, qui n'a plus que peu de temps à vivre,
S'était assis pensif, tourné vers le couchant.

C'était un vieux pasteur, berger dans la montagne,
Qui jadis, jeune et pauvre, heureux, libre et sans lois,
A l'heure où le mont fuit sous l'ombre qui le gagne,
Faisait gaîment chanter sa flûte dans les bois.

Maintenant riche et vieux, l'âme du passé pleine,
D'une grande famille aïeul laborieux,
Tandis que ses troupeaux revenaient dans la plaine,
Détaché de la terre, il contemplait les cieux.

Le jour qui va finir vaut le jour qui commence.
Le vieux penseur rêvait sous cet azur si beau.
L'Océan devant lui se prolongeait, immense,
Comme l'espoir du juste aux portes du tombeau.

O moment solennel! les monts, la mer farouche,
Les vents faisaient silence et cessaient leur clameur.
Le vieillard regardait le soleil qui se couche;
Le soleil regardait le vieillard qui se meurt.

VICTOR HUGO.

105. *LA CATHÉDRALE*

VOCABULARY

le reflet, reflection.
émeut (3rd sing. pres. indic. of *émouvoir*), moves, affects.

La haute cathédrale est grise, presque noire,
Et découpe un profil austère sur les cieux.
Une voix vague sort des blocs silencieux;
Dans leur langue gothique ils nous disent de croire.

C'est le reflet, et c'est la vivante mémoire
Des âges d'autrefois, sauvages et pieux.
On sent qu'en ce grand corps est l'âme des aïeux,
Et cela vous émeut comme une vieille histoire.

Avez-vous remarqué cette forme des tours,
Qui montent et qui vont diminuant toujours,
Pour porter le plus haut possible la prière?

Que vous croyiez ou non, vous ne souriez pas
De voir ces murs géants, semblables à des bras,
Tendre vers le Seigneur leurs sombres mains de pierre.

ALBERT MÉRAT.

106. *LA FÉODALITÉ*

VOCABULARY

le canton, district.
le lien, bond, tie.
l'insouciance (n.f.), indifference.
ménager, to spare, grudge.

La nature humaine a un besoin instinctif d'obéir. Quand un pouvoir disparaît, elle cherche d'abord à quel autre pouvoir elle se soumettra. Dès qu'on cessa d'obéir au roi, il parut naturel qu'on obéît à l'homme duquel on tenait la terre.

Tous les regards et toutes les espérances se portèrent vers les seigneurs. On était sûr de les trouver au moment du danger. On n'avait pas à attendre qu'ils vinssent de loin ni à craindre qu'ils fussent occupés ailleurs; car ils habitaient la province ou le canton menacé. Entre le comte et la population du comté le lien des intérêts était visible; le champ du laboureur était le domaine du comte; il le défendait comme son bien propre; si soupçonneux que fussent les hommes dans leur malheur, ils ne pouvaient penser à accuser leur seigneur direct d'insouciance ou de trahison. Vainqueur, on ne ménageait pas la reconnaissance; vaincu, on savait qu'il souffrait plus que personne. Seul il était bien armé et suivi de quelques bons soldats; seul il veillait pour tous; fort ou faible, il était le seul défenseur, le seul espoir des hommes. La moisson, la vigne, tout périssait avec lui ou était sauvé par lui.

FUSTEL DE COULANGES.

107. *SAINT-JUST*

VOCABULARY

un épervier, sparrow-hawk.
fondre, to swoop.
le glaive, sword.
s'en prendre à, to attack, set upon.

Saint-Just promène l'épouvante sur tous les partis. Comme l'épervier qui paraît immobile et n'a pas encore trouvé la proie sur laquelle il veut fondre, il tient, pendant deux heures, la Convention sous sa vague menace. Il ne conclut pas. Il met chacun en présence de lui-même; car il sait que la terreur, pour être un bon instrument de règne, doit d'abord entrer dans toutes les âmes. Personne n'excelle mieux que lui à tenir ainsi le glaive suspendu sur toutes les têtes avant de frapper. Quand il a fini, nul n'ose l'interroger. Chacun se demande en secret: De qui veut-il parler? Quel est le coupable aujourd'hui? Ai-je mérité sa haine? Est-ce moi? Il regardait du côté de Danton tout à l'heure. Mais qui oserait s'en prendre à Danton? Il est donc vrai qu'il y a des traîtres autour de moi! Et si l'on rencontre Saint-Just, on essaye de sourire à l'exterminateur. Car même parmi les héros, il a su faire pénétrer la peur. Celui qui tout à l'heure racontait la victoire de Geisberg écrira de Saint-Just, quarante ans après: "Son souvenir me fait encore frissonner."

EDGAR QUINET.

108. *LA CHATTE ET LA NUIT*

VOCABULARY

n'en pouvoir plus, to be exhausted.
crotté, mud-bespattered.
il est bien question de = *il s'agit bien de.*
le parti, side.
franchir, to cross.
le seuil, threshold.

La Nuit. — Qui va là?

La Chatte. — C'est moi, mère la Nuit...Je n'en puis plus...

La Nuit. — Qu'as-tu donc, mon enfant?... Tu es pâle, amaigrie, et te voilà crottée jusqu'aux moustaches... Tu t'es encore battue dans les gouttières, sous la neige et la pluie?...

La Chatte. — Il est bien question de gouttières!... C'est de notre secret qu'il s'agit!... C'est le commencement de la fin!... J'ai pu m'échapper un instant pour te prévenir; mais je crains bien qu'il n'y ait rien à faire...

La Nuit. — Quoi?... Qu'est-il donc arrivé?...

La Chatte. — Je vous ai déjà parlé du petit Tyltyl, le fils du bûcheron, et du Diamant merveilleux... Eh bien, il vient ici pour vous réclamer l'Oiseau-Bleu...

La Nuit. — Il ne le tient pas encore...

La Chatte. — Il le tiendra bientôt, si nous ne faisons pas quelque miracle... Voici ce qui se passe: la Lumière qui le guide et qui nous trahit tous, car elle s'est mise entièrement du parti de l'Homme, la Lumière vient d'apprendre que l'Oiseau-Bleu, le vrai, le seul qui puisse vivre à la clarté du jour, se cache ici, parmi les oiseaux bleus des songes qui se nourrissent des rayons de lune et meurent dès qu'ils voient le soleil... Elle sait qu'il lui est interdit de franchir le seuil de votre palais; mais elle y envoie les enfants; et, comme vous ne pouvez pas empêcher l'Homme d'ouvrir les portes de vos secrets, je ne sais trop comment tout cela finira... En tout cas, s'ils avaient le malheur de mettre la main sur le véritable Oiseau-Bleu, nous n'aurions plus qu'à disparaître. MAURICE MAETERLINCK.

109. *LA VRAIE CHARITÉ*

VOCABULARY

épuiser, to exhaust, empty. *le témoignage*, proof.
la bienveillance, kindliness, benevolence.

Il ne s'agit point d'épuiser sa bourse et de verser l'argent à pleines mains; je n'ai jamais vu que l'argent fît aimer personne. Vous aurez beau ouvrir vos coffres; si vous n'ouvrez aussi votre cœur, celui des autres vous restera toujours fermé. C'est votre temps, ce sont vos soins, vos affections, c'est vous-même qu'il faut donner; car, quoi que vous puissiez faire, on sent toujours que votre argent n'est point vous. Il y a des témoignages d'intérêt et de bienveillance qui font plus d'effet et sont réellement plus utiles que tous les dons. Combien de malheureux, de malades, ont plus besoin de consolations que d'aumônes! combien d'opprimés à qui la protection sert plus que l'argent!

Déclarez-vous hautement le protecteur des malheureux. Soyez juste, humain, bienfaisant. Ne faites pas seulement l'aumône, faites la charité; aimez les autres, et ils vous aimeront; servez-les, et ils vous serviront; soyez leur père, et ils seront vos enfants.

J.-J. ROUSSEAU.

110. *LA FORÊT*

VOCABULARY

ravissant, charming, delightful, lovely.
les graminées (n.f.), grasses.
le bouleau, silver birch.
le sein, bosom; depth.
s'exhaler, to be breathed forth.
au gré de, at the will of.
la nuée, cloud.
le bourdon, humble-bee.
la tourterelle, turtle-dove.
les accords (n.m.), chords, notes.

Comment exprimer les ravissantes harmonies des vents qui agitent le sommet des graminées, et changent la prairie en une mer de verdure et de fleurs, et celle des forêts où les chênes antiques agitent leurs sommets vénérables; le bouleau, ses feuilles pendantes; et les sombres sapins, leurs longues flèches toujours vertes. Du sein de ces forêts s'échappent de doux murmures, et s'exhalent mille parfums. Le matin, au lever de l'aurore, tout est chargé de gouttes de rosée qui argentent les flancs des collines et les bords des ruisseaux; tout se meut au gré des vents; de longs rayons de soleil dorent la cime des arbres et traversent les forêts. Cependant des êtres d'un autre ordre, des nuées de papillons peints de mille couleurs, volent sans bruit sur les fleurs; ici l'abeille et le bourdon murmurent; là des oiseaux font leurs nids; les airs retentissent de mille chansons. Les notes monotones du coucou et de la tourterelle servent de base aux ravissants concerts du rossignol et aux accords vifs et gais de la fauvette.

BERNARDIN DE SAINT-PIERRE.

111. *LOUIS XIV*

VOCABULARY

le joug, yoke.
n'avoir garde de, never think of.
la famille, *lit.* family, name given to section of classes at St Cyr.
fâcheux, troublesome, vexatious.

Il n'y a personne qui ne souffre. J'ai l'honneur depuis longtemps de voir le roi de fort près; s'il y avait quelqu'un qui pût secouer le joug, et n'avoir point de peine, ce serait assurément lui; cependant il en a continuellement: il est quelquefois toute une journée dans son cabinet à faire des comptes; je le vois souvent s'y casser la tête, chercher, recommencer plusieurs fois, et il ne les quitte point qu'il ne les ait achevés; il n'a garde de s'en décharger sur ses ministres. Il ne se repose sur personne du règlement de ses armées; il possède le nombre de ses troupes et de ses régiments en détail, comme je possède les familles de vos classes. Il tient plusieurs conseils par jour, où l'on traite d'affaires très sérieuses, souvent fâcheuses et toujours ennuyantes, comme des guerres, des famines et autres afflictions. Il a présentement le gouvernement de deux grands royaumes, car rien ne se règle en Espagne que suivant son ordre.

MADAME DE MAINTENON.

112. (*Young Horatius has been selected along with his two brothers to fight for Rome against the three Curiatii who represent Alba. He speaks thus to one of the Curiatii*)

VOCABULARY

la querelle, quarrel, cause. *mâle*, manly.
l'attente (n.f.), expectation.

Horace. Loin de trembler pour Albe, il vous faut plaindre Rome,
Voyant ceux qu'elle oublie et les trois qu'elle nomme.
C'est un aveuglement pour elle bien fatal
D'avoir tant à choisir et de choisir si mal.
Mille de ses enfants, beaucoup plus dignes d'elle,
Pouvaient bien mieux que nous soutenir sa querelle;
Mais quoique ce combat me promette un cercueil,
La gloire de ce choix m'enfle d'un juste orgueil;
Mon esprit en conçoit une mâle assurance:
J'ose espérer beaucoup de mon peu de vaillance;
Et du sort envieux quels que soient les projets,
Je ne me compte point pour un de vos sujets.
Rome a trop cru de moi; mais mon âme ravie
Remplira son attente, ou quittera la vie.
Qui veut mourir ou vaincre est vaincu rarement:
Ce noble désespoir périt malaisément.
Rome, quoi qu'il en soit, ne sera point sujette,
Que mes derniers soupirs n'assurent ma défaite.

CORNEILLE.

113. *IL FAUT APPRENDRE À SOUFFRIR*

VOCABULARY

tomber de son haut, to fall flat down.
tranchant, cutting, sharp.
bien avant, very deeply.
s'estropier, to lame *or* maim oneself.
de toutes pièces, at all points.
piqûre (n.m.), pinprick, sting.
s'évanouir, to faint away.

Loin d'être attentif à éviter qu'Émile ne se blesse, je serais fort fâché qu'il ne se blessât jamais, et qu'il grandît sans connaître la douleur. Souffrir est la première chose qu'il doit apprendre, et celle qu'il aura le plus grand besoin de savoir. Il semble que les enfants ne soient petits et faibles que pour prendre ces importantes leçons sans danger. Si l'enfant tombe de son haut, il ne se cassera pas la jambe; s'il se frappe avec un bâton, il ne se cassera pas le bras; s'il saisit un fer tranchant, il ne serrera guère, et ne se coupera pas bien avant. Je ne sache pas qu'on ait jamais vu d'enfant en liberté se tuer, s'estropier, ni se faire un mal considérable, à moins qu'on ne l'ait indiscrètement exposé sur des lieux élevés, ou seul autour du feu, ou qu'on n'ait laissé des instruments dangereux à sa portée. Que dire de ces magasins de machines qu'on rassemble autour d'un enfant pour l'armer de toutes pièces contre la douleur, jusqu'à ce que devenu grand, il reste à sa merci, sans courage et sans expérience, qu'il se croie mort à la première piqûre et s'évanouisse en voyant la première goutte de son sang? J.-J. ROUSSEAU.

114. (*The father of the Horatii consoles his son who has incurred the anger of the populace by killing his sister who insulted Rome*)

VOCABULARY

un effet, result, manifestation. *le vulgaire*, the vulgar throng.

Le Vieil Horace. Horace, ne crois pas que le peuple stupide
Soit le maître absolu d'un renom bien solide:
Sa voix tumultueuse assez souvent fait bruit;
Mais un moment l'élève, un moment le détruit;
Et ce qu'il contribue à notre renommée
Toujours en moins de rien se dissipe en fumée.
C'est au roi, c'est aux grands, c'est aux esprits bien faits,
A voir la vertu pleine en ses moindres effets;
C'est d'eux seuls qu'on reçoit la véritable gloire;
Eux seuls des vrais héros assurent la mémoire.

Vis toujours en Horace, et toujours auprès d'eux
Ton nom demeurera grand, illustre, fameux,
Bien que l'occasion, moins haute ou moins brillante,
D'un vulgaire ignorant trompe l'injuste attente.
Ne hais donc plus la vie, et du moins vis pour moi,
Et pour servir encor ton pays et ton roi. CORNEILLE.

115. *LES FABLES*

VOCABULARY

le rapport, connection.
prendre parti, to take sides; — *pour*, side with.
les jeunes gens, older boys and girls.
se défier de, to distrust, mistrust.
la pointe, sharp point, sting.

Dans l'enfance, ce n'est pas la morale de la fable qui frappe, ni le rapport du précepte à l'exemple; mais on s'y intéresse aux propriétés des animaux et à la diversité des caractères. Les enfants s'amusent singulièrement des petits drames dans lesquels figurent ces personnages; ils y prennent parti pour le faible contre le fort, pour le modeste contre le superbe, pour l'innocent contre le coupable. Ils en tirent ainsi une première idée de la justice. Les fables ne sont pas le livre des jeunes gens. Ils préfèrent les illustres séducteurs qui les trompent sur eux-mêmes et leur persuadent qu'ils peuvent tout ce qu'ils veulent, que leur force est sans bornes et leur vie inépuisable. Ils sont trop superbes pour goûter ce qu'enfants on leur a donné à lire. Ce temps d'ivresse passé, quand chacun a trouvé enfin la mesure de sa taille en s'approchant d'un plus grand, de ses forces en luttant avec un plus fort, de son intelligence en voyant le prix remporté par un plus habile; quand la maladie, la fatigue lui ont appris qu'il n'y a qu'une mesure de vie; quand il est arrivé à se défier même de ses espérances, alors revient le fabuliste qui savait tout cela, qui le lui dit, et qui le console, non par d'autres illusions, mais en lui montrant son mal au vrai, et tout ce qu'on en peut ôter de pointes par la comparaison avec le mal d'autrui. NISARD.

116. (*Burrhus, the good genius of Nero, tries to dissuade him from the crime of poisoning Britannicus*)

VOCABULARY

abject, humble. *épargner*, to spare.

Burrhus. Tels étaient vos plaisirs. Quel changement, ô dieux!
Le sang le plus abject vous était précieux:
Un jour, il m'en souvient, le sénat équitable
Vous pressait de souscrire à la mort d'un coupable;
Vous résistiez, seigneur, à leur sévérité;
Votre cœur s'accusait de trop de cruauté:
Et, plaignant les malheurs attachés à l'empire,
"Je voudrais, disiez-vous, ne savoir pas écrire."
Non, ou vous me croirez, ou bien de ce malheur
Ma mort m'épargnera la vue et la douleur:
On ne me verra point survivre à votre gloire,
Si vous allez commettre une action si noire.

(*Se jetant aux pieds de Néron.*)

Me voilà prêt, seigneur: avant que de partir,
Faites percer ce cœur qui n'y peut consentir;
Appelez les cruels qui vous l'ont inspirée;
Qu'ils viennent essayer leur main mal assurée.
Mais je vois que mes pleurs touchent mon empereur;
Je vois que sa vertu frémit de leur fureur. RACINE.

117. (*The Emperor Titus has, for reasons of state, resolved to part from Berenice whom he loves and who loves him*)

VOCABULARY

un amusement, distraction.
je lui plus, see p. 47, § 32.
funeste, disastrous, fatal.
prétendre, see p. 26, § 16.
passer, see p. 29, § 18.
chanceler, to waver.
encore un coup, once again.

Paulin. Hé quoi! seigneur, hé quoi! cette magnificence
Qui va jusqu'à l'Euphrate étendre sa puissance,
Tant d'honneurs, dont l'excès a surpris le sénat,
Vous laissent-ils encor craindre le nom d'ingrat?
Sur cent peuples nouveaux Bérénice commande.

Titus. Faibles amusements d'une douleur si grande!
Je connais Bérénice et ne sais que trop bien
Que son cœur n'a jamais demandé que le mien.
Je l'aimai; je lui plus. Depuis cette journée,
(Dois-je dire funeste, hélas! ou fortunée?)
Sans avoir, en aimant, d'objet que son amour,
Étrangère dans Rome, inconnue à la cour,
Elle passe ses jours, Paulin, sans rien prétendre
Que quelque heure à me voir et le reste à m'attendre.
Encor, si quelquefois un peu moins assidu
Je passe le moment où je suis attendu,
Je la revois bientôt de pleurs toute trempée:
Ma main à les sécher est longtemps occupée.

. . . .

N'y songeons plus. Allons, cher Paulin: plus j'y pense,
Plus je sens chanceler ma cruelle constance.
Quelle nouvelle, ô ciel! je vais lui annoncer!
Encore un coup, allons, il n'y faut plus penser.
Je connais mon devoir, c'est à moi de le suivre:
Je n'examine point si j'y pourrai survivre. RACINE.

118. *PARIS*

VOCABULARY

entendre, to mean.
un pavé, a paving-stone.
subsister, to remain, survive.
ancien, see p. 23, § 16.

On parle souvent de l'attachement du montagnard pour sa maison, du paysan pour sa chaumière; mais, qu'est-ce que tout cela à côté de l'invincible chaîne qui attache à Paris les plus malheureux de ses enfants? J'entends par là ceux qui y sont nés ou qui sont venus l'habiter de bonne heure; en un mot, ceux auxquels chacune de ses rues, chacun de ses coins, chacun de ses pavés disent quelque chose. Ne contient-il pas toute notre histoire? N'est-ce pas comme une grande maison dont nous aurions habité toutes les chambres, et dans laquelle, à chaque pas, nous retrouvons un souvenir? Où pouvons-nous passer sans avoir aux lèvres le mot du fabuliste: "J'étais là, telle chose m'advint"? Nulle trace ne subsiste de notre ancien passage! cette vaste mer, où chaque flot pousse l'autre, a recouvert et effacé notre empreinte; mais, sous cette nouvelle surface de joies et de douleurs aussi mobile, aussi éphémère que l'ancienne, nous évoquons notre propre histoire, nous nous voyons encore sourire, nous nous sentons encore pleurer.

LUCIEN PRÉVOST-PARADOL.

119. *WASHINGTON*

VOCABULARY

l'entremise (n.f.), intervention, interference.
le rapport, contact.
arrêter, to fix, decree.
entretenir, to keep (here passive in meaning).
répondre de, to answer for, be responsible for.

Esprit admirablement libre, plutôt à force de justesse que par richesse et flexibilité, il ne recevait ses idées de personne, ne les adoptait en vertu d'aucun préjugé, mais, en toute occasion, les formait lui-même, par la vue simple ou l'étude attentive des faits, sans aucune entremise ni influence, toujours en rapport direct et personnel avec la réalité.

Aussi, quand il avait observé, réfléchi et arrêté son idée, rien ne le troublait; il ne se laissait point jeter ou entretenir, par les idées d'autrui, ni par le désir de l'approbation, ni par la crainte de la contradiction, dans un état de doute et de fluctuation continuelle. Il avait foi en Dieu et en lui-même.

C'est qu'il joignait, à cet esprit indépendant et ferme, un grand cœur, toujours prêt à agir selon sa pensée, en acceptant la responsabilité de son action. Que l'occasion fût grande ou petite, les conséquences prochaines ou éloignées, Washington, convaincu, n'hésitait jamais à se porter en avant, sur la foi de sa conviction. On eût dit, à sa résolution nette et tranquille, que c'était pour lui une chose naturelle de décider des affaires et d'en répondre; signe assuré d'un génie né pour gouverner.

GUIZOT.

120. *LA MER*

VOCABULARY

une plaque, plate; patch.
l'étain (n.m.), tin.
le trait, shaft; streak.
la houle, swell.
agoniser, to be dying; linger.
le pan, face (of cliff).
blafard, wan.
la rafale, gust, squall.

Des nuages pesants glissent sur le ciel gris,
Et des plaques d'étain luisent sur la mer grise,
Qui s'éteignent soudain à nos regards surpris,
Ou se brisent en traits que la houle divise;

Jusqu'aux deux caps brumeux tout l'horizon est pris;
Parfois une lueur incertaine agonise
Sur un pan de falaise; on dirait des débris
De clarté que le choc des brumes pulvérise;

Un rayon de soleil blafard et fugitif
Sur un cap éloigné frappe des dunes pâles
Où luit le rouge toit d'une maison perdue,

Brève apparition tremblante, confondue
Dans les mornes brouillards roulés par les rafales,
Et changée aussitôt en un rêve pensif.

AUGUSTE ANGELLIER.

INDEX OF FRENCH WORDS TRANSLATED OR DISCUSSED

INDEX OF PASSAGES FOR TRANSLATION

For EU product safety concerns, contact us at Calle de José Abascal, 56–1°, 28003 Madrid, Spain or eugpsr@cambridge.org.

www.ingramcontent.com/pod-product-compliance
Ingram Content Group UK Ltd.
Pitfield, Milton Keynes, MK11 3LW, UK
UKHW012328130625
459647UK00009B/146

* 9 7 8 1 3 1 6 6 1 2 5 7 6 *